Russia & World Order

STRATEGIC CHOICES AND
THE LAWS OF POWER
IN HISTORY • *George Liska*

THE JOHNS HOPKINS UNIVERSITY PRESS
Baltimore and London

This book has been brought to
publication with the generous assistance
of the Andrew W. Mellon Foundation.

Manufactured in the United States of America

The Johns Hopkins University Press, Baltimore, Maryland 21218
The Johns Hopkins Press Ltd., London

Library of Congress Cataloging in Publication Data

Liska, George.
    Russia and world order.

    Includes index.
    1. World politics—1945–   2. Russia—Foreign
relations—1945–   I. Title.
D843.L53   327.'09'04   79-22872
ISBN 0-8018-2314-5

For Suzy
once more and always

CONTENTS

PREFACE

This book is both a return to the past and a gesture toward the future. The past is represented not only by the discussed or only intimated events of more or less recent history but also by my own earlier writings on Europe and America, which are given here a sequence. The future can be only the object of imagination and intuition that either trace out past trends or would break with them as irrelevant. My approach has always been, and is also in this book, of the former kind.

There are many intermediate shadings between soberly detached analysis and an argument that, not unlike a homily, is addressed to sentiment as well as to reason; that uses snatches of analysis in order to strengthen the intellectual credentials of the apostrophe. The present book belongs unashamedly to the latter genre. Baring one's soul, as it were, in the exercise of a latitudinously defined vocation carries with it a personal risk that, such as it is, is the obverse of a potential for social utility. I submit this volume, therefore, as a token of the private scholar's endeavor to do his public duty. Anyone who wishes a more sustained and dispassionate analysis of the specifically foreign-policy-related themes only briefly surfacing in the vaster ambit I take here for my province will find it in two recent books of mine, *Career of Empire: America and Imperial Expansion over Land and Sea* (1978), and its predecessor in the date of publication but in substance its sequel, *Quest for Equilibrium: America and the Balance of Power on Land and Sea* (1977).

More germane within the genre of "engaged" writings are earlier appreciations put forward in *Europe Ascendant* (1964), *Imperial America* (1967), and *War and Order* (1968). The balance of continuity and change in my strategic views between then and now is briefly summarized here in the Introduction. But only exposure to the earlier texts will disclose the full extent of a fundamental difference. The pervasive thrust of the writing at the height of de Gaulle's challenge in Europe and America's involvement in Asia was positive and essentially optimistic. My stated intent was to cheer on the expansive trends then still in evidence. As a propagandist from the sidelines, I failed; as a forecaster, I was in error as to the events wished for (though much less so as to warnings). Europe has not continued to "ascend" (or not in the way I saw it rising again), and the American "imperial" role was not triumphantly asserted in Asia and has not been institutionalized world-wide since. I can only hope that I am in error again as I react to the more recent developments in Europe and America. Where before I was positive, I now tend to be negative; where I strove to be optimistic, I surrender to the consolations of pessimism. The reader may wish to beware of both attitudes.

In the same mood, the reader will treat as only part of the story my sometimes harsh observations about present western Europe and today's America. They contrast with the hopeful things I take upon myself to say about Soviet Russia. When I do so, I like to think that I speak, by way of the Soviet Union, of the Russia whose long-suppressed identity begins to re-emerge from behind the iron mask—the *masque de fer* of French *histoire secrète* —in which it was concealed from the world by the autocrat of all the Soviets.

In my time I have felt in the flesh, as it were, the moral fragility of a small nation and the political weightlessness of a minor state when neither was guided at a critical moment by the responsible statesman's capacity to penetrate beyond the counsels of prudence, concerned with physical preservation, and look to the body politic's moral foundation in self-esteem. I have since inclined to view the world of international politics through the categories of the great political powers, of power and will, and of will in terms of public morale rather than private morality. The resulting outlook has been a variably romanticized Machiavellian realism, a Realpolitik unabashedly committed to the exercise of power but humanizing the calculations of immediate interest by concessions to sentimental obligations and to historic rights more than any others. When applying general precepts to American foreign policy, I have been no more able to shed an inveterate Europeanism of an increasingly obsolete kind than I can step out of character as one hailing from eastern Europe when I write about either western Europe or Europe as a whole. About eastern Europe I have never written before in a book as much or as explicitly as I do now, and my cultural biases are more than ever those of my native background when I step outside my professional expertise and publicize subjective impressions more copiously than is proper.

The questions I raise and the initial remedies I suggest are those of a political conservative and are different in outlook from what passes for "neorealist" conservatism in contemporary America. My analysis and conclusions are addressed to those who will soon influence policy, rather than those who currently make policy. They are also directed primarily to a western audience. But I would like to think of the implied call for a larger, philosophical view of relevant history in the devising of strategies as a challenge issued also to a Soviet leadership that currently tries to present itself to the American public as devoted to "peace, détente, and (improved) Soviet-American relations."[1]

Last but by no means least, I think, as I reread what I have written, of fellow east Europeans behind what used to be the "iron curtain" and still in part remains such. When I speak of issues that constitute their predicament, I do so as one whose license has been enhanced and perspective widened, but any kind of authority lessened, by having withdrawn from the reach of Soviet or any other oppressive power. I dare not presume to be speaking to them. My only ambition is to speak for them when deducing a claim on the West from a unique common genius.

In contrast with the contents, the procedure of putting the present little volume together was not a matter of spontaneous generation. The first essay was originally written in response to an assignment by the incumbent director of the Washington Center of Foreign Policy Research to "revisit" *Europe Ascendant* for the purpose of the center's regular round table discussions, in April 1978. The second chapter grew out of my inability to dismiss quickly enough from my mind the remarks I had just made, in early December 1978, as one of a faculty panel discussing directions of American foreign policy at the invitation of the student activities committee of the School of Advanced International Studies (SAIS) of The Johns Hopkins University.

If the forbearance with which my colleagues at the center and other fellow discussants received the "romantic" paper on post–de Gaulle Europe supplied the foundation, the response of SAIS students to my "reactionary" remarks on the state of President Carter's America provided the immediate impetus for releasing all hitherto restrained prejudices in fitful spells of writing, done in the main in December 1978 and January 1979. The lack of plan and the absence of premeditation will, I am afraid, be only partially obscured by the incorporation of tentative historical hypotheses and generalizations evolved as part of different efforts. The cost in the coin of form of so incremental a production is too obvious to stress. The undiscouraged reader will decide for himself what, if any, is the compensating gain in variety, the daughter of spontaneity.

A word, finally, to explain this preface. All speculative writing about politics, and not least about international politics, that is worth the writer's and the reader's effort is in some more or less remote fashion autobiographical, registering the individually variable mixes of public function and the

---

1. Such is the title (minus the parenthesis) of a collection of speeches by Leonid Brezhnev published in English in this country (New York: Harcourt, Brace, Jovanovich, 1979).

inner life. The more general the scope, the higher will be the level of sublimation and the larger may be the social interest of the product. But it is not necessary, and may be scarcely human, to hide at all times behind high-level abstractions and cryptic allusions. The moment comes when the cloak pieced together with patches of earlier conceptualizations may be protectively thrown over reflections more overtly partaking of confessions. When this happens, the grandest of cycles in intellectual growing up is closed; a return to the sources is in order.

Being a tangible expression of such a return, this book is also an offering to the memory of a nearly forgotten conservative Czech statesman who was once the paragon of my earliest youth. I find echoes, unrealized as I wrote, of what I associate him with in the parts of my argument most directly relating to eastern Europe. A leading statesman of pre–World War I Austria-Hungary before becoming the new successor state's first prime minister, he stands for the capacity of a small people's genuine elite to gain a position of respect and even influence in a larger political conglomerate that either substitutes for or encompasses a formally sovereign statehood. A believer in Slavic Russia, he further stands, well before the post-Munich conversion of his domestic political adversaries, for the effort to anchor the feasible measure of national independence in a strong and acknowledged position of the eastern great power in European and world politics. The Russia of his loyalty and imagination was a radically different one from that which has since evolved, and of which he was the most uncompromising of enemies. *Tempora mutantur;* if it is to be more than nostalgic, the most complete return to sources cannot ignore the transforming currents that make up the historical context of objectives that are at all realistic and of strategic concepts that are at all viable at any one moment in time.

ACKNOWLEDGMENTS

Since this happens to be the tenth of the both small and larger books published for me by The Johns Hopkins University Press since 1962, I should like to remedy at long last the earlier omissions and give thanks here to all those who, over the years, have made the connection satisfying and rewarding for me, even if not always profitable to the Press itself. The unfailing tolerance at all levels of my peculiarities as author, and the willingness at the highest level to bear the related risks, have had a large part in whatever merit may be found to reside in the total product of the common effort. Naming none in particular, I have all in mind and memory.

Russia & World Order

INTRODUCTION. *Changing*
Prescriptions and the Constant Premise

In earlier writings, I argued either implicitly (in *Europe Ascendant*) or explicitly (in *Imperial America*) that the United States ought to be willing and able to continue controlling the global, third-world peripheries in the imperial mode. The more effective among the third-world countries, I thought, would or should simultaneously move by way of economic development into a position that made them capable of handling the devolution in their favor of politico-military roles in regional orders. As the prolonged process unfolded, the United States would provisionally check the Soviet Union in the peripheries. And developments in the Eurasian continent, notably China, would simultaneously direct the Soviets toward seeking outlets from the eastern European ghetto into constructive all-European diplomacy. Soviet influence would become—and be allowed to become—global only as the Soviets themselves were Europeanized in policy and as they reduced their oppressive controls in captive eastern Europe in the process. American politico-diplomatic hegemony in western Europe would be countercontained with Soviet assistance as a continental western European ensemble became more independent in foreign policy around a Franco-German core. And the sum of these developments would create the basis for a loose all-European unification discreetly anchored in shared Franco-Soviet concerns about either American or German predominance.

The changed emphasis in this book takes into account the new situation created by the United States in relinquishing "global policemanship" by accepting defeat in Vietnam. That fact triggered an economic insurgence against the West by third-world forces and intensified revolutionary or regressive political turmoil in the third world. Two new givens were the result: one is a fresh license and an enlarged leeway for stepped-up Soviet penetration in the global peripheries; another is a shift of U.S. foreign policy toward détente with a receptive Soviet Union (principally in Europe and in the nuclear-strategic sphere), conjointly with a movement toward triangular balance-of-power politics reciprocated in stages by China.

The immediate urgency perceived in the West after Vietnam was to reforge a unity of policy between the United States and western Europe. Whereas agreement on this need was general, purposes were ranked differently: one priority was to contain the divisive implications of American-Soviet détente in Europe for the goal of western solidarity; another was to guard against the dangers of deep Soviet penetration into vital western positions and communications in the peripheral land masses and maritime routes and narrows. Yet another priority (favored in this essay as the prime prerequisite to reserving the future on all other grounds) was to counteract the impact of insurgent third-world actions and demands—starting with the economic sphere—on western political economies and ultimate political cohesion.

To identify the priority thus reflects an evaluation that partakes of hope while being more than hope. Any U.S.-Soviet condominium in Europe going beyond a shared interest in the politico-military evolutions in the two Germanys is the least likely prospect and the least serious jeopardy, while the Soviet global outreach holds out a promise. That outreach will expose the Soviet Union to global learning and is likely to ease Soviet Russian complexes induced by regional confinement. And, if properly managed, the outreach will do both without producing major gains for the Soviets that would seriously undermine either existing or prospective equilibrium globally and in the various regions.

Related to that assessment is an assumption: even a loose unification in all of Europe that does not "Finlandize" western Europe will have to take, under the new conditions, the longer route of the Soviets being westernized in depth rather than merely Europeanized in diplomacy.[1]

A revised strategy toward the Soviet Union implies a revision in the role assigned to China. China's role is henceforth downgraded from a strategic to a tactical one, from propelling Soviet statecraft toward western Europe (if only to minimize the dangers of a Sino-German diplomatic "encirclement") to moderating Soviet global "adventurism" (and appeasing the related American alarms). It is assumed that common Soviet and western interests would go on crystallizing meanwhile, with the Soviet Union becoming an industrial and naval power intent on upholding its needs for stability in the face of third-world demands for rapid and radical changes. Moreover, the emphasis on

---

1. See the next three pages for more on the distinction.

Soviet westernization involves, both logically and practically, an increased concern about China. The concern focuses on the long-term risk that China will return at some future date to her essentially eastern (and historically, anti-western) biases if her growth in power is not concurrently matched in the area west of her.

So much for shifts in strategic and tactical emphases. Continuity resides in an unchanged feeling, prompted by a reading of history at least as much as by investigation of contemporary incidents, which, by itself, is inconclusive in any event. The very success of the strategy applied to Soviet Russia after World War II from outside her regional Eurasian orbit has, since the late 1950s, begun to permit—and may increasingly require—a shift: from a strategy enforcing containment to one fostering decompression; from a doctrine concentrating on graduated nuclear deterrence of the Soviet Union to one expanded to embrace a likewise graduated extraregional diversion by the Soviet Union.

The pressures and phobias accumulated within Soviet Russia by either history or ideology can only be loosened by policies that look beyond the Soviet-controlled orbit to wider horizons; as a result, there is a fair chance for the already accomplished initial mellowing of the Stalinist totalitarian dictatorship to be followed by the maturation of the Soviet Union as a conventional world power. The underlying key premise here is this: a measure of external expansion is necessary for legitimating a new regime of an "upstart" power internally, and both conspicuously successful foreign policy and tacit regime legitimation must precede or attend ideological and related institutional relaxation within the Soviet Union, as well as in non-Soviet eastern Europe.

How to approach in the West the issue of more political freedoms in the East has come to involve, at a level transcending but also affecting foreign policy strategy, two possible Russian pathways toward something akin to liberalism and more than two kinds of western conservatism.

The Soviet Union can open itself up to larger currents by either the European or the western route. The terms *Europeanization* and *westernization* are not easy to differentiate. As I use the terms, Europeanization refers primarily to full participation in the European state system or great-power concert as an equal party; its cultural derivatives affect mainly or only the social elites. Westernization comprises Europeanization culturally on an enlarged social base; its additional and distinguishing characteristic is industrialization. It also has or can have a strategic connotation. As regards industrialization, the currently employed world-wide division between the North and the South has the former represented in fact by what has, since the sixteenth century, been the European Northwest and its American extension. As the European East is industrialized, it becomes the Northeast in current global terms. (Japan, as in all respects, is precariously poised somewhere in between.) Yet, the moment the Northwest and the Northeast are joined as a full-fledged "North" in economic terms, they automatically tend to be transmuted into a physically enlarged West in terms of other criteria. These include, if nothing else, historically conditioned culture traits and a key trait of political history: this or that party's identity as an agent rather than the object of long-distance, cross-cultural colonization. In these terms, a Russia that absorbed Byzantine-Mongol influences is less western culturally than are the east Europeans west of her but is more so as a colonizing rather than colonized society in modern times.

Industrialism and related global outreach tend to equalize formal status and to reduce psychological inferiority complexes relative to the West. The dual advance will also engender a degree of politico-institutional assimilation with the West in due course. Such changes will in turn tend to release hitherto latent socio-cultural aspirations to be part of the prestigious West. But not everywhere will such aspirations be sufficiently deep-seated and widespread to permit equalization to be translated into identification. Westernization of the latter kind is clearly different from its superficial manifestations in modes and techniques of living that are open to all; it differentiates eastern Europe (including Russia) from even the fastest developing parts of the global South or "East."

Thus, there are at least two types and meanings of westernization. One is westernization in social techniques and life styles consequent on—and in fact coterminous with—economic modernization. Another connotes the release (activation and expression) of politico-cultural feelings of identity with the "historic" (i.e., European or Europe-derived) West within a wider social orbit than is constituted by a few privileged individual elites. Although dependent on the equalization of political status, this type of westernization is open only to cultures that historically derive from the historic West or have had a long-term symbiotic coexistence or dialectical interaction with it. The second type of westernization is distinct from the first and is both more restrictive and more meaningful; to dispute the distinction is to reduce westernization to economic modernization and to make the term itself not only redundant but also ethnocentric.

Russia had begun to be westernized under Peter the Great, even before she started to be seriously Europeanized in diplomacy and elite culture under Peter's successors, notably the Tsarina Elisabeth. By the mid-nineteenth century, Russia's Euorpeanization had proceeded faster and further that her westernization; the latter began to forge ahead again at the end of the nineteenth century as part of an accelerated rate of industrialization and a sustained rate of colonial-type expansion. Whereas industrialization continued under the Soviet regime from early on, only the late 1950s saw a resumption of the seesaw between the two overlapping, but distinct, tendencies: diplomatic Europeanization and cultural and material western-ization.

A third possible meaning of westernization has strategic connotations. In these terms, Russia was at any time westernized only abortively when her inclusion in coalitions against European powers west of her was, from her viewpoint, exploitative, and the temporary alignments with one or another of the western powers on issues raised by the Ottoman empire were no more satisfactory. The deficiency of strategic westernization was most acute for Russia when, recoiling or not from frustrations in the West into regionally confined conflicts over or with China, she looked in vain for western support or sympathy in her eastern engagements. More subtly but no less seriously than invasions from the west (following upon those from the east), the discriminatory ways of implementing Russia's Europeanization impeded the progress of her westernization. They also held back, or made regress, Russia's liberalization.

Different kinds of conservatism are no more easily distinguishable theoretically, but also no less important practically, than are possible seedbeds of locally nurtured greater liberalism. If the latter issue is peculiar to Russia, the former is increasingly relevant for America at a time when conservative inclinations are on the rise in the West's citadel. One kind of conservatism is philosophical and, as such, materially disinterested. It is concerned that change occur gradually as a function of organically matured conditions, within the broad framework of discernibly patterned historical continuity. The contrary type is pragmatic and, in class or status terms, interested conservatism. Its adherents are concerned with upholding the existing status quo unchanged against what seems to be the most immediate threat and challenge to acquired positions.

Another axis of differentiation involves ideology. An ideologically specific conservative opts for a particular way of life, all the way from legitimist (including ultramontane) monarchism to economic, if not also political, laissez-faire. He is against whatever may be regarded as the diametrical opposites of his preferred values. By contrast with the ideologically committed, the ideologically neutral or indifferent conservative is less concerned with the tenets of particular doctrines. He is more anxious to see respected what he considers to be the natural and, in essence, immutable laws of social dynamics and historical evolution; to him, it is compliance with such laws that is most likely to assure conditions of a humanly satisfying or at least endurable social and political order at any time.

The final difference is between defeatist and defiant conservatism.[2] The first is the conservatism of one who either withdraws from competition with

2. This difference is spelled out in my book *Beyond Kissinger: Ways of Conservative Statecraft* (Baltimore: Johns Hopkins University Press, 1975), pp. 94–97. The foreign policy argument advanced there has changed since from criticizing Kissinger's overdependence on détente (now

forces that appear to be on the ascendant or entrenches himself behind passive defenses; the second is the posture of one who would rather expose the monopolistic pretensions of the new forces to a species of mobile warfare, aimed at preserving the most cherished traits of the past within a revised configuration.

A conservatism that is philosophical but nonideological, at once flexible and defiant, is least likely to foster adoption of a rigid stance in contemporary world affairs. In particular, its votary will not, and need not, fixedly oppose any and all Soviet foreign policy gains, regardless of changing conditions and threats. Nor need he submit to the opposite, liberal fallacy—that of uncritical and automatic support for the newest forces and most recent pretensions emanating from the third world, a support that all too often spells capitulation. Conservative preference for gradualism and organic maturation suggests instead that many another people or power is in line for its finest hour before the time has arrived for anything like the "African century." Such an outlook may be historicist, but it is neither racist nor neocolonialist.

Much of what precedes can be contested. But one point seems to be beyond dispute: only intellectual sterility and deferred disaster in policy would ensue if the councils of the West were to continue being seriously influenced by the wrong kinds of conservatism and liberalism, acting separately or in unwitting alliance. The former is self-consciously tough-minded when containing or keeping down one kind of East; the latter is guilt-ridden and tends to be weak-kneed when appeasing or making up to the other kind of East.

---

called "overselling") to criticizing the American (beginning with Kissinger's) conception of détente. The more recent theme, developed in *Quest for Equilibrium* (Baltimore: Johns Hopkins University Press, 1977) and briefly reformulated here, has been as follows: *if* there is to be détente, *this* is what it means and cannot but mean *if* one is serious about it as a long-term object of strategy replacing world-wide U.S. interventionism or "empire." The constancy at issue here bears not on the fundamental premise but on the feasible role of foreign policy scholarship.

Part One

THE SETTING: *The Two Europes and the Two Faces of America*

I

WESTERN EUROPE
WITHOUT GAULLISM

The future of western Europe is uncertain, because so is the surviving relevance of the political man. A question that transcends Europe is once again posed most sharply in Europe. Does the modern man—not least as a young man—still possess the thirst and therefore the ability to relate to causes at once metapersonal and finite, made to inspire as well as to discipline? Or has political rationality waned and with it the intellectual outlook, psychic disposition, and hierarchy of decisional standards that partake of as well as constrain the nonrational; that put the moral foundations of the polity above the politics of surface stabilization; and that set individual life-enhancing goals above the unconditional preservation of life itself? Has such a political rationality been wholly supplanted by the economics of a pettily hedonistic calculus? Is there an irreversible eclipse of the kind of politics that is the sum of always purposeful and, when required, forceful activities for gaining control or managing conflict; that coordinates auxiliary functions or functional realms in a way enhancing efficiency in both control and conflict? Has, in short, the *arcanum imperii* become a secret so poorly guarded as to get lost while serious minds were preoccupied with trivia?

Varieties of present ills and illusions:
unification vs. united action?

Political rationality has been eclipsed by professedly statesmanlike prudence along a spectrum extending from de Gaulle's failure to heed the full range of the French stake in Algeria to the western European response to de Gaulle himself; from America's reactions to Vietnam to the West's response, or lack of it, to OPEC. Within most or all western countries, schemes of radical social renovation have been in a stand-off with policies of only marginal revamping of established economic systems. Political oppositions have either gambled on the system's unavoidable collapse, have been co-opted into grand coalitions and neutralized therein, or have alternated with incumbents without offering a real choice. More than only metaphorically, cautious managers of portfolios have displaced inspired mentors of peoples. The peoples themselves, no longer on the march, have ceased to be well disposed toward manning the barricades of defense. No wonder, then, that governmental economism, private consumerism, and either political or criminal terrorism have taken to jostling one another in the vacuum created by one more retreat from individual *virtus* into decay of the *res publica*.

Addressed by experts, questions about Europe's future would have to ask whether petrodollars were being safely recycled and enough of the oil-derived investment was channeled to Europe; whether post–World War II Britain made an irreparable mistake by overinvesting abroad to the detriment of a stop-go domestic economy or whether, instead, the pipeline from the North Sea would undo all the past backslidings of the one-time workshop of the world; whether West Germany could or should inflate so that both the European "snake" and the snakelike sign of the U.S. dollar could start wriggling out of their late predicament; whether France would or could overtake West Germany by the 1980s in terms of mean individual income, or else was likely to outstrip either Scandinavian or Soviet-type socialism in terms of social justice for all—or most. If such questions were *the* questions to ask, the one comfort would be that they had no reliable answers.

Other forms of redemption may still be possible, although neither the redeemers nor the redemption mechanisms have been clearly visible on either the European or the American stage. However, one impression has stood out, any wishful thinking to the contrary notwithstanding: western Europe now seems past saving herself as a political entity on her own and from within.

A false dawn in the Carolingian West   The tragic hero went down, as heroes will, under blows from little men agitating small issues as if they represented fate. "Ten years is enough";[1] another ten has been more than enough. The electoral and parliamentary binds of routine Europeanist politicians have never coalesced so as to substitute a configuration of political convenience

---

1. *"Dix ans est assez"* was the outcry of protesters against de Gaulle's ten-year rule during the May 1968 events in France.

and opportunity for the creative fusion of positive passion with negative fear: passion for restored dignity, even if not for greatness; fear of being tempted by the easier road—and yet greater fear of the tax levied on self-abandonment by friend even more than by foe. In the opportunistic late-Gaullist version itself, the role that joint European nuclear capability could play in a breakthrough to substantial unity and symbolic independence was confused. It was inverted as to sequence and, as a result, subverted as to potential effect. Such a force was the most likely or the only plausible effective cause, or at least precipitant, of political ascent; it was instead held up, and thus held back, as the hypothetical effect and unavoidably delayed consequence of a prior, not to be hurried, political unity.[2]

Western Europe did not embark upon a new lease on life. She neither undid the contentious nor integrated into new forms the constructive consequences of the fact that her early dawn had also been a false start. She did not find her way back, that is, to her Carolingian beginnings in the form of a solidified Franco-German core. The prayers of two old men, Charles de Gaulle and Konrad Adenauer, in a German cathedral went unheard; the remains of France's last regal Charles do not rest at the old emperor's feet in Aix-la-Chapelle. After the "A" of Adenauer came the "B" of Brandt; there has been no one since to infuse an updated political meaning into the "C" standing for Charlemagne.

What could have been an indissoluble Catholic marriage between the two founders of the modern Occident was denied America's blessing. It shrank thereafter into a civil union of convenience, riddled with trial separations and repeatedly poised on the verge of psychic divorce. On the ruins of *Westeuropa,* it became a major object of *Ostpolitik* to deflate French leadership in Euro-Soviet rapprochement. Like the earlier French one, the German initiative was instead destined for being fitted into Soviet preference for direct accommodation with the United States as a mere subtheme. A more or less discreetly anti-German motif is always latent in a Franco-Russian flirtation. The motif surfaced in the latest spell, but with no substantial effect; it was dwarfed and offset by the U.S.-related tactical objectives of the courtship between the two continental European wing powers: De Gaulle sought an effective counterpoise to American influence and the Soviets a leverage on American readiness for détente. The more definite outcome of the failed Franco-German

2. The dynamic effect that a joint western European nuclear force would exert on political unification was the central operational (as distinct from analytical) thesis of *Europe Ascendent*. A similar point was made more recently by Michel Tatu in an article in *Foreign Affairs* (July 1975). The issue may resurface as U.S. nuclear protection and (consequently) diplomatic veto power decline in Bonn's perceptions and the diplomatic Soviet option and economic optimism erode in those of Paris. This would leave only the self-induced Soviet veto to overcome.

marriage has been to replace interwar suspicions of German intentions with contemporary unease over German capabilities.

The intentions were politico-military; the capabilities were economic. But the German problem, if nothing else, is alive and well. Germanophobia has begun to vie again with anti-Americanism for the status of the emotional compensation and release favored by elite Europeans. The two complexes may fuse eventually into one if the half-century-long background duel between America and Germany over succession to the British empire were to eventuate in an unconcealed Americano-German condominium in the residual West. Signs have not been lacking that it might do exactly that. For the past hundred years, well-wishers no less than suspecters of unified Germany have counseled the modern Huns to abandon martial gods for the exercise of mercantile genius; to give up the idea of conquest for the pacific imperium of commerce. The Germans have listened, learned, and, at long last, heeded the counsel with a vengeance. The "good" Germans seem to have finally triumphed over the "bad." They did so under the posthumously triumphant signs of a different, liberal Prussia, with some aid from the life styles of one and only Bavaria. The fear of the two hegemonies, American and Soviet, has given way in consequence to resentment over German crypto-hegemony.

Characteristically, it was a West German politician who was hailed most recently as neo-Gaullist. But Chancellor Schmidt's strictures and independence moves were no less characteristically addressed to the inflationary economic rather than the hegemonic political policies of the American alliance leader. Less driven than even the increasingly relaxing Germans, the French (outdone by the Italians) have been responding to the lure of an ideal polity after American interference helped bar the way to real power through Franco-German reconciliation in depth. President Giscard, too, borrowed from de Gaulle, most prominently when claiming France's African policy as a presidential preserve. Yet even in the limited sphere, he too has reduced the political component—the hierarchical-feudal relationship—in favor of over-archingly commercial concerns. The erosion of de Gaulle's bequest in foreign policy was most striking, however, when the incumbent official leader of Gaullism engaged, for the edification of an American audience, in anti-Soviet fulminations more plainly rightist *à l'américaine* than authentically Gaullist.[3]

And the British? Their decline in foreign politics has been from three great strategic options with global implications to three possible tactics relative to Europe alone. The optional strategies once were hegemony over, balancing of, and insulation from, Europe; the choice among them was regulated by

---

3. See Jacques Chirac, "France: Illusions, Temptations, Ambitions," *Foreign Affairs* (April 1978).

changing emphases on either securing the British Isles from Europe or paralyzing Europe for the sake of a greater and safer empire. The tactical alternatives have since comprised, more as a threat than a fact, (1) the diplomatic subversion of any continental association that would exclude Britain or be vetoed by the British; (2) economic separatism from Europe *à l'écossaise,* floated (as Britain was into her last great victory in World War I) on streams of oil; and (3) captive moral sponsorship of a U.S.-German politico-economic duopoly as its legitimizing, if junior, partner.

Of such stuff no reascension of western Europe was likely to be made. *La guerre impossible, la paix ennuyeuse,* de Gaulle is reported as having once complained: the prospects of rebirth have been receding along with the fading of the galvanizing threat of instant, if honorable, individual and collective demise. They receded because successive generational layers were burying ever more deeply the older inherited, austerity-bred criteria of what constituted the good life and what made the good citizen. Wild careening toward ephemeral weekends in the country has come to be mistaken for vitality, and the cult of sun-drenched vacations has been filling the otherwise vacant temple of civic religion. When this happens, the only remaining question is whether the sickle will in due course undercut the thorny rose or the rose will flourish after the social soil is hammered level by a sturdier instrument.[4]

Fresh light out of the East or the farthest West?   What is to be done? If western Europe is unable to return on her own to her beginnings, could a reversal between the West and the East restore vigor and redress a historic wrong as well?

At Europe's dawn, an initially primitive West outstripped and overcame in due course the more prosperous and sophisticated Byzantine East. At one time or another, Germany was unified by Prussia, not Frankfurt; Italy by Piedmont, not either Venetia or Tuscany; Yugoslavia around Serbia, not Slovenia or Croatia. And Russia was fashioned out of Muscovy, not out of either Kiev or Novgorod.

The political potency of economic inferiority suggests a query. As the goose step reverberates from east Germany into the countinghouses and playgrounds of the Federal Republic; as unspoilt nature, raw humanity, and simple belief in the existence of an ideal political life survive disillusions in Europe's marches in the east, might not seeds of eventual salvation for Europe survive there underneath moribund ideology and lushly growing bureaucracy? It just might be that eastern Europe's centuries-old longing to be a full and equal part of Europe, to be accepted in her western part as more

---

4. The metaphor refers to the emblems of the French Communist and Socialist parties.

than always a nuisance and (from before Sobieski to Stalin) occasionally the military savior, would wrest from the West's disarray the substance and the mandate for a decisive east European contribution to Europe's future.

The contribution would have to be vital if partial moral conquest were to do duty for total military victory and permit discounting the geographic source and social-philosophical auspices of such a victory. Alternatively, if the not-yet fully degenerated political idealism among eastern European intellectual elites were to combine with the practical materialism of the proletarians in a genuinely classless upheaval, an eastern Europe that had substantially transformed Communist rule might yet qualify for decisively accelerating Europe's lagging progress toward some form of unification.

As for western Europe, the ghost of Eurocommunism lately haunting her distributed about equal terrors in Moscow and Washington. It may do so again. Will or could Eurocommunism be a more clearly definable and effective synthesizer of the East and West in Europe than any direct impact from the east—not only as Russia was Europeanized, but as Communism was de-Asianized? Another and different new start might then offer itself. Instead of Frankish Carolingia, the point of departure would be the Communist revolution *as if* it had taken place, and since mellowed, in socially and economically ripe Germany in 1918 and not in retrograde Russia a year earlier; as if the Prague spring of 1968 were not needed to recall the peoples' spring of 1848. Bridges could be built and socio-political systems integrated between eastern and western Europe while a Berlinguer or post-Berlinguer doctrine for the latter coupled humane Communism with commitment to both political and economic communitarianism, and while U.S. doctrine and policy allowed for consolidating Soviet sway in eastern Europe economically in exchange for political humanization of that sway.

If there is no *lux e tenebris,* finally, and if eastern darkness were to reclaim instead all efforts to dispel it from Europe's western flank under radical auspices, could a spark flying from the Far West breathe new life into occidental *ignis fatuus* under essentially liberal signs? In order to do so, western Europe's recoil from the post–de Gaulle moral and economic morass would have to meet halfway with America's reascent from post-Vietnam dejection. Moreover, the reascent would have to avoid the route back to parochial conceit, bred by ages of American insulation from outside hindrance to the capacity for increasing power without sacrificing good conscience. It would have to lead forward to a larger, interallied conception of a still-necessary imperial role for the West in managing interstate order.

New threats or dangers have been the unsuspected consequences of America's self-inflicted defeat in Asia. OPEC has laid siege to the industrial western city and a Soviet-Cuban alliance has probed the African periphery. The late American diplomatic strategies and political attitudes have been, in the main, mechanisms for coming to terms with one of two ills: the overadvertised demerit of an allegedly imperialistic intervention, or the still-suppressed sense of collective ego diminution from a national failure as unprecedented as the nature of the test itself. As the newest show in town, the grand diplomacy of triangular balance of power reduced the Vietnam tragedy to the status of a mere curtain raiser; the new stress on military hardware issues made possible the continuation of conservative hawkishness by other means; the reemphasis on human rights promised to carry the cold war-damaged liberal ship around the cape of good intentions toward utopia—just as their support of the cold war/imperial engagement had previously done penance for the liberals' backing of the wrong party to the Spanish civil war; and an ailing U.S.-Soviet détente provided materials for querulous rhetoric that replaced risky reengagement of physical resources.

The hidden purpose was on all scores the same: to gain a psychological respite for the body politic and to discover an optimum framework of policy for rehabilitating damaged foreign policy elites or qualifying new aspirants. The agitation in the corridors of power did little more than occupy the *entr'acte* before the dramatic theme would again begin to unfold in earnest on the global stage.

Atlantic confederacy for intervention vs. alliance for integration   A restoration of public morale and of elite mandate is likely to require, first in America, a resolute response to a threat as meaningful to the public at large as it is manageable by the governmental agents. Such threat is not, for the moment, military and does not come from the Soviet Union in Africa any more than in Europe. It is economic and, by extension, moral. And while it occurs in the third world, it is ultimately lodged within the West. If OPEC did not unleash the economic aggression that others would imitate if they could, that aggression would have had to be wilfully incited. At some point, in danger of strangulation from the outside or of asphyxiation from within, the West may rediscover the resolve for an act of self-defense that would arrest slippage, refurbish dimmed values, and confer upon it the undeserved boon of yet another new beginning.

If and when this happens, it will be imperative for western Europe that she be not again saved, and further infeodated, by America; that she not pay for yet another demonstration of Atlantic interdependence with the near-depleted treasure of European independence; that she not make up for passivity in the face of threatened ends with protests against means, and for lack of action by a surfeit of accusations. America's postwar empire, if it revives, ought to be multilateralized; America's infantile nationalism, blending inefficient patriotism with complacent chauvinism, should be imperialized; and Europe ought to be decolonized psychologically, lest she also fall behind the emancipated objects of her own one-time imperialism in the all-important sphere of elite mood and public spirit. Change can happen only if an Atlantic confederacy forged in active military intervention replaces a stillborn Atlantic community invented by political rhetoric, and if a partnership-in-risk committed to the recovery of safe resources makes redundant yet another grand design made in Washington.

Only a show of firmness abroad might preempt mass support in Europe for yet stronger internal reactions to enforced lowering of expectations, ending the capacity of functionally overextended and politically weak middle-class regimes to prolong tenures by sating ever greater consumer appetites.

In preparation for such an occasion, the encouragement will have to come from America, while the execution, should it come, must be in fair degree European. The shared experience could not avoid being bracing for both partners. A steel bath taken together might alone undo, at least in part, the consequences for western European morale of America's Suez betrayal. A truly new Europe and a true western alliance might then be born and again exert political, alongside economic, magnetism beyond the Oder-Neisse line.

American logistical support for the French and Belgian paratroopers sent (in May 1978) to deal with an Angola-based invasion of Zaïre has been a step, if a very small one, in that direction. Earlier, post-Suez western disunity was alive in the reactions to the 1973 war in the Middle East and the subsequent oil crisis. When western European governments denied over-flight rights to U.S. miliary supply planes headed for Israel, they turned the tables on the United States for its lack of solidarity with the embattled English and French in 1956. The basic reason was the same: to curry favor with the Arab powers; the difference was that the American motivation had been mainly political, while the European motives were by then solely economic.[5]

Failing a resolute western response to the economic threat, no direct military threat was likely to stimulate soon either unity or revival. To be

---

5. The Middle Eastern situation in a yet later period, following the Egyptian president's visit to Jerusalem, illustrated vividly the dimension of will as it relates to the issue of war and peace and the price nations are prepared to pay for the latter. It could still be believed in the late spring of 1978, but not a year later, that Sadat's feat of psychological peacefare would *not* do for the Israeli psyche what improved military performance in 1973 had done for the Egyptian soul, and would not prepare the soil for a separate peace on terms that restored Egypt's territorial integrity but further reduced both Egyptian and Israeli political and economic independence.

Only on the still outstanding West Bank issue did Prime Minister Begin seem to cling to what had previously appeared to be his more generally applied posture: that he would have peace only if it confirmed Israel in the possession of a mini-empire in the Roman style, complete with armed transfrontier colons and both indebted and infeodated "friends." In defiance of liberal American dogma, Begin seemed to act on the correct assumption that history did *not* teach clearly that security based on power and territory was any more fragile than peace based on bracing, a threat has to be intensely felt as one that is both relevant and manageable. A military attack from the east in Europe was not felt to be likely. In addition, postheroic west Europeans were certain to experience an actual military assault as an event that could not be managed at a reasonable cost and ought not to be met by resistance at all costs for the Europeans.

Low-cost conventional resistance would be sufficient and, therefore, possible only in a virtually simulated conflict that acted as a cathartic release from accumulated tension and was a catalyst for restructuring the psycho-political environment of deadlocked negotiations. In any larger conflict, effective military resistance in Europe would almost certainly have to be in some form nuclear. It was likely to spare the heartlands of the reciprocally immunized superpowers and place on the United States the onus of deciding to initiate the first strike. An American president would then act less as a surrogate for the Europeans than as an imperfect substitute for a doomsday machine. The nuclear means of defense may have been bestowed by providence on mature and sophisticated industrial societies just in time as the only feasible safeguard against rougher barbarians; it was apt to consummate in practice the unwillingness of such societies to defend themselves at all. The paradox is regrettable for American planners. The irony is that for a different mentality to be perpetuated, western Europe had to be unified and repoliticized around a separate nuclear deterrent while martial values had not yet wholly disappeared with the disappearance of the World War II generation. Such a development was strenuously opposed by successive U.S. administrations.

The key military-strategic problem for the United States, for U.S.-European relations, and for Europe's future was not henceforth how to limit conflict in the European theater by means of American and Soviet self-

---

protestations of good will and that before haphazardly assembled peoples—Israeli no less than American—could become nations, they might first have to prove themselves fit to endure the ordeal of empire.

While the Israeli and Egyptian parties to the negotiations had been waiting for the maturation of the American willingness to open an expanded—and, in due course, virtually unlimited?—line of credit to both, their will to reach agreement expressed a sober estimate of each nation's capacities to endure further hardships of any kind. But their tactics and pronouncements also reflected a well-founded estimate of the West as a political culture that places the comforts of appeasement above all other values and shrinks back (in bad conscience?) from acts of sturdy fortitude, including those it might share in only by proxy. As a means to offset the mood, dramatizing Soviet inroads in the area has been tempting, but no more unimpeachable than to calibrate by narrowly oil-related requirements of Saudi moderation or survival the degree of pressure to exercise on Israel's will to sacrifice on the altar of instant peace. A measure of accepted Soviet regional presence was as much of a precondition to stabilizing a comprehensive settlement as the scope of appropriate concessions on non-Egyptian issues was implicit in the security advantages Israel chose to derive from an initially separate pacification.

restraint. It was instead how much the United States would have to expand such a conflict in order to stay in the running for a later and decisive intercontinental phase of a duel with the Soviets. That phase was not likely to be part of or immediately follow the engagement inside the mutually adjoining western and eastern continental European *glacis* of the super-powers; it would more probably only climax an intervening spell of a simplified, Orwellian balance of power and confrontation between their heartlands.

The main options for an American president would be correspondingly polar and simple. He might commit American strategic power to completing the destruction of the west European industrial production base. The object would be to delay Soviet readiness for the final round while the United States withdrew provisionally into a garrison state behind the screen of a neo-Stimsonian doctrine of nonrecognition of the fruits of aggression. Or the president might concede western Europe relatively intact. The expectation would be that cultural softening and moral decomposition would ooze eastward as part of the material influx, that incorporating western Europe into what was once and might then again be called the socialist common-wealth would do for the Eurasian Soviet empire what reintegrating westernized Kiev had not quite done for Russian orthodoxy based on Muscovy (and what, *ex hypothesi,* Eurocommunism failed to do peacefully in the period before the conflict).

The Soviets would face a comparable key question. Ought they or ought they not to˙expand the intra-European conflict, not so much westward as eastward toward China? Leaving Chinese industrial and nuclear capability intact would risk losing the war politically in the process of winning the first stage of the military battle with the West. It would risk setting the stage for either an unstable three-power balance or a rigid Soviet encirclement as the first-stage outcome locked China more firmly than before into the American alliance and removed any remaining American qualms about turning China into a first-class nuclear power before the Soviets had time to integrate a restored western European potential into their armory.

Such a scenario may be far-fetched. But it is more plausible than are scenarios for a successfully managed, limited conventional or nuclear war in Europe that is more than warlike simulation for a diplomatic purpose. If so, common military *action* outside Europe (be it Africa or its Middle Eastern extension) is all the more superior in the political potential it harbors for the West than is any conceivable coordination of military *capabilities* for joint defense. This is not the least true at a time when technocrats of defense proliferate subtly unmanning scenarios of the most arcane, presumably force-economizing, kind.

Varieties of dangers and remedies:
economic threat and political rationality

An economic threat is most serious over time if it fluctuates in intensity—rising one day in the form of one-commodity embargoes and more broadly based revolts against the status quo while subsiding another day into the pursuit of only moderate adjustments of western-style economic order. Nor is its internally debilitating impact any less if economic superiority is overrelied upon in relations with a militarily strong great power such as the Soviet Union; if military recourse is limited to politically and economically feeble countries such as former French Africa and abdicated in relations with economically overassertive states; or, comprising all the above, if the world is perceived overwhelmingly through the prism of economic values and instruments giving rise to something like economism.

Such being the multifaceted nature of the economic threat, it is not enough to prescribe or implement specific responses to it. More important is to modify the fundamental attitudes of the parties threatened. The setting for specific actions and general attitude has been conditioned, among other things, by the failure to consummate prior approaches to European unity, including the Gaullist. The drive and the chances for a politico-military European unity subsided as the economic threat from outside Europe rose. It is possible that, at least provisionally as a result, progress toward European unification ceased to be an urgent immediate goal and became only one optional means to an effective western response.

Beyond functionalism and diplomatic strategy for unification   In the early 1960s, a potentially fruitful sequence seemed to be unfolding in Western Europe: from an economically prepared liberal-constitutional phase of unification efforts to a conservatively innovating phase characterized by diplomatic strategy.[6] Since then, conditions have changed sufficiently to prompt measures yet more dramatic than diplomatic strategy: united military action

6. That was the main thesis, or cardinal premise, in the author's *Europe Ascendant: The International Politics of Unification* (Baltimore: Johns Hopkins Press, 1964). The following discussion refers repeatedly to that book when the earlier conditions and assumptions are differentiated from the more recent ones. As is possible to infer from the discussion, the Gaullist strategy was originally identified as one that employed spectacular thrusts, disintegrative of existing NATO arrangements, with the aim of compelling a loose unification *within* a diplomatically confined European area (partially separated from the Anglo-Saxon powers) and *around* the French nuclear and a Franco-German political nucleus. The strategy leaned on largely realized preconditions (enumerated in what follows) and aimed at increased independence in defense and foreign policy for western Europe and at a progressive removal of the East-West division in Europe as a whole.

as the last resort. The liberal-constitutional first phase, centering on the European community idea, had been pan-Atlantic in bias; the second, or strategy-centered approach, identified with Gaullist France, was anti-Atlantic in spirit. The latest perspective is again western, while continuing to be like the Gaullist approach complementary with a longer-range pan-European one. By the same token, to emphasize a common U.S.-European military action is to remain skeptical about the virtues of mere institutional consolidation[7] and to stress more than ever the social contract forged in joint effort.[8]

It is no longer enough to rely on the potential of mere military deployments, such as a U.S.-Soviet nuclear stalemate, to facilitate a diplomatic strategy by reducing European confidence in American deterrence or defense. The focus changes correspondingly from conviction and compulsion to coercion. Economic interests and political responses can converge in a shared conviction inspiring the design for unity characteristic of the liberal-constitutional phase. It will require a diplomatic strategy to compel unity to move beyond the degree achieved out of conviction, in preference to even less desirable alternatives arising out of the existing—e.g., NATO-type—relationships being deliberately disintegrated by the strategist. As for coercion, it is implicit both in the threat of economic aggression and in forceful response to such aggression. The progression is thus one from ostensible freedom in creating institutions, via a necessity that has been diplomatically contrived from within, to an extraneously imposed, near-physical necessity to act.

In the supranationalist phase, functional integration responded to positive economic inducements and either prepared or coincided with cooperative institutions building. The Gaullist strategy added to the functional stimulus and objective a diplomatically staged impetus toward concerting and executing an independent foreign policy by the west Europeans. Both kinds of incentives and goals have been yet more recently superseded by a species of normative imperative for a joint redemption from distress, including the economic one, for the entire West. It would be too much to say that the latest need and needed response replicate those of post–Roman Christian Europe facing economic disintegration and economically (as well as otherwise) induced disarray.[9] It is not too much to say that the latest need is for a revised interplay between power and norm, as action replaces capability in the dimension of power and morale takes the place of morality in the normative realm. The Marxists ask: is capitalism viable without the prop of a massive armaments industry? And the liberals ask: is representative democracy

7. *Europe Ascendant,* p. 82.
8. Ibid., p. 50.
9. Discussed in *Europe Ascendant* at the beginning of the second chapter ("The Conditions of European Unity"), pp. 21 ff.

compatible with imperial exertions abroad? To these queries it is becoming urgent to oppose another interrogation: can the civic bases of an affluent liberal-capitalistic democracy survive unless armed action restores from time to time the commitments traditionally rooted in austerity?

New threats and old problems with responses   A basic change in the quality of dominant threat constitutes one kind of authentic revolution in international politics; failure of commensurate response may be only falsely represented as marking a forward evolution in dominant rationality. The key threats that legitimately conditioned the earlier approach were politico-military: Soviet nuclear blackmail more than aggression; divisive even more than redundant nuclearization in western Europe; Franco-German disunity as much as a debilitating American hegemony. The related assumption was that economic growth and integration were positively even if insufficiently underpinning the potential of non-Communist Europe to become again a political power as well. That assumption failed to anticipate the economic dislocations that have transpired since and the related danger of politically divisive and psycho-logically degenerative approaches to material self-preservation by insecure or improvident governments.

The United States was unable to provide either assured or adequate protection against both the military-political and the economic threats. But it was invariably opposed to an independent European response: first by separate nuclear force (outside the only fictitiously separate and independent multilateral nuclear force—the MLF), later by separate economic deals (with the Middle Eastern members of OPEC). The U.S.-sponsored association of oil consumers resembled the MLF project in that both favored continued leadership of a United States that needed both the least. In addition, both favored a steady rise of a West Germany best able to absorb their costs, to the detriment of France and her initiatives. The risk in each case was that the West would be polarized within itself well before assuring effective protection against the outside.

Related to similarities in response were parallels bearing on responsibility for response. Opposing abuses of oil producers by means of economic reprisals is on a par with counterforce nuclear strategy, in that challenge and response are qualitatively identical in both cases. Matters are different when threats of a military response are supposed to deter another oil embargo or a continuing price escalation. The resulting qualitative disparity between source or kind of aggression and kind or target of retaliation is then the same as it is in countercity nuclear strategy. Disparity between action and reaction requires extra political will to compensate for any material inadequacy or moral dubiety inhibiting the response. Yet in both the military and the economic contexts the west Europeans were reduced to only a supporting role: conventional military in the nuclear setting, only auxiliary in the economics of recycling and investing in the oil setting, while they questioned the efficacy of American acts for their defense or liberation and had reason to fear the effects on their independence if such acts were efficacious.

Beneath the surface that encourages easy analogies, the difference between the two threats is cardinal. Whereas the military menace has been hypothetical, the economic threat has been present and real. A hypothetical military threat has, moreover, a greater potential for eliciting a politically creative—including multilateral—response than does an effective economic threat. The latter is more likely to invite materially self-serving and politically self-saving unilateralism. The response to the economic threat may, therefore, have to be militarized on occasion before the consequence of either threat or response can become politically productive. This is not least true for actors that are politically dependent, as are the west Europeans. Their economically defined interests will be more divisive, and their responses more erratic, than the militarily or diplomatically strategic interests and responses of actors enjoying a high measure of autonomy in the international system, as the Europeans did before World Wars I and II. The economic pressures on political dependents may be no greater than the existential pressures on independent powers; however, the constraints on them are fewer, regardless of whether inhibitions come from environing structures, internalized rules of action, or the immediate risks attaching to short-term opportunism.

The eclipse of political and rise of economic rationality   So to argue is to reach beyond one kind of rationality to another. When practicing economy of force, economizing rationality will automatically search out for a means of limiting the application of force in any one instance and time period. Political rationality will, by contrast, give equal consideration to calculated acts of terror or the deliberately fostered impression of awesomeness for more concentrated dramatic effect at less final or aggregate cost. Economizing rationality will also prefer incremental acts of continuously adjustable and reversible organization of resources (e.g., the Marshall Plan, NATO, MLF, SALT, and the like) over an irreversible assumption of risks in diplomatic maneuver or military action. The *conceptual* consequence is to domesticate the approach to foreign policy by transferring thither from the more permissive (i.e., domestic) system dubiously applicable postulates and practices. The postulates concern routinely manageable risks and replicable opportunities; the practices are centered on marginally adjusting compromises. The *practical* result is to subordinate foreign policy goals and methods to domestic imperatives or to construe the external goals to fit the internal needs. Such an economically conditioned integral domesticism was manifest in the western

European approach to the Middle East and Africa in particular; it increasingly determined western approaches to international issues in general.

The declension from political to economic rationality may be a function of growing sophistication or just social aging. Accordingly, politics first was the proper stance of the founding fathers of the new states-minus-nations—such as, most recently, Nkrumah and Sukarno—unmindful of developmental or any other economics. The intermediate stage is a balanced approach to political economy by mature societies such as that of multinational western Europe in the mid-1960s or binational Canada relative to the Quebec issue, up to a point. The balance is discarded in favor of all-out economic rationality, or economism, in old countries governed by frightened or fatigued regimes that aim to diffuse opulence while often promoting localized anarchy or terror. Post-Fascist Spain and post-authoritarian Portugal individually and post-de Gaulle western Europe as a whole may belong, or be on the way to belonging, to that category.

In the interwar period, political rationality was overshadowed in interstate relations by its normative component of a special, formalistic kind. The result was the League of Nations syndrome. Political rationality revived in the post–World War II rediscovery of power politics but had to compete with its technical military-strategic component of a peculiar, economizing kind. While anything but receding, strategics has been lately challenged for primacy by integrally economic rationality. Economism escalated with the need to formulate responses to OPEC and, in part, also to the Soviets from a declining political base. It reflected the new style of devious coercion effected by OPEC in regard to the West and implemented the attempt by the West to check the Soviets in Africa and elsewhere (i.e., by manipulating technological transfers and the most-favored-nation clause). The trend reflected a shift in the most likely locus of cataclysmic upheaval, away from a nuclear holocaust. It also promoted the shift of chief danger to the collapse of western morale and will, a more-than-formal aspect of the normative dimension.

During the cold war, political rationality was applied self-consciously. On occasion it was applied somewhat simplistically, as when exaggerating—especially in connection with foreign aid for third-world liberal economic development—the utility of an overburdened economic factor as an instrument of power and control for essentially conservative ends. No equivalent political challenge has so far replaced the sources of the cold war. The void has favored a reaction in favor of unchecked utilitarianism in both private calculations and the formulation of public policies. Postwar liberal thought reacknowledged the central role of power in the reigning version of political realism, if mainly for the purpose of reining in the wielders of power. Partial rehabilitation has yielded again to virtually unqualified condemnation of the use of force as an instrument for both contriving and controlling social change.

Sources of past failure and future prospects:
ideas vs. implementation

What factors and errors turned the prospect of Europe's de Gaulle-style foreign policy ascendancy into a prelude to domestic anarchy in 1968 and stagnation since? Gradually eroded or suddenly gone from among the key factors—or material conditions of unity—was the domestic base, the diplomatic leverage, and a firm sense of goal.[10] This left only the neo-Victorian international setting, expanded by the appearance of a new collective economic great power, and succession to Europe as the stake competed over by a changing array of fragile middle powers (including, for a time, the neo-Persian empire).

Adverse developments and avoidable errors   Reestablishment of authority within states was seriously set back after 1968, weakening one prerequisite to interstate unification. As a self-styled social revolutionary girded with the tricolor, de Gaulle followed in the steps of the "white revolutionary," Bismarck. The erosion of his rural base was dramatized by the sudden eruption of an urban-intellectual would-be proletariat that was both ultrared and denationalized. The defeat of that attempt at revolution did not revive in full the earlier trend toward stable authoritative government by the executive power. Partially as a result, leveling for a so-called new society replaced, as the operative slogan, upward movement of renewed Europe in the international hierarchy.

The damage was in the end limited because diplomatic leverage had collapsed even before the erosion of the domestic base. American foreign policy after Kennedy demoted the Grand Design for Atlantica to second place behind a Great Society for America before becoming inconclusively engaged in Asia. This reorientation was attended by the Soviet shift from France-in-Europe to the U.S.-in-Germany as the preferred partner in détente—if not yet entente. Under Lyndon Johnson, the vacuum of U.S. reaction to de Gaulle's strategy either restored or only reemphasized American incapacity to lead for an alternative. More importantly, apathy proved lethal for the strategy, where Kennedy's earlier opposition had been energizing. When frontal resistance dissolved on the American side and indirect support faded

10. The "material conditions" are set out in *Europe Ascendant* on pp. 46 ff. For the "neo-Victorian" era of (essentially) multipolarization, see *ibid.,* pp. 8–13, and for "succession to Europe," pp. 13–20.

on the Soviet side, the result was to compound the standing handicap of the master strategist, weakness in his own deployable resource. Encountering a void, de Gaulle's strategic thrust became a quixotic gesture, a *baroud d'honneur* for a cause waiting to be put to rest by the policy reversal of Adenauer's successor. Moscow would not provoke the United States in Europe diplomatically while aiding Hanoi militarily in Asia; the Bonn of Erhard went "all the way with LBJ" while taking the first of its unrequited small steps toward Pankow.

One more ingredient of the strategy was relaxed by the resumed momentum toward British membership: the political confinement of continental western Europe, differentiated from the maritime Anglo-Saxons. The breached confinement was wholly disrupted when the slowdown in economic expansion reintensified dependence on the United States. An era came to a close while the equilibrium-hegemony issue gravitated from a de-crystallized political to a disintegrating economic sphere.

Adverse developments actually occurring (war in Vietnam) and reverses in the making (U.S.-Soviet détente, Britain's inclusion, the Arab-Israeli war and its related oil crisis) reduced the bearing of any error by the chief strategist. De Gaulle refused to adopt for western Europe Bismarck's prediction about unified Germany: once in the saddle, she would learn to ride. His one real resource was the French nuclear asset. He finally refused to employ it for compelling unity within the narrowest west European frame around nuclear defense, preferring to risk the alternative of political atomization. It does not matter whether he feared more that Germany might unseat the French horseman or that it might upset the Franco-Soviet team work—and with it the East-West applecart. De Gaulle was likewise unable to achieve what Bismarck had managed on the next larger scale. He failed to span the hiatus between a western European (Bismarck's north German) and the all-European (Bismarck's all-German) solution, in part because he seemed unwilling to decide between a Soviet-centered and a satellite-centered approach to eastern Europe. But if his sentimental journey to Warsaw was still among the causes of failure, the later worldwide wanderings from Phnom Penh in behalf of neutralized southeast Asia to Montreal in behalf of French Quebec merely expressed failure among the ruins of the strategy's largest, global setting.

Soviet and American wing-powers and Europe's central values   To what extent does or must frustration of the hypothesized Gaullist scenario for European unification invalidate presuppositions about the wing powers, Soviet Russia and America? Past failure does not dispose of the notion that the unity idea would spread eastward "in intensified form."[11] Within the range of three

---

11. *Europe Ascendant,* p. 110.

main Soviet options or alternative postures—détente with the United States for nuclear arms control; partnership with western Europe of a weakened and Europeanized Soviet Russia; and preeminence in all of Europe of a strong one[12]—the second has been more visibly fading than the other two. It faded along with the prospect of a Sino-European or specifically Sino-German squeeze on the Soviet Union. Even a moderately upstaged U.S.-Chinese normalization made the west Germans fear that precipitation in that quarter would spell provocation of the Soviet Union. Western Europe was simultaneously ceasing to qualify as a privileged receptacle or attractive magnet for Soviet concessions on the subject of control forms in eastern Europe. She was turning instead into a moral vacuum that was neither threatening nor attractive diplomatico-strategically. The greater the vacuum, the more eligible the western part of the Continent was for realizing the third Soviet option by transferring eastward, away from postindustrial United States, the capacity for protecting it against economic (as distinct from nuclear) blackmail.

A major shift in relative power and pull might transform two loosening blocs in Europe into two communicating vessels, with the natural consequence for the initially disparate socio-economic substance or governmental forms. Any convergence, to change the metaphor, might spring less from mutual attraction than from parallel recoil from different parts of the non-European world. It might be aided further by any remaining capacity of the west Europeans to participate vicariously in the upgrading of the Continent's power and prestige in the world at large: faced with a choice between several kinds of barbarians, the west Europeans may end by choosing their Russian cousins.

What about the American wing power? In the early 1960s, it operated amidst declining military pressures on NATO. The automatic reaction of the leading ally was to look for compensating ways of reaffirming diplomatic hegemony *within* the alliance. The tendency called forth, and in principle ought to have favored, de Gaulle's separatist response to alliance integration and its integrative intent for a separate European association. The more recent setting is one of increased economic pressure from the third world. This has created different dilemmas for both the leading ally and the subordinate allies, dilemmas that might be corrigible only by updating the American, or innovating a joint western, imperial performance *outside* the alliance as part of a reconcentration within it.

To deemphasize instant politico-economic unity in western Europe is to stress a higher or prior object: the revitalization of a political civilization that grew out of Europe. This civilization can be defined as one that ultimately

12. Ibid., p. 114.

rated ideal over material values; was actively creative or Faustian, rather than passively enduring and pervasively otherworldly; was deferential vis-à-vis ideas (including its sustaining idea of self) more than toward men and, since men incarnate ideas unequally, was elitist rather than egalitarian; and, since it was keyed to realizing its potential to the full, was liable to subordinate individual self-determination to collective self-realization if and when the procedure and the achievement clashed in irresoluble conflict. It is thus a civilization that cannot long survive prolonged political apathy. Nor can it long endure side by side with the renunciation of one set of goals (transpersonal ideal) and the gratification of only one set of needs (material individual).

While the economic strength of western Europe was rising, it served as an impetus to downgrading intraregional functions and institutions as the main determinants and expressions of unity and, along with an enhanced role, of more-than-economic strength. Regional and economic horizons were replaced, first and foremost by de Gaulle, with global and politico-diplomatic perspectives as the chiefly inspiring and controlling ones. With the rise of economic difficulties and economically induced disunities, it has become necessary to regress, beyond even the narrowly regional and functional ambit, to intrapersonally manifested modes of recovering group integrity, as the preliminary to attempting any further significant progress in integration.

It is possible to rediscover an older self in the act of meeting a contemporary challenge. Yet impatience can be a still greater academic pitfall than fundamental error. Is it not too soon to abandon the stress on strategic action by the inspired leader and adopt a politico-fundamentalist approach only a moment in time after the neofunctionalists have moved from economically conditioned automaticity in the personalist direction?[13] The time required to close the lacunae between normative ideas, idea-implementing strategies, and supporting structural conditions is even less easy to predict than it is to guess at the operative connections between the several components in the abstract and outside time. Among the requisites of a working Wilsonian world view were antiwar public opinion, economic interdependence, and intangibility of territorial states. Some of these have been surfacing only recently; the world view may merit some disinterment; but we are still far from a working collective security. By the same token, it is quite possible that functional integration will slowly grind its way ahead in the absence of an economic upheaval. That does not mean, however, that a diplomatic strategy from within western Europe is about to effect even a loose

13. See Roger Hansen's review article of the relevant literature ("European Integration: Forward March, Parade Rest, or Dismissed?") in *International Organization*, Spring 1973.

political unification; it is least likely to do so if no psychological shock from outside the sphere of either manipulative or managerial foreign policy generates a fresh impetus.

European unity in and for individual freedom and collective independence may still prove to be an *idée-force* for the future, waiting for the gap with reality to be progressively narrowed and then quite suddenly closed. But that same idea may also prove to be no more than a myth, distorting facts in order to accredit a fiction. As such, it may be headed for regression as its formal aspects—to wit, its institutional shape and geographic scope—are dissolved in the global politics of economic interdependence and ethnic-cultural communalism, or as its effective thrust fails to simultaneously breach and assimilate the eastern way of imposing political dependence while dispensing with spurious transnational overlays.

Postscript 1. A Meeting of Europe's East with the West

For the West to survive as a leading power and civilization, it must reacquire a purpose, if no other than to renew itself in a way that expands the benefit it has long derived from individual east European exiles. Because such exiles are individuals, they personify the striving of eastern Europe toward the West's political ideals and models, as well as her divergence from many of the western modes of social life and individual feeling. Because the individual exile has removed himself from the social contract, he lays bare the points of contact and the lines of cleavage between West and East.

Eastern Europe is neither pure West nor integral East; nor is the political exile from eastern Europe either an emigrant or an immigrant: there are not two different words for "exile," one denoting departure and another arrival. Eastern Europe is suspended between West and East; the exile likewise lives poised between the land of birth and the land of refuge. His rejection of what proved intolerable in the past is vindicated when he transforms the hurt into energy for crystallizing that hurt in positive thought or action; his present is bearable only so long as progressions (as the exile learns) keep pace with regressions (as he remembers). Between the memory of a stealthy flight and the expectation of a proud return, the political exile acts out his role as the supreme winner and the supreme loser in history's revolutions. He wins as the man of character who defines himself by the individual potential he has realized: whether he returns to his homeland or not, he will have been greater in the end than he was meant to be in the normal course of events. He loses as a common man who lives in order to have his share of panhuman possibilities: stranger if he stays, he will be more bitterly so if he returns.

The exile neither emigrates nor immigrates. When leaving his native land, he leaves behind the right to find a new home for the spirit. He is the eternally recurring Comenius of politics, trying to teach the settled nations the whys and wherefores of things that made him what he is and exalting, either in counsel or censure, what can only thus become partly his. He may swear loyalty to a foreign prince but can fulfill the oath of allegiance only if he denies himself the comforts of assimilation. The failure to adapt fully to either society or culture that is not his own is made of both refusal and inability. It is also the exile's repayment for the grant of refuge. Since he has received, he must give. And, in order to offer a return in kind, he must give something singularly his own. He is the sympathetic witness, seeing from the outside while dwelling within. Only thus can he look through his peculiar prism and say what may be said because it need not be listened to.

The exile from eastern Europe to the West will fulfill his function only when the conditions have passed away that make him into a legitimate political type; when he yields his place to cultural misfits and socially irrelevant aberrations from eastern Europe, akin to the one-time American expatriates to Europe; or when his unique identity has been dissolved in the mass phenomenon of psychological mutilation, alongside America's inner emigrants of today.

II
THE UNITED STATES
WITHOUT IMPERIALISM?

Post-Gaullist western Europe has failed to recapture *élan vital*, despite some institutional and economic moves forward—to wit, in the main, direct elections for the European parliament and projects for monetary union. But neither has America pushed on after Vietnam with her heralded greening, despite attempts at moral uplift from presidential and other pulpits. There has been instead a marked graying of America. The dullness has been one of a prematurely grizzled middle age, lacking even the kind of resignation that can pass for serenity and undeserving of the sense of the vanities that can pose as wisdom—both being the pallid, but honorable, rewards of having given one's full measure when still youthfully buoyant and filled with hopes. This monochromatic quality of life has come from avoiding the many-faceted contrasts, from blending into the intermediate hue the blacks and whites, that stimulate existence. In the field of foreign policy, those contrasts included America's overconfident outreach into the world and the bitter condemnation of that enterprise at its climax.

National experience prepared Americans for the insidious ordeal of unrelieved tedium even less than an older civilization and a heavier past had prepared Europeans. The so-far hidden war that broke the post-Vietnam peace has increasingly been between the qualities and the defects, the ideals and the self-deceptions, that characterized two eras of America's brief history. The earlier era of pretended innocence preceded World War II, the cold war, and the product of those two conflicts—the American empire; the more active period witnessed a forced-draft growing up and incidental corruption. The longing of late has been for a return to the values and the valuation of self, faintly and in part wrongly remembered from the earlier era; that longing has been given voice rather than real validation by Jimmy Carter's campaign for the presidency and its early exercise. The subsequent dulling of that aspiration has tended to confirm every possible suspicion that an unreal dream was about to give way to an awakening that would match, and might outdo, the just-survived nightmare.

Varieties of postempire experience: will-to-power and ways of power

Only in a longer retrospect will it be possible to say with confidence whether there actually was an authentic American empire. If there was one, it grew out of competition with the Soviets and was a substitute for the receding national power and colonial empires of the west Europeans. Many of the structures and much of the dynamics that denote empire were present; in the testing hour of truth, however, the forms and functions of empire proved to be deficient in spirit. Lacking has been the determination that makes structures endure a decent span of time and makes the dynamics produce a decent measure of devotion—to the task of empire management on the part of the nation's natural elites, and to the empire itself on the part of its dependents.

Residua of empire and the costs of its abandonment   What has remained, for the time being, as the residuum of an apparently receding empire? First, the multiethnic character of an imperial agglomerate has been compressed again into the domestic microcosm, and the microcosm has been further diversified by Asian refugees from the consequences of what was also America's defeat. It was possible to question the force of the moral imperative for a mass reception of fugitives fleeing from what was also *their* failure and coming to what was not necessarily an inferior substitute for success.[1] But any

---

1. Let me explain myself. There is every possible humanitarian ground for admitting refugees from a tyrannical or unpredictable regime, but there is neither an obvious criterion of selection nor a convincing limit on the numbers of the fugitives to admit on such charitable grounds. The rationale loses its solidity without acquiring structure when it shifts from a humanitarian to a political basis. It is no obvious duty for a retreating imperial power to carry off haphazardly assembled refugees from defeat in the last baggage train. Those who had sided with the subsequently defeated foreign power did so presumably for reasons of their own; the foreign power owes them nothing outside an effort proportionate to theirs.

Were the opposite principle to be admitted, the partisans of the foreign intervenor could only "win": they would either consolidate their positions in the home country by victory or escape the consequences of defeat into a psychologically precarious position but materially a not necessarily inferior or less secure one in the country of refuge. Since they could not but win, their incentive to prevent local defeat would diminish. The equations of contribution and cost as between the imperial power and its dependents would be deranged in consequence, and the

such questioning was made irrelevant by the promptings of bad conscience, not least on the part of the Americans who contributed most to the defeat.

Another residuum of empire was an oversized foreign policy and security bureaucracy; it had grown along with the so-called imperial presidency and survived in size the atrophy of the imperial function. The inherited bureaucracy served the nation both well and ill: it absorbed as the object of blame the nation's immediate frustrations with the flaws attending empire, but it has also threatened to accentuate, by its penchant for routine, the postempire trend to define foreign policy in terms of operationally manageable, tangible issues of economics and defense. Even the drawback was a virtue, however, when it acted as a counterweight to exercises in moralizing abstractions by a seemingly deimperialized chief executive.

No presumably hard-headed descent from high policy to low politics, however, any more than the soaring presidential fancy, could obscure the most important permanent residuum of the late empire. The potentially beneficial legacy was the loss of Americans' illusions about themselves and the world, and the fading of the world's illusions about America. Only the future will tell whether the loss was crippling or cleansing, and only later will we know whether the fading led to a more solidly based respect for America or whether it shaded off into a rejection of the American example as misleading and of America's very existence as, on balance, harmful. When existence and impact have been traced far enough into the past, Europeans may figure prominently among those injured by opting for a seemingly less costly alternative to painful intraregional adjustments to the ebb and flow of national power.

Much will depend on America's capacity to recover some of the drive that propelled her to empire, even as she revised the shape and size of her orbit of action. Thus far, the manifest alternatives to empire have proved to be no less costly, if different, in cost, than global policemanship. Some of the costs are material. They have included the consequences of the license that the loss of

---

psychic cost of defeat would compound the cost in prestige for the imperial power that acknowledged the expanded responsibility and of necessity could only partially implement it. The two consequences would immeasurably increase disincentives to future interventions, at an incalculable systemic cost.

There is a point at which protection is clearly owed to individuals who go beyond the call of duty or outside the compass of decent humanity in their contribution to the defense effort. The problem, then, is how to select them and how to time their evacuation. The problem is not solved by stigmatizing delays in such evacuation and the resulting disarray. Cf. Frank Snepp, *Decent Interval* (New York: Random House, 1977). The superficially plausible arraignment, by the Central Intelligence Agency operative, of the resident U.S. ambassador's delaying tactic on evacuation out of Saigon is fundamentally false—or, at least, false from a "higher" political viewpoint; nor is the dilemma overcome by indiscriminate and disorderly last-minute evacuation *en masse*.

awe before American power seemingly gave the oil-producing countries to turn the tables on the West for its alleged past exploitation. The briefly feared, and so-far contained, economic undoing of the West could still be put back on the agenda, not least ironically by the political undoing of the so-called moderates among the oil-producers, who are unable to master the many appetites aroused by their inordinate new wealth.

Other material costs were implicit in making peace in the world from a position of greater, if mainly self-ascribed, moral strength than real national strength. If it was only contemplated to buy out the white Rhodesian (and later South African?) settlers in Africa, the Israelis had actually to be bought out of the Sinai. They may have to be removed at cost from the West Bank in the next phase, and, if premature peace proves to be a prescription for terminal disaster, from the Middle East in the concluding phase.

To buy out the victims of half-negotiated and half-imposed pacification may be more uplifting than to sell out the victims of an ultimately abortive counterinsurgency. Yet to promote a peaceful order in the first manner as a means of saving lives or shielding American fortune, at least in the short run, resembles the second manner in that it, too, makes demands on American material resources. It is not necessarily immoral or unfeeling, moreover, to hold that there are circumstances when the expenditure of a nation's treasure is raised to a higher moral plane by the readiness also to spill the nation's blood. For a great power to lose a war waged in behalf of a dependent ally offsets the client's heavy loss by some, if lighter, loss incurred by the patron; the disparity in loss is justified by the disparity in stakes and interests. Engaging dependents in an even but potentially disastrous course of peace carries within it no potential for a comparable exoneration.

Compounding the material costs and the moral risks are the political costs of relinquishing global rule making for local peacemaking. These costs are inherent in the shortcomings of alternative foreign policies. Two strategies have been offered and favored as replacements of empire: building world order and developing détente. In the dominant interpretations, world order has chiefly economic connotations, and the strategy is addressed mainly to the third world; the idea of détente has chiefly arms-control connotations in relations with the Soviet Union, as part of a triangular interplay including China.

Enthusiasm for the world-order strategy has fostered images of world-wide interdependence between the industrial and the industrializing countries in economics and affirmations of equality of all states in politics. The actuality has been less benign. Inconclusive bargaining over a new global economic order between the more conflicting than consonant economic interests of the North and South was kept in line by relative capacities for economic blackmail, if by anything. Calls for equality among the new states and for the South as a whole were attended by the resurgence of hegemonic international politics in the third world, contained only because all indigenous parties were short on usable politico-military leverages. Western utopians, some of them in high places, foresaw the spread of the Swiss type of functional interlocking of diverse ethnic groups in mutually beneficial national and regional communities—first to the Middle East and from there beyond. In actuality, much of Africa and some of southeast Asia were indigenously predisposed to tribally inspired genocidal barbarism within and between ethnic groups, owing even temporary suspensions to the infusion of effective power from the outside.

Lately, the major-power intervener has increasingly been the Soviet Union, rather than the United States of America. The passing of initiative was as much due to America's post-Vietnam psychological and strategic disengagement as it was to the Soviet commitment, consequent on the Cuban missile crisis, to deploy more widely the means to world power. More lastingly dangerous than Soviet interventionism was American illusionism. Nothing else could sustain either the official or the academic notion that disengagement could be unattended by some dispossession; that even the smaller measure of actual disengagement from empire than advertised did not have to be made up for by a new balance, comprising substitute engagements by others. And if substitution by lesser regional powers (by way of devolution of responsibilities) was both weak and weakly promoted, reallocation of power in the form of influence and shreds of control between or among the greater world powers was bound to be all the more prominent.

Out of such self-deception first grew the misconception of détente and thereafter its spreading repudiation. The only viable meaning of détente was one differentiating the thaw from the cold war. The two superpowers would continue to limit competition over geo-political stakes to areas outside each other's reserved domain. But they would also dovetail a competition thus constrained with two new and interrelated factors: (1) the reconstruction of the strategic-nuclear plane in the direction of arms-controlled parity and (2) the (implicitly consented-to) corresponding redistribution of access and influence in the world at large.

In actuality, two successive American administrations rose to ever higher rhetorical heights when condemning one and all Soviet encroachments and implantations, at first notably in Africa. They chose to ignore two features bearing on the just-stated two-part definition of détente. One of these, Soviet penetrations in western Africa and in the Horn of Africa, took place in areas that the United States had, by previous conduct, transformed from an American reserved domain into the political equivalent of what international lawyers call *terra nullius:* land belonging to no one and, as such, free for effective occupation by anyone. Whereas Angola was made ownerless (in terms of a great-power presence) by prior American failure either to sustain the colonialism or to control the decolonization of the Portuguese ally and dependent, Ethiopia was cast adrift by the yet grosser failure to advise effectively and to conserve a foremost vassal of the American empire, the Abyssinian emperor.

Failure to practice, in the days of American preponderance, the measure of romanticism in behalf of clients that both strengthens and redeems empire was followed by the collapse of political realism when the search was supposedly on for an alternative to paramount power, in the form of balanced or diffused power. A realistic try at détente required, as its second defining feature, a strategy of linkage between the SALT negotiations to control strategic arms and the Soviet bid to construct a salt-water navy and acquire their own overseas empire. There was, however, no visible readiness to go slow on accepting parity in the abstract strategic domain if the Soviets went too fast too far in the geo-political arena. Instead, U.S. policy was one of disjunction and denunciation: disjunction between tolerance for strategic parity (or worse in some judgments) and intolerance of any Soviet move in the direction of complementary parity in the geo-political theater; denunciation of all Soviet successes while failing to count any Soviet setback and regression.

The failure to pursue a uniform strategy for both of these two vital arenas, with the aid of tactical linkage between them, could not but open up a conceptual gap within America's foreign policy. Once opened, the gap was doomed to widen, since it was then harder for the two parties first to evolve and then learn to apply updated rules of the game for the détente phase. The place to evolve and modify rules is still the geo-political ground and not yet (pending a nuclear exchange) the stratosphere; failing new rules, new facts cannot but heighten controversy. The controversy could not be stilled, and the conceptual gap within the policy could not be significantly narrowed any time soon, by the single and only apparently simple expedient of playing the Chinese card in triangular diplomacy. Nor could responsibility for the consequences of failure be effaced by any future disposition to meet the largely self-made challenge of a revived cold war in bilateral relations.

The impossibility of building a world order quickly and at little cost around the nonexistence of an ordering world power, together with the refusal to pay for disengagement through redistribution of global real estate, denoted an absence of both political realism and a sense of history. History in the shape of struggle for power among great and small states was supposed to come to an end whenever the United States chose to withdraw from the game, while keeping the gains of its prior winning streak. Realism disappeared with the rejection of both the expenditure of resources for implementing effective empire and the long-term risks implicit in any strategy of balancing power for later concert or deferred confrontation among great powers.

Carter's renovatio *and America's ward politics*   The repeal of history and the disavowal of realism signaled an almost unavoidable rebirth of a species of spiritual imperialism. That not-too-original American variety of action in and on the world meant a change for the American presidency, as practiced by Jimmy Carter's immediate predecessors. Depending on one's view of things, the chief executive either rose or sank from the role of imperator to the stance of inquisitor, the supreme guardian of doctrinal—specifically, liberal-democratic—orthodoxy. The American president would again sit in judgment over the nations, currently as to their practice of human rights and state power. And he would ordain peace among the peoples in the Middle East, in southern Africa, and beyond.

The newest inquisitor was better equipped than his role models had been, before America's entry into either of the two world wars. Yet even he, as both censor and pacifier, lacked the indispensable complement of the office: the executory arm of readily available secular power to intimidate the hesitant and extinguish the sinners. In his peace-imposing persona, he also lacked a valid moral basis. The right to impose peace derives from either a community of fate, the coercion by force, or the exercise of function. The first condition is present when one section of an ongoing community moderates another; the second is given when a victorious power dictates (a moderate?) peace to the vanquished; the third obtains in one of two circumstances—first, when an unabashedly imperial power undertakes and is unquestionably able to police indefinitely the consequences of a peace imposed as part of keeping order, and second, when two condominial great powers impose local pacification as both a condition and the outcome of their cooperation. The value for the universe of either of the two last-mentioned types of order can then be held to exceed any possible costs of imposed and enforced local peace for the parties immediately concerned.

Neither of these conditions has been present—or present in full—behind President Carter's all too-forceful mediation in the Middle East; neither of them has made less than presumptuous the Carter-Young approaches to southern Africa. The campaign for instant results has preempted longer organic developments. It has also intensified divisions within the parties to the various conflicts, as well as divisions between parties. Unless the peacemaker has inner assurance of the present and future capability and the will to coerce any future violators of a decreed peace at a cost that the disarmed victims of a violation can bear, he displays nothing so much as conceit. It is not surprising if the moral presumption is coupled with intellectual vanity: the age-old, ingrained conviction of the layman that he possesses the secret of shortcuts to political outcomes that have been impeded by professionally deformed specialists and passionally blinded participants. The shortcuts addict cannot but deny, or at least downgrade, the real long-term threat to vital interests, and to lives and fortunes, that is immanent in foreshortened approaches to quick solutions wrested from transient opportunity or transitory opportunism. The slightest delay or hesitation of the leader responsible for an embattled people will assume in the eyes of the foreign policy layman the quality of caprice. And the only partially idealistic pacifier will all the more hysterically denounce the pause before the leap from insecurity into uncertainty, the more he thinks and acts ahistorically and unrealistically. Such was the attitude of the American president after the U.S.-Israeli-Egyptian summit at Camp David in 1978, whenever the look of things changed for the worse once negotiations moved out of Franklin Roosevelt's Shangri-La.

While administrations come and go, Americans in and out of government will have to undergo some change of heart if they are to (1) adjust their course; (2) merely revise instead of reverse the commitment to an ordering role; and (3) incur as well as administer the constraints implicit in henceforth both a possible and unavoidable equilibrium politics among the major powers. They must also acquire or reacquire a missing component. The so-called will *to* power continues to be in plentiful supply so long as power can be won and held cheaply. More acutely missing has been a matured appreciation of the ways *of* power: not only how capabilities can be deployed as an act of instant policy and husbanded as a matter of political economy over the middle term, but also how powers tend to polarize in function of changing splits or schisms and how preeminent power gravitates over long period of times and across vast spaces within or outside a civilization.

It is not wholly irrelevant to recall that the American political intelligence either mismanaged or failed to bow before the impossibility to adjust peacefully, within a finite time frame and in a straight line of development, the key event of national history. That event, falling between the providential gifts of embryonic political nationhood and of world empire, was America's own South-North schism and shift in the center of gravity. The nation's political aptitudes have all too long continued to be tutored and exerted in the arena not so much of world as of ward politics, wherein a certain form of political realism and will-to-power sharpens the tactical, but has no room for the historical, sense. At no time, not even during the straightforward cold war clash with the Soviets and the Chinese, had Americans the occasion to contemplate seriously their attitude toward the exercise of power for a long-term purpose that had not been defined for them by the acts of adversaries or imposed upon them by the accidents of existence. From such self-interrogation, when both questions and answers must be self-generated, Americans recoiled more readily and instinctively than from the actual wielding of power. They disarmingly enjoyed the last-mentioned sport so long as the home team was winning and the out-of-town audience was not too hostile.

By keeping aloof from any serious engagement in the historical drama, Americans have avoided two extremes without evolving an original compromise. They neither did, nor did they need to, deploy the obsessive preoccupation with power of, say, modern German aspirants to the political kingdom when overreacting about evenly against the grosser features of their past balkanization and the subtleties of outside opposition to their globalization. Nor have Americans learned, and had the time to develop, the civilized deprecation of therefore no less assiduously nurtured power. They were no match, that is, for the more worldly among the late British incumbents of empire. A refined embarassment over past modes of acquiring superior power complements in such a case a keen practical sense of the difficulty to retain the advantage by the original means in the future. Since they lacked a settled attitude toward acquiring and keeping power, Americans inevitably also missed an elementary, if commonly overlooked, point about the ways of power. They failed to distinguish, in the attitude of others, betwen the period before and the period after attaining the position of acknowledged power and legitimized influence. They failed also to see that a nation or elite behaves one way when trying to force its way forward from behind and another way when reduced to maintaining a position on the strength of immaterial defenses and deterrents erected *pari passu* with the fading of material, or also moral, superiority. Nor did the American political mind always differentiate sharply enough between the smallest and the biggest arena, the world and the ward, and between the immediate specific stakes and long-term systemic objectives.

The laws of power, the axioms of the physics of politics, are few in number and, once abstracted from the flow of history, simple to state. For that reason alone, they often fail to gain intellectual authority with practitioners who are self-consciously either tough-minded or sophisticated. Nonetheless, these axioms should be respectfully taken into account, especially when the task is to isolate the comparatively secondary or impermanent, residual peculiarities in the behavior of one's opponents, be they cultural, ideological, or any other. Pointing to the distractions and brevity of political office holding in America is not an adequate answer to demands for a policy concept that has continuity because it reflects historical continuities. The trouble is as often with men as it is with institutions, with lack of commanding perspective as with oppressive routines.[2]

Varieties of strategic challenges and options: reactivation and reapportionment

The act of relating the short to the long view, the opportunistic to the historical perspective, takes place within concentric circles of ever more

2. Part Three makes clearer the meaning of the preceding remarks. The observations that immediately follow echo points made in Chapter 1 in a different context.

outward- and forward-reaching tactics and strategies. An immediate need has been to assess anew the costs and the risks of rehabilitating the American image at home and abroad by reactivating the capacity for politico-military engagement in the third world. The higher strategic task was to decide whom, and on what grounds, to oppose the least or accommodate the most among the many competing aspirants to greater power and influence.

Specific political crises and failures of effective response   Addressing the immediate need directly and the longer-term requirement indirectly meant effecting two changes in the Atlantic-Pacific arena. It may or may not be a paradox that the full satisfaction of the immediate need involved an only remote, if desirable, possibility, while it was an immediate necessity to make a beginning on the longer-term strategic objective. The first change, to recover the power to intervene, would ideally entail restructuring the American empire, or what was left of it, into one both smaller and more widely shared than its predecessor. Making all of the trading and industrial nations of the West, and possibly also Japan, capable of jointly intervening overseas is to aim at a working league or confederacy. Such a confederacy stops short of being a confederation, but it is more than a wasting coalition for peacetime organization and hypothetical military-strategic planning. If cooperation takes place where it matters, it will inhibit competitive economic loss-and-gain calculations and reciprocal diplomatic upstagings; it will save the western allies from repeating what they did during and following the 1973 war-and-embargo crisis in the Middle East.

The second change bears on reapportionment among the great powers. Its one component is discarding anti-Soviet rhetoric in favor of carefully selecting areas for demonstrating resolution. Applying pressure or force so as to pace the geo-political outreach of the Soviets is to make their expansion stay in step with offsetting internal and external evolutions, without denying—for all that—Soviet entitlement to overseas influence as a matter of unchangeable principle. The other component of the second change is to use the process of managing the Soviet egress from the inland ghetto as a means of reassuring China as to America's capacity to have her writ run in places of her choosing, without—for all that—allowing the Chinese to dictate the ways of American self-assertion against the Soviets, even as they tacitly reserve the right to arbitrate the duration and location of America's involvement.

Occasions for moving on both the narrower or the broader front were not lacking as the Carter administration itself moved into high gear. One suitable opportunity for joint western action may have presented itself in Africa in the early days of the South Rhodesian internal settlement between the whites and the blacks. Even if it did not, the case against supporting the settlement was not as clear, and its rationale ought not to have been as ideological (or, relative to the African "moderates," as opportunistic) as the American official stance seemed to indicate. So long as southern Africa could be plausibly earmarked as part of the West's reserved domain, drawing Soviet-equipped Cubans into a head-on clash in company with some blacks (virtually any blacks) or conspicuously deterring them from interference was superior to bewailing interminably the unopposed Soviet-Cuban successes with too many black Africans.

Other occasions, for actively promoting or preserving the conditions of viable détente and reapportionment, arose in Iran and in Indochina. Both were apparently missed, and their being missed mattered more than any longer-term outcomes that were not directly caused by American action.

In the southeast Asian conflict between Cambodian factions, the administration's impulse was to oppose Hanoi as the patron of the rebels and by implication defend the Phnom Penh incumbents, if both only verbally. Yet there was little ethical merit in defending the bigger domestic evil in order to impugn a lesser international one, in upholding genocidal tyranny against aggression. More to the point, it was impolitic to miss the opportunity for reducing the Soviet monopoly of influence in a Vietnam that did not yet constitute a reserved domain, least of all in the eyes of Hanoi; sympathetic reticence (if nothing more positive) on the Cambodian issue would have inserted the American presence in Hanoi diplomatically, just as prior reconstruction aid to the former foe would have done so materially. If the policy was impolitic, it was amateurish diplomacy to miss the opportunity for showing the new Peking leaders that, despite their spectacular turnabout (which was somewhat suspect also because it was not the regime's first since 1949), the United States continued to have its own policy, just as China insisted on having hers. It would have been statesmanlike to secure, via enlarged access to Hanoi, a tactful but elastic leverage over Peking on the Taiwan issue in particular—compensating for the new distance from the Nationalists—and on the course of Sino-American relations in general. It was always naive to assume that the stake of the U.S.-Vietnamese war was anything less than Hanoi's domination in all of formerly French Indochina. It would have been worse to believe, in the Cambodian context, that the war's battlefield outcome could be reversed by United Nations or any other kind of rhetoric. The argument had been advanced at the time of the American intervention in Vietnam that the intervention was unnecessary because of a Vietnamese nationalism and regional imperialism that were hostile to China, and that it was harmful because forestalling the outbreak of Sino-Vietnamese antagonism. The argument has since been proved technically correct, irrelevant as it was historically. So long as the United States was an imperial power, it had reasons implicit in its fundamental role and posture to oppose, as a matter of highest global strategy, any and all regional imperialisms inimical to unrestricted American access outside the narrowly defined Soviet orbit. Since the argument was technically correct, however, it was in the later contingency unsuitable for its one-time proponents, and not very sensible for anyone else, to oppose the validation of Vietnamese regional imperialism. It was least sensible to do so for spuriously practical reasons having to do with the ethics of the Vietnamese aggression and the expediency for the United States of appearing to condone that aggression, in disregard for Chinese feelings.

Now that the United States has come to be "loved" again by China's multitudes, it had better take care to retain the respect of China's masters. If romantic Sinophilia without realism did not add up to a policy in relations with another great power, the revolution in Iran demonstrated the failure of realism without a dash of political romanticism in the relations of unequal allies. For a moment, it looked as if American policy makers had learned at long last, even if perhaps too late, the uses of unflinching client support in running even a shrinking empire and would stand or fall with the Shah.[3] Yet once an easier exit from the crisis was seemingly offered by the last Shah-appointed government, the one-country approach prevailed once again over the one-system approach. As before in other situations, the United States would cooperate with virtually any halfway willing successor regime in order to hold on to a country, regardless of the systemwide repercussions of abandoning a dependent regime to its fate or failing to punish its destructors.

More was at stake, however, than either the Shah's autocracy or even the so-called arc of crisis in the Indian Ocean area. At stake was the key premise of American disengagement and of U.S.-Soviet détente. Both rest on the supposition that middle-sized local surrogate powers, acting as receptacles for the devolution of previously American responsibilities, are increasingly able to maintain regional order. Iran as run by the Shah was not the most prominent test case of the policy's viability; it was *the* test case and exemplar. *That* Iran had to be upheld even at serious risk—and not only an Iran that did not go immediately Communist or promised to start pumping oil again. That Iran was, however, dismantled by the outgoing Shah's premier-designate in his very first public statement, before being embraced by the Carter administration none the less warmly. That Iran having fallen, neither Israel nor Egypt nor even a limited reinsertion of American military presence could adequately substitute for it, and least of all without other and potentially great risks and costs. The situation in the Persian Gulf area reverted to a U.S.-Soviet zero-sum game, regionally *in esse* and, by extension, globally *in posse*. At the very moment the administration's makers of foreign policy were celebrating the completion of the global triangle by finally normalizing with China, the

---

3. On "empire romanticism," see the author's *Career of Empire: America and Imperial Expansion over Land and Sea* (Baltimore: Johns Hopkins University Press, 1978), p. 306.

situation was allowed to be detriangularized in a vital region. It was repolarized, moreover, in conditions of radically diminished U.S. ability and willingness to hold up its end of the simplified balance.

In the light of the very high—if deferred—risks, anything worth trying in Iran was worth risking. There were measures worth trying so long as the United States could assist and count on the Iranian *military* to keep street riots from assuming the appearance of a social revolution; so long as it had an *economic* leverage for thwarting any potential successor regime to the Shah's by way of the choice it would offer the Saudis either to fill by increased production the supply gap created by the West quarantining Iranian oil exports for a time or else have the United States become manifestly powerless to defend friendly conservative regimes in the area; and so long as American policy makers were prepared to drive the religious *political* opposition inside Iran into a stark choice between "godless" Communism and U.S.-sponsored "satanism," between the Soviet route and the Shah's ways. Just as playing one card does not make a game, so on-again and off-again carrier rattling does not add up to any effective, including gun-boat, diplomacy. At the very best, it appears to prevent what was not really in the cards anyhow: the destruction of West Pakistan by India during the Bangladesh crisis in the Nixon-Kissinger era; Soviet intrusion into an Iran that an effective policy kept roped off as U.S. reserved domain in the Carter era.

Larger cleavages and the need for effective responses   Reapportionment, at issue in third world geo-politics between East and West, was also implicit in the so-called dialogue between North and South over changes to be made in the economic world order. The capitalistic world order probably requires some reforming. This could still be done, however, on the analogy of a yet more universal and likewise reform-needy medieval institution, by tightening up disciplines rather than fundamentally recasting the dominant theology. There was room for more awareness and a clearer definition of what could be done and what could be tolerated within and between all the concerned economies. Both awareness and definition could be inculcated by persuasion or, persuasion failing, by more forceful means. But there was neither a pressing need nor a solid basis for either postulating or institutionalizing politically unadulterated economic interdependence between, and economically unaffected political equality within, the northern and southern groupings.

Any grand new policy will have to heed two tendencies and try to contain them, also by pitting one against the other. One is the tendency of aggregations of economic power to self-liquidation, the other of politico-military power aggregates to overextension. Economic primacy or originality liquidate themselves as skills and assets are diffused to imitators who are anxious to become economic competitors and end up being political rivals; superior military force or presence are overextended as they are deployed against multiplying resisters impatient for a chance to become imitators. Anyone looking toward a surcease from having to manage economic equations with political or military assistance ought to keep shy of an *a*historical materialism—i.e., a reliance on the miraculous healing power of worldwide plenty in a situation in which, since even the now affluent, small part of mankind was materially deprived and insecure for nearly all of its known history, the past teaches us little or nothing (while the present sends out warning signals) about the psychological and political consequences of assured material abundance for human behavior.

Economic and politico-military factors of power are always interdependent in the last resort. But the manifestations of that interdependence have been different for states where the coercive power surplus grew primarily out of land and the labor of the peasant, and the states in which the surplus of coercive and manipulative power was mainly gathered in from the seas and the enterprise of the manufacturer and the merchant. In our time, the fluctuating ascendancy and the competitive interplay of these two types of states have been overshadowed by the striving of nearly all for the mercantile variety of power within a technologically revolutionized war-making setting. But even if the two kinds of power and the difference between them no longer unequivocally suggest policies, they are still perceptible in two sets of interplay. One consists of the unevenly politically tinged economic competition among the several Atlantic-Pacific mercantile-industrial allies, each of which embodies a different amount of residue from the continental-rural type of domestic economy and external politics; the other consists of the unequally economically tinged politico-military rivalry of the three world powers, each of which incarnates a different degree of progression beyond the land-bound political culture. The classic cleavage and the different contemporary mixes are largely ignored by current doctrine. They nonetheless continue to create problems in adjusting conflict and orchestrating strategy.

Even while the functionally defined schism between the sea-oriented and land-based powers rose and receded, the orbit of the geographically denoted East-West division has continued to expand until encompassing the Unitd States (and Japan?) in the West and, next to eastern Europe and Soviet Russia, China and the third world in the East. In the process, the main line of demarcation in Europe has shifted back and forth between the westernmost part of eastern Europe outside Russia and the western boundary of Russia herself.

The world system, the balance among three or more great powers, and—as the inner core of both the system and the balance—America's relations with the Soviet Union: all of these can be managed differently for different purposes. One such, and not the least significant, purpose is to determine not only where the principal line of East-West division will be but also how deep it will be because of the fact that it is or is not relieved by cross-cutting differentiations and associations. However, any pragmatic mapping of day-to-day strategies is incomplete if it does not keep in view the longer-range, second purpose: admitting Russia to the status of full-fledged world power and finally receiving eastern Europe into full citizenship in Europe. The two objectives and related tasks are interconnected, if only because they are partly or potentially conflicting. They constitute the one unfinished business of the European era of world politics. Many facts and more appearances to the contrary notwithstanding, that era is not wholly over so long as the major powers in the world are the United States, Europe's spoiled daughter, and Russia, Europe's rough-shod Cinderella.

Only a one-sided view of history can find a lasting obstacle to the East-West merger in Europe among the memories and complexes that derive from the several partitions of Poland and were amplified by the Soviet seizure of eastern Europe. The first victim was the self-appointed outpost of the West against Russia, while the second was an anti-Soviet *glacis* conceived but unconsolidated by the West; both sets of events—the partitions and the seizure—were made possible by western weakness powerfully assisted by indifference. Only a narrow view of political dynamics can assume that keeping Soviet power confined within either the multiethnic national compass or the regional orbit is likely to promote a gradual and peaceful internal transformation toward greater civil liberty, even as the regime's legitimation is impeded, and its prestige curtailed, by denials of foreign policy success. And only a culturally self-satisfied view can ignore the vital infusion which the "spirit of Russia,"[4] still latent underneath Marxist-Leninist orthodoxy, can effect in the desacralized mentality of a West severed from both of its traditional expressions of religiosity.

Varieties of moral experience: political religion-substitute and politicized religiosity

Just as the commingling of the secular and the spiritual themes in the medieval West's ideal—and in part reality—was broken apart by the rise of the secular territorial state, so the wars of religion were part of the final birthpangs of the nation-state. The erosion of faith through its climactic affirmation was only lately matched, first of all in western Europe, by the

4. This is the title of the multivolume classic by Thomas G. Masaryk (New York: Macmillan Co., 1955 [vols. 1 and 2]; New York: Barnes and Noble, 1967 [vol. 3]). The bias is the author's. On the Russian "soul" see Wladimir Weidlé, *Russia: Absent and Present* (New York: Vintage Books, 1961), chapter 6.

exhaustion of the quasi-religious national and political loyalties that had largely replaced, even as they had in some places relaunched, the older faith. The secularized form of devotion succumbed to its own terminal excess when totalitarianism superseded mere nationalism, attending if not the birth then the difficult infancy of industrialism in politically unfulfilled societies. In America, the political religion-substitute remained confined to the creed of patriotism that stopped short of the cult of the national state; its dimming, no less marked for burning low from the beginning, has been almost inevitably attended by the recrudescence of demonstrative religiosity. It is a religiosity which, when posing as a return to early Christianity, is really much more and is more often a neurotic reaction to late industrial society—its real stresses, unreal promise, and lack of a satisfying political framework.

Tragic rebels and pathetic rebellions against postpolitical normalcy   It is possible to view, and it ought not to be impossible to depict, the latest stage of social evolution in terms of two opposing border phenomena, each covering a spectrum of shadings but reducible to a common denominator. One spectrum comprises the more or less demonic prophets of political religion and the other the more or less saintly proponents of revived religiosity with political implications. Within the first spectrum, the centrist Charles de Gaulle is flanked on the extreme right by Adolf Hitler and on the extreme left by Mao tse tung. The three differ in ostensible ideologies, in the effective means for implementing their designs, and in personal and political ethics. Their common denominator is to be found in a single two-faceted attempt to stem the progression of petty hedonism and raise or preserve collective morale by summoning their countrymen to a more exacting commitment, thus reducing the modern individual's spontaneous gravitation toward the pole of material satisfactions.

The appearance of this kind of political leader, the nature of his appeal, and—not least—his failure add up to what may be the outstanding event of the present century because it reveals a mutation covering the span of several centuries. The fact that these three men emerged has been nature's mechanism for testing the shifting balance in the material possibilities and normative preferences of men and societies. The fact that they failed to reverse or even to halt the shift in that balance has been nature's way of showing, beyond all possibility of contemporaneous cavil and retrospective doubt, that the assortment of possibilities and preferences has undergone a major, and not easily or fully reversible, change. Moreover, the fact that all three shared latter-day embitterment—whatever other forms were assumed by their reactions to the resistant quality of the human material they sought to mold into the shape of their vision—was the same nature's way of signaling the presence of personal tragedy. The task the outsized shakers and shapers pursued was one which, even when its prosecution was not more widely destructive, destroyed in the end their political base and, at least for a time, their reputations. Their effort at social creation was thus, in an important sense, self-destructive.

Being the indispensable barometers of changing social climate, the vain resisters to one kind of change help the survivors understand what they are and where they are headed; the costs of their effort and the gain from their failures can be properly judged only from the opposite extreme of the new normalcy they have diagnosed, have rebelled against, and have summoned others to a recoil from.

The quintessentially non-American rebellions against normalcy do more than illuminate the passage from a still recent past to the present. They also place into high relief another kind of revolt, portentous for the future, that reflects a more advanced, postindustrial stage of such normalcy in America. That revolt took on a particularly gruesome form at about the midpoint of the Carter administration in a group act of physical self-immolation by members of an expatriate American religious commune in the jungle of Guyana. The social and political significance of the mass suicide lay less in the towering horror of the act, however, and more in the spectrum of which it was but one, if extreme, pole. That spectrum spans not only the physical distance between Georgia and Guyana but also the moral distance between a political "reverend" and a religious president.

The differences between one kind of politically ramifying religiosity, Jimmy Carter's pietism blending with populism, and the other kind, Jim Jones's fundamentalism degenerating into the basest form of socially masked fascism, are too obvious to need stressing. Instead, the most striking superficial parallel is between the American "dad" and the German "fuehrer," in death even more than in life. But there is also an undercurrent of similarity between the two opposite poles of politicized religiosity in contemporary America. Both kinds make an appeal against the moral ambiguity of political society and action as they are and always have been. And the receptivity they arouse is to the promise of a leap out of that system into higher spirituality, out of social or political corruption into panhuman compassion. Both the message and the response are themselves highly corruptible, however, not least because keeping the message potent will require additions of ever stronger stuff for an ever more bemused audience. The more the appeal is to the better side of human nature, the easier will such politicized religiosity be inverted into acts or attitudes that are radically irreligious (Jones) or impolitic (Carter). Unless or until the would-be renovator admixes ever more pragmatism with his predication in the act of applying his tenets to the real world, little or nothing will shield him from hysteria or, at least, petulance. For Jones, hysteria resulted when the outside world seemed to be girding itself for war against a false prophet's private paradise. In Carter's case, petulance rose to the surface when the outside.world refused to receive the law on schedule from the inspired peacemaker and world reformer.

Carter-style politicized religiosity with a social conscience is, at its best, the answer of the heart to the cult of the State and its Reason. It opposes its own flaws to the different flaws of the political religion-substitute without reliably matching the latter's strengths under stress. Being essentially sectarian and thus the obverse of both stoicism and statism as the contrasting (aloof and involved) reactions to the crisis of polity, socially politicized religiosity is the public creed *par excellence* of the America of the common man. The Reason-of-State doctrine, on the other hand, blends easily with high-church acceptance of man and the world as they are and as the sectarian, low-church approach would have them not be. Also for this reason, the doctrine has always been in the minority and lately more than ever on the defensive in such an America.

Search for cost-free morality and the price in public·morale   In post-Vietnam America, the religio-political outlook and culture that helped carry Jimmy Carter to the presidency signaled a momentarily irresistible urge and a temptation. The urge was to find release from the greater material demands and from the more clearly revealed moral risks implicit in the cold war/imperial phase; the temptation was to revert to the earlier, not too exactly remembered, experience of relatively cost-free morality internationally and reward-rich materialism domestically—with only marginal redistributions propping up both. The forgotten point was that, whatever may be true of rare individuals, few societies and nations can be reborn, and none instantly by an act of will.

Innocence, once lost, is past recall, and all that remains of it is a form of arrogance. One aspect of that arrogance has been the reluctance—or outright refusal—to build consciously upon cold war/imperial experiences and accomplishments. Their place has been taken by an updated replay of two themes in a not-yet-mature America's attitude towards world affairs. On one side is moralism without substantial supports; on the other side is a concretism that is at home mainly or only with tangibles—be it the economics of the price of world order and local peace or the technology and strategics of nuclear deterrence or war. Fading again was the previously developed measure of sensitivity to the middle ground between moralism and concretism, the higher form of realism that appreciates the weight of intangibles and redeems its distrust of any direct application of private morality to the affairs of state with the most earnest concern for the effect of political action on public morale.

For America to go on graying while indulging in the fantasies of early youth (even as western Europe yielded to the indulgences of disabused age) carried with it an obvious danger. A vacated role might well be claimed at some future date by a foreign leadership less impressed by the change in social and moral orders than by ultimate continuity in the stakes of power—a leadership, moreover, that managed one way or another to overcome the preference of its subjects for a life more happy individually than heroic collectively. The current interlude may or may not prove to be an interregnum; it betokens, in either case, the unreadiness of any other major power to issue the classic challenge and the reluctance of all peoples to pay the price of implementing that challenge. And it is to that interlude more than to anything within themselves alone that Americans—and westerners generally— owe their relatively risk-free opportunity for deciding at ease what elements of what past they would mold into a new formula for their future.

It is not likely that the interlude will last indefinitely, and it is not certain that it will end in a wholly new kind of world politics (or economics or community), rather than in an updated configuration and incumbency of world power. Moreover, were a wholly new world politics to be forthcoming, it is no more certain that it would be beneficial. However slowly have evolved the traditional—or classic—state and state system, man's psychic make-up and adaptability to radical change in social environment have evolved yet more slowly, regardless of his rash desires. The blessings of universal peace and prosperity might well prove to be too much of a good thing too soon, and they might unhinge man's always precarious inner equilibrium.

The territorial state—and the competitive system of states—made a not always duly valued contribution to mental health: they both helped mightily in keeping man alert by casting over him the pall of terror and in holding him upright by offering the pull of transcendence. The state-among-states was a focus for anxieties and a guardian against fears; a mere attenuation from time to time of either anxiety or fear set off spells of repose that could pass for felicity. And the state thus situated was the occasion for commitment to values and goals that were no less personally fulfilling for being metapersonal. When the state and the conflict of states have ceased to drain off the more violent urges and to crystallize the objects of such urges, formless barbarism and aimless terrorism will fill the vacuum. When the secular order has ceased to provide subjects worthy of an aspiration that goes beyond the private self, the impoverished self will reach after other modes of exhibiting devotion in what has become a stateless society rich with new evils, real or imagined.

Postscript 2. The Hero and the Antihero in America

In America's future there ought to be a middle point between the essential Carlyle and the essential Carter, between hero worship and implicit wholesale rejection of the heroic values. America's trek from World War via cold war to world empire does not offer a formula. But it supplies an illustration of the dialectic between the individual who personifies, and a society that is uncomfortable with, the dichotomy between physical or moral heroism and a likewise constituted cowardice. Individual and collective reactions to the McCarthy phenomenon at the height of the cold war illustrated the attitudinal dichotomy and, within it, the nonheroic side. The real war and actual empire showed the social dialectic in ways exemplified by the Patton-Nixon syndrome.

Patton's part, as represented in the dramatized motion picture version of his wartime career, consists of two revealing acts and situations: the general's physical manhandling of one type of soldier and his sentimental glorification of another type. The American public reacted to the first event with massive outrage: its culture did not admit of cowardice, but only of the all-too-human inability to deal with stress. The second event takes place when the general, in the midst of human and material devastation, imprints a kiss on the forehead of the wounded tank commander who has just led a fight to the last man and beyond the last shell; and when, routinely asking for God's forgiveness, Patton expresses ecstatically his "love" for what he sees. If not artistically imagined, the exclamation certainly went unreported at the time. Had it been, the great American public was poorly prepared to grasp the meaning behind the blasphemous remark.

I shall suppose that Patton is not (and is not meant by the film maker to appear to be) a sadist. And I shall stipulate that the soldier's heroism need not be reduced to psychological or social conditions qualitatively identical with those causing (or explaining) cowardice. What the military leader loves, then, is not the massive size of violent death and destruction encompassed by war, but the exercise of power and will. That exercise only climaxes, in different ways for the leader and the led, in the phenomenon of war and in the opportunity that war gives for acts of noble courage—mostly moral for the leader and the public at large, also physical for the men directly under fire. Everything is enlarged: propensity to good as much as to evil; capacity for great deeds as well as for small evasions. Moreover, only the pursuit and the exercise of power, or of publicly significant functions, has that magnifying and intensifying effect. Unless it occurs on a level where wealth and power merge, where wealth is amassed as a means to power rather than as a way to greater ease, the pursuit of material goods merely degrades. In the end it compels everyone, willingly or unwillingly, to do things that a good or noble man would rather not do—to depart from one's highest hopes for, and estimation of, one's self. And the pursuit of happiness? That pursuit, if central, *does* elevate—but only the demands made on life in lieu of oneself. It corrupts more subtly than the pursuit of material goods does and in the end tends to destroy more perversely.

Such a view of Patton, and of the film bearing his name, must have had a role in Richard Nixon's reported admiration for both.[5] The admiration may be dismissed as a case of late adolescent, and essentially private, hero worship or the affinity may be accepted as one that expresses an intimate aspiration by a public figure. Such aspiration implies a definition of the qualities that a man (and certainly a man who is president in the age of America's global power) ought to have some share of, and yet larger sympathy for, not least if he is to compensate for the inherited obverse tendencies of the society at large. Only if he does will he be able to bend these tendencies in a direction that befits the newly acquired majesty and unavoidably assumed miseries of great power and imperial responsibility.

The pathos of Richard Nixon was that he was neither great nor big enough to narrow the gap between two kinds of ethos. One is the ethos of a *civil* society born and bred outside the most acute tensions of a contentious state system; the other is an ethos that would enable Americans to continue their late but real, essentially politico-military contribution to a minimally ordered *international* society that can be humanized only gradually.

So much for pathos. The tragedy was that the shape of Nixon's dream about what he and America ought to be and ought to dare was out of touch with flaws that inhered as much in the American society as in Nixon himself. The dream was finally deformed by the flaws in both. The feature that redeems the pathos is that Nixon knew what he ought to try for; what conditions the tragedy is that his trying may not be America's last.

It is in the nature of America's only brief and somewhat shallow and uninstructive history that, when she came to the large arena of world power, the more ambitious among her presidents who were not the world's homemade inquisitors were, by and large, imitators of European models. The memory of Churchill was present with John Kennedy who, thinking he knew "why England slept" in the 1930s, would rouse America to transfer the liberal empire, British-style, to a yet bigger stage. Similarly, compelled against all his instincts by a differently aroused public to beat a retreat, Nixon would model himself on de Gaulle when easing an apparently impossible empire out of a seemingly unwinnable war into a commanding role in global equilibrium. The fact that Richard Nixon did not reach out to his middle-American constituency with the demand for an effort exceeding one needed

---

5. It is not important for the argument, but may be revealing of Nixon's estimate of the continuing value system of middle America that, if I correctly remember from one of his conversations with David Frost, he denied having viewed the film repeatedly. My views on "power" are expounded more fully in a contribution ("Morgenthau vs. Machiavelli") to the *Festschrift* for Hans J. Morgenthau, *Truth and Tragedy* (Washington, D.C.: The New Republic Book Company, 1977), edited by Kenneth Thompson and others.

for a superficially honorable peace, that he did not seek to parlay the provincial chauvinism of the average American into a performing patriotism of the highest kind, were measures of his limitations as would-be heroic leader. These failings also confirmed his quality as an imitator, mistaking de Gaulle's and France's impossibilities for his own and America's. We touch here on a crucial difference: imitation of the model by the admirer is not the same as the intimate identification with the hero. Only the latter springs rightfully from a feeling of intimate kinship and equal worth.

So much for one, obsolescent view of men and nations. Yet the warm reception that a disgraced Nixon was given by members of the Oxford Union in the last days of 1978 was one event permitting doubt that such a view had become completely irrelevant. The jeering crowd *outside* the union was mainly American; insofar as the demonstrators abused Nixon for the Christmas bombing of North Vietnam and the Cambodian invasion, they were the spiritual heirs to the Oxonians of the 1930s who had taken an oath not to fight for king and country. But the ovation for Nixon by the sons and grandsons of those Oxford oathmen at the close of his appearance points in a different direction—assuming the warm response was more than a sporting tribute to a kind of moral courage prompting the ostracized leader's public reappearance, more than yet another sign of the European political mind's inability to grasp the depravity inherent in Watergate.

Beyond the differences in political culture and capacity for moral outrage looms the still greater difference in lived experience. The Americans of a certain generation continue to work off the experience of Vietnam and Watergate, even as still younger Americans already begin to sense the oppressive absence of goals and stimulants that comes from the apotheosis of private and public virtue being unattended by reasons and occasions for exhibiting *virtus*. The young Britons, on their part, have lived long enough with the social and individual consequences of a final, seemingly irreversible retreat from power and mission. Their historians have been hard at work to come to terms with the loss of empire. When the last word is written, read, and accepted by the intellect, however, the deeper instinct remains unconvinced. It could not help showing some recognition to an American politician who tried to keep imperium for yet a moment longer in the possession of the West.

Part Two
THE ISSUES: *The Polarities and the Dual Threat*

III

THE WEST
AND EASTERN EUROPE
BEYOND COMMUNISM

Power tends to travel, and paramount power travels conspicuously. Its general direction has been west-northwest since it started moving from Mesopotamia to the eastern and central Mediterranean. From there, preeminent power gravitated in the aftermath of Rome's fall via the Carolingian realm (German and French) and the Castilian (Spanish) realm to Britain and on across the Atlantic to America. Within the United States itself, power has already begun to move away from the eastern seaboard westward. If the trajectory remains in force, it cannot but traverse the Pacific to the land masses of either Russia or China; one or the other (or both in succession) could then look toward bringing Japan into her orbit of influence—or more than influence.

Varieties of migration and divisions of power: pathways and polarities

Power has gravitated as a function of many factors. Material and institutional innovations will be diffused and exploited unevenly, even if ultimately spreading far and wide, and two- and multiparty conflicts will have lopsided outcomes even when players roughly conform to the rationality of the balance of power. Uneven diffusion and critical defeats will precipitate the organic rise and decline of individual powers because of a still wider range of reasons. The ebb and flow of power occurred historically within more stable lines of basic divisions that transcended specific conflicts while constraining their enactment. One line of division that reemerged in early modern Europe was between powers essentially maritime and powers essentially land-based (it displaced the antecedent cleavage between chiefly spiritual and chiefly secular or temporal powers); another division was that between powers essentially western and those essentially eastern. Both of the still globally operative lines of cleavage are fluid and have shifted with varying issues and relationships.[1] And although the fields of forces they delimit are more surely separable analytically than practically, they do introduce order and structure into sporadic interactions that have little contemporary meaning and even less capacity to instruct as to the future.

The ancient land-sea power division antedates even that between Sparta and Athens. It moved forward when early Rome confronted mercantile seafaring Carthage. And, eclipsed by the land-rooted feudal political economy (only marginally qualified by Norman-Byzantine-Moslem naval interplays), seapower challenged land power again successfully in modern Europe and the contemporary world.

The East-West line of division in turn preceded, but was perpetuated in, Rome's interactions with the East. It was extended to the present by the interplays between the several actual or would-be successors to both western Rome and eastern Rome (Constantinople), ever since the very early days when, also on grounds of dogma, the Holy Roman Empire and the Roman Papacy were at odds with Byzantium over the nonromanized European East north of the Danube.

Within each of the fields of forces, moreover, there has been a near-continuous succession, as incumbents of the same kind or location of power

1. Thus, France is essentially a land-oriented power, despite her maritime provinces and mercantile features. And she is historically more of a land power in attitudes and policies vis-à-vis the truly maritime western powers such as the Netherlands and Britain, while being relatively more of a sea power when compared with Germany. Long a land power only, Germany must also be considered an eastern power when it comes to past interactions with Britain over seapower and overseas colonies. But the same Germany is to be counted as a western power relative to colonization in the eastern Slavic lands (themselves constituting western Slavs relative to Russia) and a central power in relation to an all-European balance of power or concert.

Russia is invariably eastern (except potentially in comparison to China), including relative to east-central Europe, and essentially a land power with maritime ambitions and capabilities ever since Peter the Great. Whereas England was Russia's counterpart antagonist on the land-sea power axis, she was not a primary one on the East-West axis, while the two sources of antagonism have tended to merge in U.S.-Soviet relations.

Finally, in the beginnings of Europe, the East was maritime-mercantile and the West was rural and —except for the Northmen—sea-shy. The change occurred gradually with the opening of the Atlantic, while the Mediterranean was the arena for mixed or amphibious powers and politics, illustrated in the Spanish-Ottoman interaction. Venice was the prototypical sea power in the regional context, facing the Hungarian land power across the Adriatic at the peak of her seafaring prowess.

followed one another.[2] The lines of succession are not without interest in any attempt to stake out the gravitation of power. However, of yet greater moment are the diverse interplays within the two fields of action and conflict, and the differences between them.

Interaction between East and West and between land and sea powers in Europe   Within the East-West field, the primary act and original aim tended to be some form of ideological (religious or cultural) conversion. Since both power and civilization were uneven in the two parts of Europe, conversion was attended by mixes of military conquest and economic colonization. And since the West evolved faster than the East from essentially familial-dynastic (or genealogical) determinants of policy and events toward geo-political norms of statecraft, conquest and colonization were superseded only slowly in the East and between East and West by sustained politico-military competition among consolidated greater powers.

So long as religious conversion was at issue, it was the western Church (and the Holy Roman Empire) and the eastern Church (and the Byzantian Empire) that competed over who would christianize the pagan populations extending spatially all the way to Kievan Russia, and who would incidentally influence them in matters temporal. When the religious issue was updated within a later

2. The long line of contacts and conflicts in the land-vs.-sea power category comprises those between Phoenicia and Assyria, Athens and Sparta, Carthage and Rome, Venice and Milan (in the Italian setting only), the Dutch or the English and Spain or France, Great Britain and Russia or Germany, and, in our time, the United States and Soviet Russia (while the Asian side show or foreplay pitted Japan against China and Russia). In the East-West category, intimated by the ancient conflict between the Greeks and the Persians, division led to confrontation between the western and the eastern Roman empires. The West's later "new monarchies" (displacing the Holy Roman Empire of the Germans and including Spain) acted as either successors or only defenders of Rome against the Moslem (including Ottoman) empires from the East, themselves acting as either oppressors or successors of Constantinople.

In the present era, the United States, acting as the defender of Germany and successor to Britain, confronted and was confronted by the Soviet successors to the Russian tsars and, through them, to Byzantium. China may one day replace Russia as the main eastern power after retracing Russia's Petrine and post-Petrine material and Marxist-Leninist ideological westernization. There is thus a line of succession running through the several duels and confrontations. It runs among the sea-based powers from Phoenicia to Carthage and from Athens to Venice, the Dutch, the English and the Americans; the land powers extend from Assyria, Persia and Sparta to Rome and, in modern times, to Spain and France and on to Germany and Russia. The western line encompasses the Greek city-states and Macedon, the western Roman empire, the Carolingian and Holy Roman empires, and the new or northern European monarchies (France, England, Spain) which, evolved into nation-states, gave way to the United States. The eastern line in turn comprises Persia, the eastern Roman empire (Byzantium), the Ottoman empire, Russia, and China. All lines of succession correspond roughly with the overall west-northwest direction of power gravitation, with one important exception: the eastward power shift that began on the European continent in the seventeenth century with the passing of preponderance from Spain to France and has gathered speed in the following centuries.

Russia into one of cultural and ideological orientation entailing conversion for the losers, the contest was between the so-called westernizers and the Slavophiles. A comparable contest unfolded in a more subtle key within Germany, reflecting the eventual translation of the geographical East-West cleavage into an ideological one between liberalism and autocracy. This contest was forcefully extended before and after World War I to the fragmented area between Germany and Russia, in the form of rival drives or pressures by proponents of the several authentic or orientalized versions of western socio-political ideologies. Less markedly keyed to conversion but no less ideological was the earlier contest between western Christianity and Islam. It too was mediated through a power-political conflict, between the Spanish and Austrian Habsburg and the Ottoman empires, to begin with.

Conversion efforts tended to produce long-lasting stalemates, while conquests ended in provisional ones. Both kinds of stalemate permitted or promoted more or less enduring diversions of the eastern actors, away from the East-West relationship further eastward: thus, Poland deflected her principal energies from the Holy Roman Empire toward Lithuania and Russia (or Ruthenia), the Ottomans intermittently toward Persia, and Russia beyond the Urals and toward the Far East. The eastward diversion was necessitated in some instances by western desertion of nearer-eastern resisters (such as Austria, Hungary, and Poland) to Mongol or Turk invasion and conquest from the farther East.

At a later stage, diversion would also follow from deadlocks within the eastern European subsystem or the all-European system, involving the by-then consolidated eastern great powers (Austria, Prussia, Russia). Instead of being caused by western desertion, the later eastward diversions were facilitated by the relative decline of the western great powers in terms of land-based power, following their successful overseas diversion further westward and southward. While the all-European system expanded as a result, East-West tensions were at least temporarily and superficially attenuated at a cost to the lesser nationalities.

Both desertion and decline signaled western aloofness from eastern Europe, even when it did not betoken outright indifference. And both aloofness and indifference, both relative ascendancy and decline, reflected the growing trend for the western powers to be primarily involved in the land vs. sea power field of forces and conflicts. Conflict along that line of division was first and foremost over material assets, augmenting and augmented by commerce and colonization. The new stakes delimited an economic and global arena that rivaled the previously dominant intra-European politico-military arena for primacy in determining policies and policy outcomes and in crystallizing competition and order. Conversion as stake or object either was or became secondary before the onset of modernization, as overseas catholicization by Spain gave way to the proselytizing and civilizing methods of the maritime Protestant powers (the Netherlands and especially England) and to the yet later French efforts at cultural assimilation.

Like efforts at conversion and conquest within Europe, overseas colonization involved stalemates of unequal duration, not least when the Dutch were displacing the Portuguese only to be challenged by rival English seapower and when maritime Britain encountered in France the first rival land power with oceanic outreach. The stalemates and the supersessions permitted a late extension of the land-sea power cleavage eastward, while the seeming overall success of colonization prompted bids to share in its benefits. After France, tsarist Russia and imperial Germany became the prime aspirants to maritime outlets, with the result that intra-European hegemonical conflicts were from time to time temporarily diverted to the less portentous competition overseas.

There is a sense in which the East-West and the land-sea power divisions resemble the early European cleavage between secular and spiritual powers. In the abstract, the East and the West are like medieval emperors and popes, in that they stand for different mixes of secular and spiritual elements. And the land-sea power cleavage is like the earlier one, in that it reproduces the tensions between the known earth and the world beyond what is familiar, if (again) in a different form. In chronological terms, the pope-emperor contest in the West (and its eastern and northern European extensions) had to fade before room could be made for the two more singularly secular contests. But in terms of specific stakes, the papal-imperial contest was replicated in the land-sea power sphere by the riches of the transoceanic colonial world replacing those of Italy, while the continuing contest over the allegiance of Germany shifted from the papal-imperial to the East-West sphere when it engaged the Russian "third" Rome as one of the key condenders.

Differences between East-West and maritime-continental force fields in the past and present   The overlaps between the two continuing divisions and the antecedent, now-effaced one are largely symbolic. They are of little importance for policy. The same is not true for shifts in power among key parties to the continuing divisions. Such shifts resulted—at least in part, and in a complex relationship of cause and effects—from the strictly secular force fields overlapping in action.

Within the globally expanded land-sea power field, the power advantage has shifted from continental to the maritime-mercantile states and, among them, to those with an ever bigger territorial base; one reason for this is in their greater capacity for institutional innovaton and economic and technological inventiveness. Within the East-West field, the flow of decisive power, civilization, and prosperity moved in the Christian era first eastward, from western to eastern Rome and to the Moslem polities. Subsequently, the flow changed direction westward and northwestward, first on a European and then on a global scale. At a still later stage and within continental Europe only, an eastward undertow began in the narrower sphere of military-economic power and, to an extent, also in the elusive sphere of intellectual creativity. That subcurrent flowed from Spain to France, to Germany, and on to Russia in modern times; as it gathered strength, it also neared the area of possible confluence with the dominant world-wide power flow running northwestward. A continuing consequence has been to leave unclarified, and thus confusing, the question of whether to perceive great-power rivalries in more or less ideologized geographic terms (East vs. West) or in more or less structurally induced functional terms (land vs. sea powers).

Such shifts of power are of more than merely historical interest. They suggest tendencies that either manifestly continue or may resurface in the future. Therefore, awareness of them can usefully affect present policy. The same is true for other features of the two fields of forces and conflict and for the differences between them.

Changing parties to the land vs. sea power cleavage remained locked in an ever-renewed standoff, for reasons embedded at least as much in structures of power and system as in individual policies. The rival powers failed to evolve a uniform system of norms and standards for the politics of aggregating self-sufficient power and containing preponderant power. Nor was it possible to evolve mutually acceptable methods and frameworks through which to equalize access to the material foundations of power in both territorial and oceanic environments. As a result, the nominal identity of the essence of power (combining economic or material and politico-military components) was translated into an effective polarity between two different mixes of the elements of power—and, consequently, types of powers—when Europe's continental-maritime orbit widened with her expansion overseas.

In the East-West setting, the difference between nominal and effective features did not bear primarily on the quality and configuration of power; it conditioned instead the diffusion and the transformation of institutions and ideas. Nominal convergence tended to produce effective divergence as institutions and ideas moved outside the originating West and were either only intensified or also deformed in the East. Eastern conditions were intrinsically different, and the impact of the diffused ideas and institutions was either premature or unduly deferred. An early change was in the quality of the Roman emperorship as it moved eastward, first in its spirit and then also physically to Constantinople; the mutation only prefigured analogous changes in the nature of feudalism, urbanism, nationalism, and, in our time, Marxism. Formal assimilation or adoption of an idea or institution by the East merely alienated it politically and psychologically from the West, as outward reception by some bred in-depth rejection by others. However caused, the cleavage was only secondarily expressed in politico-military conflict over material stakes.

Nor were the tendencies to polarization in one field of forces and action and divergence in the other field the only features that differentiated the fields. So did the kinds of conflicts, their origin and expansion. Since the land- and the sea-based and oriented powers differed most in physical situations and economic conditions, their conflicts began over specific stakes and capabilities. Differences in ethos merely aggravated the quarrels when those differences were raised to the status of outright antitheses as part of the materially and functionally defined conflicts being protracted or escalating.

The opposite was, to an extent, the case between the geographically differentiated eastern and western powers. The primary stimulants to hostility (or so-called psychological distance) between them were differences in culture and ethos, which were at least in part original as well as materially engendered. Largely innate hostility found release in conflicts that could be initiated over symbolic or substantive issues, over true faith or territorial frontiers. Those conflicts were only gradually intensified and expanded as they were caught up in the amplifying dynamic of their geo-political matrix.

Conflicts over specific assets within the land-vs.-sea power category tended to evolve into unbridgeable schisms for first structural and then ideological reasons—e.g., between England on one side and Spain, France, and Germany, ever more acutely in succession on the other. To about the same extent, profound ideologico-cultural schisms within the East-West sphere (e.g., between Christian and Moslem powers, between Poland-Lithuania and Muscovy, and between tsarist Russia and the West) shaped the beginnings of conventional conflicts. At least in some cases or for a time, such conventional conflicts took precedence over the initial schisms and moderated or defused them.

The just-described different characteristics had likewise different results. The land-sea power conflicts tended to erode both of the changing parties to it and to be ultimately resolved by the unevenly timed, but finally reciprocal, dispossession of both (Rome's long survival to Carthage in antiquity is an exception). Moreover, the succession of such schisms destroyed, in the end, the international system centered in Europe. Conversely, neither the eastern nor the western cultural and geo-political wing was able to subdue permanently or to destroy lastingly the other wing. This was so despite cross-currents in power shifts within the global and the continental European sectors, fluctuations among individual powers, and divergences in the careers of ideas and institutions. The land-based and sea-based powers were unable to get at one another in their respective elements for the decisive assault and the final kill; yet they ate all the more effectively at the roots and dried up the sources of their respective types of power. The obverse has been true so far for the East-West line of division. A seemingly decisive defeat of an individual power or the eclipse of a region has tended to be only the prelude to its regeneration.

If nothing else, the differences between the two fields of action suggest that some positive consequences might attach to any contemporary dilution of the land-sea power schism, after four centuries of emergence and dominance, in favor of updated East-West interactions. To be noted, and prized, is the bias of East-West interactions toward deideologizing a conflict, as well as diversifying an originally bilateral conflict, once it was processed through a sufficiently crystallized international system. Another positive bias is toward fluctuating shifts in power and influence, making adverse trends or outcomes reversible, and toward resolutions of conflict that are consistent with national or regional regeneration. And yet another good point is the tendency for diversions to occur in opposing directions: farther eastward for eastern powers and westward for the western powers, away from East-West confrontations and stalemated efforts at conversion. The latter trend has been manifest in Soviet Russia's deflection of ideological (and other) hostility toward China as the main enemy; a parallel deflection by the western powers of some of the confict energy spared from the post-World War II East-West confrontation has tended to intensify economic and political competition among them.

Both deflections could reactivate the land-sea power dimension as a governing one. The U.S.-Soviet-Chinese triangle covers the entire spectrum of maritime-continental power types, while U.S.-west European-Japanese relations involve only, or mainly, mercantile-maritime powers or issues. The two patterns could become differently, and disruptively, intertwined— not least via the weak links in the second. But, for the present and immediate future, it is or ought to be possible to control and contain the extent to which an irreconcilable land-sea power conflict would develop into an unmanageable, system-disrupting schism. It ought likewise to be possible to exploit some of the more beneficent traditional features of the East-West interaction and to contain its malignancies. Foremost among the flaws is the tendency for diffusion of nominally universal institutions and ideas from the West to be inverted into eastern alienation in effective practice, not least as a result of poor timing. The occasion is one when East-West interaction is resumed within Europe, moderated between the United States and the Soviet Union, and expands globally to comprise China (to the east of a more fluid than fixed line of demarcation) and the third world (as either physically or only figuratively a part of the East).

It is for the statesman to shape all of the complex equations and overlaps— politico-military and economic, functional and geographic, cultural and social, ideological and pragmatic—that impinge on international politics and can be only schematically abstracted into discrete fields of interaction. It likewise simplifies, although it does not solve, the task if the "Russian factor" is treated as analytically central, even when not all of actual strategy and tactics is either directly or circuitously keyed to the greatest nonwestern, nondemocratic power. To reach out instead for a governing principle of action to the geo-political and functional peripheries, the political and economic raw materials, is to resume the fixation on the world beyond in ways leading to utopian conception and frustrating policy.

Varieties of political predicaments in eastern Europe: national aspirations and regional realities

In shaping the future of the East-West issue, it is important to oppose to geo-cultural cleavages as many countervailing lines of differently defined divisions and alignments as possible. It is essential, however, to make sure that in ever more respects, even if not instantly in all, Russia—even *qua* Soviet Russia—becomes part of the larger West.

Among the parties liable to being most directly affected by the course and outcome of the shifting mix of confrontation and conciliation between the Soviet Union and the West are the "men in the middle" of European history. They are the western Slavs, the Czechs and the Poles, precariously placed between Russia and Eurasia to the east and Germany and Euratlantica to the west. They stood together only occasionally when the German drive eastward coincided with the weakness of a Russia in the making. They tended to stand apart from one another when facing toward either Germany or Russia as the effective threat or a seeming refuge. And they have felt alike and acted alike (if not simultaneously) most recently only when Germany was subdued and Russia rose to be supreme and became suppressive over both. At the best of times, any political unity was only superficial and negative. Yet, in common with all eastern Europeans, however defined, if the western Slavs failed to share political orientations, they did share the most elementary, profound, and positive human traits. Whereas politics tended to divide the eastern Europeans even as they directed their expectations unevenly toward the West, the shared nonpolitical traits (having only implications for politics) have either only differentiated or also divided them from the modern West, starting, for that purpose, at the Rhine.

Shared fate and diverse fatalities of western Slavs between Russia and the West   Within eastern Europe, Czech ambivalence toward the greatest Slav nation has occupied a middling and vacillating position between the Russophilia of the Bulgars and the Russophobia of the Poles. The latter have tended to oppose to the Russian Orthodox their own Catholic brand of the messianic vocation and to Russian autocracy their rival ambition to be the region's great power. The full range of Polish irredenta vis-à-vis Russia is the eastern European analogue of French revanchism vis-à-vis Germany at its height, as the Poles, earlier than the French, had to endure a reversal of expansionist fortunes in favor of their eastern neighbor. The Czechs were unable, but for a brief medieval moment, to lead from strength. Thus they looked alternately westward and eastward for support and, finding reliable safeguard nowhere, sought consolation in a moral claim on humanity at large. They have based the claim on serving as the guiding beacon of light for others in times of their own darkness: all the way from the finally suppressed Hussite reformation (opening a breach for triumphant Lutheranism in Germany); through Munich (generating the basic tenet of American cold war foreign policy); to the Communist seizure of power in 1948 (coresponsible for NATO); and on to the Prague Spring of 1968 (reinforcing Euro-communism).

Throughout, the moral strength and political weakness of the Czechs lay in attempts to occupy a third position, moderate and moderating, tolerant and tolerated, between ideological extremes and related strategic rivalries of the moment: reformist Protestantism and Catholic counterreformism before 1620, Soviet-brand eastern socialism and western capitalism before 1948. On each occasion, the Czechs lost a form of political independence and had to resume the painful ascent toward its alternative, a vitally contributing, and as such respected, position within a larger power conglomerate. The formula, successful in the earliest context of the western Luxemburg dynasty, was mismanaged (after a briefly promising, late sixteenth-century spell and despite belated efforts before and during World War I) by the centrist Habsburg dynasty; it has since become a major challenge for the statecraft of the successors to the Romanovs in the east, testing their capacity for prolonged survival.

Such a Bohemia, and later Czechoslovakia, become yet another eastern counterpart of France—but, unlike Poland, the counterpart of a France which, as the index of moral forces in politics, was most imposing when the idea she stood for was severed from the power of enforcing it abroad. The solution of the "Czech problem" was in such a conception made contingent on the state and the fate of the world at large. It could not be effectively approached by anything as pragmatic as the interwar Franco-Czechoslovak (or Soviet-Czechoslovak) alliance; in the last analysis, the approach through power politics vitiated the ideal formula. By contrast, Poland's integral resurrection, when her martyrdom is not equated with the Redeemer's in the messianic view, could be more readily visualized in more concrete terms. It could be seen as keyed to the distribution and hierarchy of material power in central and eastern Europe (or, when excluding Russia from Europe by the decree of Polish historiography, Eurasia). Association with Russia could be accepted, if at all, only on specifically nonnational, ideological grounds—and even then only on the grounds that it made Poland the next-highest ranking socialist state in eastern Europe (pending the ethnic decomposition of Soviet Russia), rather than relegating her to a comparatively inferior status in the larger capitalist system.

Stabilization vs. suppression in eastern Europe and Soviet Russia   Even ambivalence toward Russia has turned into animosity for things Russian in most of eastern Europe, undoing the too-partisan attempts at persuasion (and the fearful ones at self-persuasion) in the opposite direction immediately after World War II. A differently lopsided view, from a likewise demythologized West, cannot aspire to do more than contain the oscillations of the needle in the politico-affective compass within a practical range. It is part of an attempt at objectivity to isolate the long-term gains derived for non-Soviet east Europeans from a situation that is perforce self-liquidating as to its worst Stalinist-regionalist features, if one continues to assume a prolonged future for international politics.

Soviet-wrought freezing of eastern Europe into relative immobility had positive consequences in at least two domains. In the national domain, the extraneously imposed quietus permitted the end-of-war expulsion of ethnic Germans from outside the quintessential (pre-*Drang nach Osten*) Germany to evolve from an act of reversible retribution into an organically resorbed condition; it allowed the time and fostered the receptivity for the full integration of the German "colonizers" into, notably, the Federal Republic. The political gain for stability in central-eastern Europe as a whole is altogether inestimable; it could not have been had for free in any but an ideal world. The economic gain for West Germany, both short-term (additional labor force) and long-term (less of political embarrassment for trade and related ties with eastern Europe), has justly offset the economic loss always borne by countries prepared to barter material skills for ideal homogeneity.

The other, or cultural, gain from Soviet dominance likewise has had an economic cost. One-power domination allowed eastern European nations to consider the price, in terms of group integrity and intimacy, of the obverse (western) dispensation of organizational multilateralism and corporate multinationalism.[3] It ought not to be, but has so far seemed to be, the lot of lesser countries with well-defined cultural identity and finite capacity to

---

3. Even if apocryphal, de Gaulle's reputed dictum when taking France out of NATO ("Paris is not a hotel") has acquired since a rich meaning for the inheritor of that particular distinction (Brussels). On the different predicament of one small nation, I wrote previously in "Czech Tragedy: A Broken Record," *Interplay*, October 1968, and "Czechoslovak Independence and the Great Powers: Retrospect and Prospect," M. Rechcigl, Jr., ed., *Czechoslovakia Past and Present* (The Hague: Mouton, 1968).

absorb diversity to be either defenselessly wide open to the many or forcefully closed off by the one. Pending the development of a superior formula, and so long as the alternations in "freeze" and "thaw" in the forms and degrees of Soviet domination in eastern Europe continued to display an overall trend toward attenuation, there was something to be said for suspended animation and a pause for informed observation on that particular score as well.

The gains are of uneven significance in terms of time long enough to matter when measured by the standard of history (while stopping short of that of eternity). But they are gains even if the freeze should prove to have failed in finally extinguishing the embers of internation (or interethnic) rivalries and animosities among the lesser eastern European breeds. Moreover, the obverse of imposed freeze is exported ferment. While Soviet Russian domination has slowed down the rate of change in eastern Europe, the comparatively more western, prosperous, or liberal eastern European societies have injected a potentially accelerating impulse into Soviet Russia proper, reproducing the ferment once flowing into tsarist Russia out of the Russian-controlled parts of partitioned Poland. Such insidious outside influence will speed up change inside Soviet Russia in due course, even if intermittently it more than arrests the process; it is most likely to do so when left alone by western strategies aimed at non-Soviet eastern Europe directly.

The ferment complements the potential benefits that accrue from the more conspicuous freeze within Russia herself. The internal freeze is one that the secular ideology of Communism imposed on the agitation (between westernizers and Slavophiles), which had made up the near-theologically formulated, irresoluble dialectic within the orthodox-autocratic Russia of the tsars, uncomfortably exposed to liberal heterodoxy from the West. The congealment had been advocated by reactionaries of the right before it was effected by reactionaries of the left; it has not prevented—and may have sped along—social transformations inside the Soviet Union. These include the changing balances between agriculture and industry (the *mir* and the metropolis) and between the Russian and the non-Russian nationalities. The consequently updated new tendencies have no more pointed in one direction than did the earlier ones. But even if the Soviet regime deliberately fosters an ethnically and culturally neutral global or Eurasian orientation for appeal and advance in all directions, the transformation may still inflect Soviet political and economic attachments ever so slowly and partially westward (while continuing to resurface what is specifically Russian). If occurring, the development would be a function of spontaneous extrapolations of favored trends (e.g., industrialism) as much as an implementation of defensive reactions against disturbing trends (e.g., waning of the Great Russian majority).

Varieties of social culture traits between eastern and western Europe: moods and mentalities

While it lasts, the alienation of eastern Europe from the West manifests itself differently from that of the Asian (or other) East. The latter's grievance in relation to the West is one against domination and material exploitation; the former's grievance is against cultural neglect or politico-military and diplomatic exploitation. The Asian's compensatory sense of superiority is cultural, most conspicuously in the case of China; the eastern European's (if any) is broadly speaking, spiritual. The differences are important, not least because the alienation of the eastern European is not doubled with animosity; therefore, it is apt to yield more readily to the healing effect of material equalization and political rapprochement or co-optation.

Forms of political intelligence and the balance between reason and emotion   The eastern European's many-sided imitation springs from the desire to identify with the West; it is not aimed primarily or, for rival regimes, most of the time at superseding the West. The position of the typical eastern European relative to western culture resembles that of the Jew in Gentile society; both must exhibit outstanding individual quality or achievement if they are to qualify for something akin to equal and full membership in the larger, tone-setting community.[4] If it is to be borne with anything like equanimity, a position felt to be inferior in relatively concrete or tangible ways will perforce be compensated for by self-attribution of some kind of superiority in harder-to-identify, more elusive qualities. It is easiest, but also self-defeating if treated as sufficient unto itself, to look for such superiority in a higher or deeper spirituality. This was historically the mechanism of the American Negro facing an overwhelmingly superior white civilization, and a resurgence of traditionalism and religiosity in the third world may generalize that mechanism. With marginal exceptions (e.g., the old-Russian Slavophile), the east European's sense of special excellence in intangible qualities is of a more limited, this-worldly kind.

One area of possible compensation open to the eastern European has been that of political intelligence. He may feel his to be more tactically agile

---

4. It is this similarity of position that, among other objective givens, helps reconcile, notably on the social elite level, the phenomenon of aggregating eastern European anti-Semitism in pre-World War II eastern Europe *(on a souvent besoin d'un plus petit que soi)* with the easy rapport between eastern European and Jew on the interpersonal level. This rapport transforms the phrase "some of my best friends . . . " from an indictment of man's supposed hypocrisy into a descriptive commentary on a human reality that takes the edge off the more negative reciprocal stereotyping.

and strategically systematic than the westerner's: agile because it is attuned to and trained on more labyrinthine, unpredictable, and (in case of mistake or failure) personally dangerous national and regional politics; systematizing because it is keyed to intrinsically volatile relations and anarchical or chaotic conditions, which need to be reduced to comprehensible order intellectually as either a preliminary or an alternative to any attempt to master them even partially in practice. Fundamentally different from the systematizing drive are both of the preeminent western types of political intelligence, the peculiarly Gallic and the Anglo-Saxon. The first is strongest at critical clarification; it tends to perceive pertinent reality in terms of contrasting categories as an antecedent (or, again, an alternative) to either viewing or shaping that reality in keeping with the logic of either a rational or an ideological world view. The second tends to oppose prudential judgment to mental agility and a tentative pragmatism to dogmatic systematizing.

The Gallic approach is only superficially similar to the eastern European. Since the constituents facing the latter are either undifferentiable or unattractive, to be transcended rather than encompassed, the intellectual process is essentially intuitive from beginning to end, and the intellectual temper is idealistic or even romantic. By contrast, the Frenchman's political system will be formally realistic in that intuited premises and methodically isolated constituents are rigorously or logically related to the envisioned cosmos. One difference in background is that between primeval chaos to be ordered or a radically uncongenial order to be reordered, and the break with an organic (monarchical?) order and tradition to be rationalized. A consequent difference in results is between an excess of fertility, easily generative of a political fantasy that is itself susceptible of corruption when applied (from Hegel to Hitler?), and an intellectual skepticism and rigorism that, expressed in institutional formalism (from First to Fifth Republic?), is either inapplicable to political reality, because it is too "rigorous," or remains unapplied, because intellectual skepticism translates into practical sterility.

If the eastern European political intelligence reflects a lack of acceptable tradition, and the Gallic a yet fully unassimilated break with tradition, the more seasoned and less imaginative Anglo-Saxon political intelligence has matured over longer interludes of relative stability and order, requiring no more than nursing basically acceptable trends and adjusting marginal differences and conflicts between groups and interests. As such, that intelligence is differently self-defeating when faced with breaks in continuity that amount to crisis. True or false, adding up to types or only stereotypes, such differences are also potential complementarities within the larger body of an essentially activist western political culture. Estrangement between its western and eastern branches is more likely to occur on the deeper substratum of political intelligence, having to do with the relationship of reason and sentiment.

The distinguishing feature in that regard is the eastern European's need to live unashamedly within an emotively defined, romanticized universe—all the way from the Germanic penchant for philosophic profundity to the vast soulfulness of the Russian. Out of that need grows the courage to manifest personal emotions as a routine matter of daily interaction between individuals, without the constraints associated with western (or any "high" or "mature"?) civilization. Implicitly rejected is both reserve (or restraint) as a dictate of the approved social manner and the sole reliance on reason as a canon of the only valid method for arriving at socially significant truth. The rejection of restraint is an expression of the individual's confidence in self and his trust in the other: the self-confidence denotes a superior indifference to either "form" or "face," and the trust denotes the generous attribution of feeling—the common denominator between self and other being a shared and mutually tolerant humanity that prizes communication above self-control. The second refusal is to be wholly and solely rational. It derives from the instinctive grasp of the justice of the philosopher's demand for the fusion of reason and sentiment in cognition and, relatedly, the view that only the subjects of knowledge peculiarly in need of that fusion are vital.

Displacing the quest for the difficult combination eastward will intensify it in the manner usual for such diffusion, be it of ideas or of institutions. The deformed result can readily assume the extreme form of pitting unrestrained, mythologizing emotionalism against would-be rationalism in what is then but a sterile polarity (e.g., in the westernizer-Slavophile Russian dichotomy). There is no need to dwell on the dangers of suppressing reason in favor of irrationalism in politics. But such dangers are also only more readily discernible, because more directly manifest in action, than is the opposite danger: from either a repressed or an atrophied sentiment, when the search is for both "truth" and the "good life" in social and political relationships.

The readiness to exhibit emotion, insofar as it denotes ultimate self-confidence, leads to moral courage and derives from historical consciousness. Uninhibited display relates to moral courage at the level where moral cowardice is rooted less in the fear of retribution by others than in the recoil from the exhibition of self; different as the motives are, they will imperceptibly merge in a society that frowns on the conspicuous display of ego. At a farther remove, the lack of inhibition relates somehow to the subject's intimate awareness of past collective trials and regenerations. From thus internalized group ordeals stems, in the very last analysis, individual immunity to social or any other disapproval of spontaneous acts and unrestrained expressions.

Fluid lines of affinity vs. alienation and the lengths and lessons of history   The eastern European's immemorial charge of the westerner's impoverished emotiveness can and did take many forms. On the continent of Europe the main East-West line runs in this respect with the Rhine rather than with the

Elbe or the Oder rivers: there is, in this respect, no essential difference between the Slav and the Teuton. The cult of reserve begins properly with the French bourgeois, reaches its peak in the English idea of the gentleman, and, like everything British, becomes a bit second-hand in America. The issue is complex, however, and secondary lines of division are variably located on this issue as well. In political internation relations, the differentiations account for a paradox: the violence and the intensity of ongoing conflicts tend to be in an inverse relationship with their long-term effect on mutual comprehension and communication between the adversaries at what can only be called the deeper level; affinities in nonpolitical sentiment tend to cut across, and are often directly contrary to, the alignments of outflanking statecraft. The Slav and the German, despite age-long hostilities, understand best one another's ultimate unfamiliarity with the Gaul or the Anglo-Saxon; the long-past climactic conflicts with England leave the French with more lasting complexes about *outre-Manche* than the German "hereditary enemy" and close neighbor has managed to inspire more recently; the Continentals *en bloc* have been either Anglophobe or Anglophile in feeling (or "Angloman" in fashions), but never quite at ease with the British; despite, or because of, their attempts to persuade themselves otherwise, the British themselves have an even greater problem than the continental Europeans in dealing with Americans and find common ground with the former on that score if no other.[5]

The reason for such affective differences and related confusions are doubtless many, all the way from questionably innate group traits to the timing and rate of, say, feudalization, urbanization, commercialization, and industrialization. What has also mattered in relations between west and east Europeans (as demarcated by the Rhine) is the kind of history of each: its relative success and failure; its being completed, detoured, or, to all appearances, permanently truncated when projected against the model of the rounded historical career derived from the western experience.

Being more sensitive than sensible, more impressionable than coolly impressive, can merely reflect either forceful arrests or artificial accelerations in what passes for the normal historical flow. As between Europe and America, however, at issue is less the kind of history than its very existence in the sense of felt individual experience and vicarious memory. History consists for the American of highly intellectualized or civic-mythologized

5. In private relationships, East-West demarcations are symbolically manifest in such things as forms of greeting (note the diminishing directness and use of the fraternal kiss among friends and relatives, also within Europe alone), the notion of friendship (note its expanding inclusiveness and concurrent devaluation, notably but not only as between Europe and America), and likewise the differential social tolerance of, and meaning assigned to, personal aggressiveness.

beginnings or transitions (the founding fathers, the civil war), several canonizations (notably Lincoln's), and isolated episodes prompting either self-congratulation (saving the world in two world wars) or one-sidedly construed events inducing more or less delayed self-laceration (e.g., slavery, the Vietnam war). Such elements simply do not add up to a shared tragic experience; nor do they constitute an organic whole. But both are needed to make up for America's natural handicaps of huge geographic size, vast numbers of people, and cultural heterogeneity when it comes to having the innermost sense of community.

Being more truthfully *geschichtslos* than the lesser Slav nationalities,[6] the Americans are—or appear to the eastern European as being—also emotion poor; they seem to suffer, in the literal and intimate sense, from the unpardonable sin of self-inflicted mutilation, a coldness of the heart. Inability to freely exhibit an irresistibly felt and socially prized individual emotion is not made good by collective manifestations of feeling. It is the former that appears to account for any deficiency in moral courage, and discomfort upon contact with the demonstrative display of such courage has afflicted American society at more than one juncture.

Filtered through such a perception of America, her recent ordeal in Asia assumes the magnified stature of a missed occasion to create authentic history for America. The occasion was one for standing alone and steadfast for a cause that mattered intrinsically less than did the consequence for self-esteem of seeing through (or not seeing through) a task once begun. The opportunity for forging effective nationhood was missed in the mistaken belief that the occasion was instead one for testing or proving something that has no being outside a very particular and partial political and moral imagination. The instant consequence has been the current "graying" of America—the premature aging of one who has not lived to the full extent of his powers. And, finally, that same perspective suggests that the graying West in its entirety cannot do very well and for very long without reabsorbing the capacity for intense feeling and freely expressed emotion.

It is a lesson from all of history that an emotively impoverished West will not be able to meet, on a basis of mutually communicable humanity, the collective sentiment of other cultures as they work out their newly active (not least West-related) idiosyncrasies. If such is the lesson, this must be counted among any blessings of the more limited European history: that its tortured course in the eastern marches has miraculously preserved for the Occident nations, which, though ancient by modern standards, have remained naively young in heart.

6. Karl Marx's term. *Geschichtslose Völker:* peoples without history.

Postscript 3. The Kremlin and a Western Escorial

As the operative West is now being enlarged at its Iberian extremity (and in some respects seems to extend for the moment yet farther westward to include Japan), it ought to be correspondingly expanded eastward, with a view to stabilizing both the lopsided intrawestern and eventual global equilibrium.

At the beginning of the modern European era, Spain moved ponderously across the ocean to the new world in the West. She imparted in the process the first shape to Euratlantica. Soviet Russia reaches out similarly to the third-world peripheries at the outset of a true global system from continental Europe's other extremity, which is also the heartland of Eurasia. Spain was consolidated as a state and reached out for oceanic empire after freeing herself from Moslem dominion within the peninsula and while mitigating Moslem danger from without, in North Africa and the Mediterranean. First the Tartars, and more recently the westward European powers, constituted a comparable setting for Russia's territorial consolidation and continuing expansionist drive.

In both instances, the ordeal of forming state and nation engendered, and the drive for empire confirmed, a compulsion to realize ideological uniformity and orthodoxy—Catholic in Spain's case, first Greek-Orthodox and now Marxist-Communist in Russia's. However, an implacable urge to extirpate heresies within the orbit of rule affected only uncertainly and spasmodically the course of expedient policies outside the orbit. Conflicts with differently constituted powers were no less bitter for that reason. They stimulated in both countries a revulsion from Europe and the desire to be part of Europe. Being part of Europe despite a measure of "foreign-ness" meant for both Spain and Russia being a preeminent part, at least in the initial stage of fusion; Europe's refusal to deny to both what was more readily conceded to other powers in succession fostered in both Spain and Russia the posture, and eventually produced the cult, of a unique and spiritually superior individuality.

The symbol of Spain's lofty defiance was the Escorial; for Russia it was, and still is, the Kremlin. Both combine the tangible and intangible attributes of sovereign residence, church, and fastness; both housed in their time secretively exercised power, deployed ostensibly for the greater glory of a creed and actually directed to acquiring more power against the state's real or suspected enemies.

Spain's exercise of power and defense of empire opened up a chasm between a vast military machine and an unproductive economy. The machine was kept going by the initially rising supply of American silver and by the gradually impoverished peasant's and townsman's subsidy; the national economy decayed in agriculture and stagnated at the industrial foundation. The chasm grew and finally became unbridgeable. Many discern a similar gap and a similar widening chasm within and beneath the total structure of Soviet power, between its military superstructure and its economic and technological base. In the relatively short run, the West would be the loser if analyses along this line are mistaken for predictions. And it would not necessarily benefit in the longer run if the analyses were proven correct, with results for Russia matching the lot of declining Spain. Spain had to wait centuries before she could try, in our time, to find her way back into Europe by the route of material prosperity and institutional renovation. Her prolonged absence from the European balance of power was far from beneficial for that balance, especially when Spain's decline proved to be only the first of a series in the West and the point of gravity continued to move eastward on the Continent. Neither would Russia's absence from the Eurasian or the global balance be an unmixed blessing under comparable conditions.

As Soviet Russia moves out of her land-locked confines toward the seas, the dark beginnings of Muscovy may come to press less hard on the Russian spirit; the lingering shadows may lighten as the dawn that had intermittently seemed to rise over St. Petersburg, facing westward and toward the world's waters, becomes lasting. So long as that evolution is possible, it ought not to be foreclosed by a western policy premised on the belief that such evolution is questionable as to method, intolerable as to cost, and impossible as to result.

So long as the internal evolution is not completed, however, and its provisional and partial outcomes can be reversed, the West must also keep its options open and its powder dry. For it to be able to do both, the western command post of last resort must be again the seat of realistic policy, sometimes secretive and sometimes consensual. And it must become the source of propaganda for a political religion that is compatible with the public creed of preimperial America without being identical to it. Moreover, the sophisticated fragility of the graceful structure at Lafayette Park must, for purposes of effective foreign policy and domestic persuasion, be squarely emplaced within the protective walls of the pentagonal seat of military power. Only then can the three vital attributes of leadership be lodged in an updated version of the Escorial, facing with equal fortitude and matching authority America's Cortes on one side and Russia's Kremlin on the other.

Unless and until power again includes employable military power, and the qualities that make up civic patriotism in changing circumstances are reunited with power behind far-sighted policy, the decay and decline of the West will become an ever more real possibility. It will even grow likely, owing to conditions and attitudes that are diametrically opposed to the deficiencies and excesses that finally brought down imperial Castile. There was too little of the entrepreneurial spirit in the Hispanic realm; such a spirit has tended to dominate the political instinct in the West. A surfeit of the crusading spirit in the dominions of the Catholic kings submerged heroism gradually in physical exhaustion, and the exhaustion itself was finally distilled into a quixotic apotheosis of the heroic code. The agnostic West has tended to sublimate its ambivalence about heroic virtues into the cult of the antihero. Yet, finally, if exalted religiosity climaxed in the too thoroughly purifying Spanish Inquisition, the West's policy-making center has seemed again inclined to make up for the passing of any kind of faith by an inquisitorial moralism that lacked both implementing and staying power.

IV

THE SOVIET RIVAL
AND THE SILENT ENEMY

Beginning with the 1960s, the principal difference in strategic options within Europe has been whether to get at Soviet intransigence via cooperative approaches to receptive eastern European *regimes* or whether to try to get something for the eastern European *peoples* via a strategy recognizing Soviet primacy and right to veto unacceptable change in the area. The more recent choice for the larger stage has been between two different strategies. One would get by the Soviet Union and focus more attention on the global periphery in an effort to redevelop there some leverages on Soviet conduct; the other would emphasize getting along with the Soviets by means of direct accords over the central strategic balance. All of these strategic emphases have acknowledged the central importance of the Soviet Union, if to different extents. All have aimed to combine containment with some relaxation in U.S.-Soviet relations, while proceeding by different routes and anticipating success at more or less remote points along the several routes. And success would ideally mean for all some loosening of regime stringencies within the Soviet Union and the Soviet bloc, if with different degrees of priority.

The usual compromises produced the customary tactical mixes, drawing on both of the successively prominent strategic options. Avoiding a clear choice also meant reducing the chances for a striking success through and for any one strategy. If no clear consensus was achieved around any strategy, it may also be because all have been premature. It is not necessarily the case, however, that it would be equally untimely to start relating the premise of ultimate Soviet centrality to a possibility (or prospect?) bearing on the global periphery. The possibility is that the Eurasian Soviet heartland would progressively assume a less competitive—because more congruent—posture in its relations with the West, not least or primarily with respect to the rimlands and outlying islands and continents. It would be provisionally sufficient to agree—and to agree on the reasons for agreeing—that a current major-power adversary may usefully be the principal focus of one's grand strategy without being necessarily viewed (and unwittingly confirmed?) as by far the principal long-term threat.

Varieties of conditioning structures: cleavages and deformations

Three polarities have been seen to operate in European and western history.[1] One has pitted the spiritual power against secular powers; another has opposed land-based to sea-and-trade oriented powers; and yet another has juxtaposed western with eastern regions. To each of these polarities corresponds, if only roughly, a more abstract duality (or, when it is sharpended, antithesis): to the first, the normative duality of morality (corresponding to spiritual power) vs. pragmatism (corresponding to secular power); to the second, the functional duality of military-political power (typical of continental powers) vs. economic power (characteristic of maritime powers); and to the third the psycho-cultural duality of reasonableness and reserve (attributable to the West) vs. willful emotiveness and release (peculiar to eastern Europe).

Both the concrete and the more abstract pairs share one quality: each pair constitutes ideally a whole of mutually correcting and complementing parts. But, in the real world, the tendencies actually operative are less favorable. The powers and geo-political segments making up the concrete polarities tend to subvert, absorb, or incorporate one another. Were this tendency to be consummated, it would logically terminate in a fusion of the powers or regions; more likely in practice would be the hegemony of one of the powers or regions over the other within each pair. The potentially most damaging tendency is different for the more abstract dualities. There the constituent values, attitudes, and functions are always at risk of being disjoined from one another within each pair and being individually deformed into logical opposites.[2] And, in practice, there is a risk of systemic chaos ensuing when too wide a gap has opened not only between the deformed attitudes or isolated functions within each pair but also, and mainly, between these and the partially independent configurations of power and inertially tradition-bound rules of conduct.

---

1. See chapter 3, pp. 58ff. for background.
2. See p. 83 of this chapter for elaboration.

Traditional schisms and separability of economic and politico-military roles   The conflict-saturated reciprocal subversion between the secular and the spiritual powers went through periods of virtual fusion under the hegemony of one of them (e.g., caesaropapism or Erastianism, papal imperialism or monarchy) before being appeased in the West at least by separation (of church and state). The land-vs.-sea power schism was fully revealed in the Euroglobal setting only when it ceased to be possible to separate the economic and the politico-military (world) orders, and the leadership roles in each, without incurring radical instability.

The new situation arose when economic primacy gravitated to a seafaring power with a sufficiently big territorial and resource base to qualify it also for systemwide politico-military dominance—to wit, when London succeeded Amsterdam as the economic center and British naval power was combined with a balancer role in Europe. Before this happened, first Venice or Genoa and then the Netherlands could be the centers of an emerging world economy while having only local, regional, or auxiliary significance as politico-military powers; Portugal could be briefly such a center while wielding superior military (naval) power only in the overseas periphery; and France or Spain could predominate in the central system politico-militarily on the basis of essentially only a parochial economy. With British ascendancy, the so-far only locally manifest tendency of economic and politico-military power to merge produced wide-ranging conflicts between the sea-based power and the competing preeminent land powers, aimed at reciprocal subversion.

The two types of power were henceforth disjoined only within narrow limits as to scope and duration. Thus Great Britain could delegate a measure of central-systemic leadership in Europe to a continental power, to defeated France in the early eighteenth century and to victorious Germany in the Bismarck-dominated late nineteenth century, while clinging to her primacy in world economics and the peripheries. In the longer run, more normal was the reverse striving of the politico-militarily dominant continental power also to achieve economic (and related colonial) ascendancy or, at least, parity world-wide. This was true for France up to Napoleon I or III, for Germany after Bismarck. Efforts to find an enduring equilibrium in separation were relatively more successful in the state-church relationship, in some parts of the world at least. The same efforts to separate power politics and economics produced only formal theories or policy fictions. Thus extreme advocates of economic liberalism would segregate free trade or economic interdependence from politics; then too, some western policy makers have tried unsuccessfully to draw a distinction between OPEC as only an economic complex and the Arab member-states as politico-military powers.

Spells of more effective separation punctuated reciprocal subversion or efforts at such subversion in the East-West relationship. Typically, deliberate conversion and colonization flowed from West to East, while in periods of western neglect conquest was replaced by a spontaneous eastward diffusion of political and cultural norms and institutions. Reverse efforts at conquest from the East westward took place at the very beginning and the very end of the European system (with the midpoint exception of the Ottoman thrust from outside that system); beginning with Justinian's from Byzantium and provisionally ending with Byzantine-Stalinist Russia's, such armed efforts tended to follow more or less effective eastern assimilation of western techniques and to express divergence from the West in the application of western ideas and institutions. However, the two segments of Europe were also intermittently separated and tensions between them eased thanks to the recurrent centrifugal diversions: westward across the Atlantic by western powers and eastward toward Asia by eastern powers. But a lasting separation was the impractical, and more often than not defensive, goal of politico-cultural ideologues: from late Byzantines through Russia's Old Believers to her early Soviet Communists in the East; from frustrated Counter-Reformation militants through eighteenth-century radical rationalists to interwar political defeatists and appeasers in the West.

Crisis in the secular-spiritual relationship has moved generally eastward, in favor of a contested secular predominance in eastern Europe and of resurgent religious forces in the third world, with imponderable long-term effects on overall East-West relations globally. But the most immediately threatening derangement in contemporary politics is located within the compass of the residually surviving, modified land-vs.-sea power polarity, in the incipient drift toward a disorderly separation between economic and politico-military power, between leadership in world economy and in the global political system.

America's imperial phase created the possibility, now fading, that the world economy and the global politico-military system could be ordered around one core power. Such hegemonic fusion would outdo even the leadership-equilibrium approach to order, as exemplified by Britain's nineteenth-century roles in the balances of both power and payments. In principle, the economic and the politico-military orders can be fused or parallel. But in neither case can they exist long without a center of gravity for both or one for each. In practice, the two orders are no longer likely to coexist effectively for any length of time under not only different but also divergent leaderships, least of all if there are no settled rules for coordinating routine operations and no settled practice makes it possible to predict whether economic or politico-military considerations will primarily determine policy in specific cases or types of conflict and crisis.

Separation under competing leaderships cannot be lastingly stable, at least on the global level, for good reasons. Enduring politico-military power depends now on a dynamically growing and multifaceted base. In addition, economic power requires the backing of politico-military power in conditions where most states refuse a meaningful division of economic labor (e.g., between raw materials-producing and manufactures-producing countries), and where a growing number also demands a precipitate redivision of economic spoils.

There is thus at least a minimum requirement: if leaderships for equilibrium within the world economy and in the politico-military order are to be vested in different powers even provisionally (and then peaceably), these powers must not be acute antagonists over geo-political stakes. In such a perspective, leadership in the world economy might conceivably gravitate to a western Europe organized (or not organized) around a German crypto-hegemony and related (or not related) to a Euro-Japanese axis. Primary responsibility for the politico-military framework and ultimate underpinning of the economic order would rest elsewhere: with either the United States, a Europeanized Soviet Union, or conventional balance-of-power interplays on a U.S.-Soviet axis or within a great-power triangle including China. In this model, western Europe (and Japan) would update and magnify the late sixteenth-century role of Amsterdam. This city and the Netherlands at large were economically active world-wide but militarily so only within the immediate regional setting or in only an auxiliary capacity. And they depended for security either on a *modus vivendi* with a major dominant power (Spain or France) or the balance among several locally and globally interacting military states or empires (the Anglo-Spanish-French triangle).

A different, possibly yet more precarious and provisional, arrangement would divide leadership in the two spheres between the United States (economic) and the Soviet Union (military-political). A prerequisite is that the two had reached an accommodation as to their respective roles and latitudes for initiatives and gains in the two spheres. This arrangement would update and globalize the Anglo-German relationship in the Europe of the 1870s and early 1880s. Two parallel, economic and politico-military, leadership equilibria replace in such a scenario the classic land-sea power schism: two coordinate centers replace one embattled stake, and long-term evolution can provisionally proceed without disruptions resulting from incompatible structures of resources and interests. It is not easy to meet the preconditions, however. One is that the preeminent mercantile actor is either not yet or no longer capable of matching or outdoing the preeminent military actor in the latter's sphere or special competence. Moreover, the economic leader does not or cannot try to confine the military leader lastingly in that role. And the latter is either satisfied with levying a tax for protection or forbearance on the mercantile leader in the present or is prepared to wait to succeed only gradually to economic leadership, too. To do so, he can look to the very same tax for reinforcement, as well as to the natural processes of power gravitation and reciprocal generation, since military-political power will tend to attract or engender economic power and vice versa on the part of rising states.

An equilibrium system taking shape around two centers of gravity is contingent on redistributing assets in both the economic and the military-political spheres. An orderly reapportionment depends, in turn, on updating traditional disciplines both within and between unevenly developed economies and on evolving new rules for accommodation between unevenly saturated major powers in the geo-political arena. A new order might begin to evolve as Soviet Russia (and, one step or several generations behind, China) becomes more vulnerable in the economic sphere (also to third-world raw material producers) and less dissatisfied in the geo-political sphere (also in the third-world peripheries). In other words, Russia (and China) would have to acquire a vested interest in defending the restructured international hierarchy, and they would have to leave to moderated future competition the determination of when (or whether or how) leadership in the two spheres of the dual equilibrium will gravitate and for how long and on what terms that leadership can be divided.

Successive American administrations have proceeded on different assumptions with strategies that were apolitical as well as ahistorical in conception and ineffectual in practice. One part of the approach has been to separate artifically the geo-political sphere from the strategic-nuclear and, secondarily, naval sphere: concessions of accomplished parity in much of the military sphere were offset with denials of legitimacy to any Soviet movement toward matching politically significant results or payoffs.

The other part of the U.S. approach has been to link, no less artificially, the Soviet employment of the conceded military power with the American employment of economic power. The overt intention has been to barter Soviet access to American economic and technological resources for politico-military Soviet abstinence in the peripheries. The so-far sterile underlying idea has been gradually to integrate the Soviet Union into mainly the institutional and economic constituents of the international system. A sustained attempt to buy off the Soviets as potential disturbers of global stability in the short run would complement scattered efforts to buy out the lesser obstacles to localized American peacemaking;[3] the two complementary transactions would be implemented with the aid of essentially identical (i.e., material) and isolated (only economic or only hardware-military) means. A feared result has been a Soviet Union that gradually acquires military

3. See chapter 2, p. 35 on "buy-outs" vs. "sell-outs." The equivalent of the hardware approach to détente with the Soviets has been the heightened reliance on arms sales for securing political and economic access to countries in the third world. The argument does not dispute the role of domestic economic concerns and technological needs in disposing the Soviets to détente.

primacy by way or outside of successive SALT agreements on arms control, and a United States that increasingly relies on economic primacy within an increasingly uncontrolled world economic system.

The first (currently Soviet, politico-military) kind of power aggregation has been traditionally subject to an innate tendency to overextension. It has been so subject particularly when the power is unchecked by either effective (in the present context, U.S.) opposition or concerted accommodation, systemically safeguarded by a wider diffusion of power. The second (currently American, economic) kind of power aggregation has already displayed its built-in tendency toward self-liquidation by near-automatic erosion and diffusion of distinguishing assets. This tendency is especially potent when it is unchecked by effective and, if need be, armed safeguard of access to vital resources and outlets.

The "man in the middle" between superpowers splitting up contentiously the ultimate unity or, at least, interlock of ordering roles would henceforth be not only non-Soviet eastern Europe but historic Europe as a whole. A disorderly fission risks straining her along several lines of force and function between the "farther" West and the "nearer" East, between Europe's henceforth not-so-much spoiled as disillusioned daughter (America) and alternately rough-shod and silver-slippered Cinderella (Russia).

Deformed attitudes and effects on societies and civilizations   Artificial separation between nuclear strategics and conventional geo-politics, along with dis- orderly divergence of economic and military orders, have not made up the sole threat to the West and its stake in world order. Nor was the initial trend toward a cleavage between U.S. economic and Soviet military primacy independent and sufficient grounds for a possible division between America and Europe. An additional, partly originating and partly contributing source of the malaise has been the deformation of policy-relevant attitudes in the West. Deformed in different degrees are both constituents in each of the paired abstract dualities noted before: morality vs. pragmatism, economic vs. military-political power, reasonableness vs. emotiveness. They became deformed as they were disjoined from one another and from the operative, or at all operable, international system.

Interactions between spiritual and secular powers, land and sea powers, East and West, as concrete entities, were creative as well as disruptive in either the same or different areas of historical experience. They certainly helped propel the Euroglobal international system in its evolution and expansion, as well as ultimately eroding its (European) core. By contrast, no discernible advantage has flowed from the more abstract paired attitudes or attributes being disjoined and polarized, with ill consequences for their capacity to correct or complement one another. In the absence of such correctives, morality will be deformed into moralism and pragmatism into opportunism, with only a negative long-term effect on international relations. American moralism reappeared in the spiritual (or moralizing) imperialism-without-executing-arm of President Carter's foreign policy mode; opportunism pervaded the methods of ward politics injected into world politics: twisting arms (e.g., in Middle Eastern peacemaking and Panama Canal treaty making) in the pursuit of momentary tactical or other advantage, yielding on symbolic essentials (e.g., when finally normalizing relations with China), and consistently overrelying on economic clout (e.g., when applying poorly assorted linkages to issues involving the Soviets). A corresponding deformation was manifest in western Europe when official foreign policy tended toward the low-grade trader's cynical amorality, and private values veered toward the opportunism implicit in petty hedonism.

In both parts of the West, through official or private materialism, one deformation was thus infiltrated by another, located in the functional domain of economic vs. military-political attributes of power. This deformation was carried over into attitudes in the guise of politically unconstrained economism, in which issues were viewed and remedies prescribed in narrow economic terms. A correspondingly exorbitant militarism was more subtly in evidence: it was relegated to the preserve of single-minded nongovernmental advocates of military preparedness and of one-sidedly arms-accumulating third-world dependents, while finding a more official expression in a highly professionalized fixation on military hardware and abstractly speculative military-strategic scenarios—both questionably pertinent to the immediately critical conventional politico-military realities in the world at large.

The final duality, capable of being intensified into antithesis, opposes reasonableness to emotiveness. It has the most complex ramifications as it extends from the sphere of individual action through the socio-cultural setting to the political arena. Reasonableness and reserve are politicized in the self-constrained exercise of the Reason of State. Such an exercise is commonly equated with political realism. Its correspondent in the socio-cultural sphere is a political nationalism moderated by a historically long-accomplished coincidence of state and nation. By contrast, emotiveness and its release are politicized in a political romanticism that is fed, among other things, by a communal or folk nationalism which merely strains toward a yet unrealized (or an only recently realized) unification with or within a state. When not checked by reason and reserve, political romanticism will degenerate into messianic and/or totalitarian excesses. Results are no better when reasonableness is not inspired by emotion and reserve is cut off from release. Political realism will then degenerate into a mix of concretism (fixation on tangibles) and technological rationalism (including the theoretical strategics of nuclear deterrence and war fighting); moderate nationalism will decay on the mass level into an alternation between chauvinism and cynicism about politics and, on the elite level, into self-consciously progressive objectivity, if not backward-leaning altruism.

Moralizing ersatz imperialism has not blended with ward politics any better in post-Vietnam America than authentic Gaullism was sufficient to sustain France's efforts at world policy in the aftermath of the Algerian war. Neither mix amounted to an adequately inspiring antidote to either petty hedonism or insatiable consumerism. In highly industrialized societies, frustrations that are not continuously relieved by policies sensitive to both psychological and material needs can be released violently in collective explosions only at long intervals, and those frustrations will then be discharged for questionable or undefined political objectives. One such explosion occurred in France in May 1968. In-between mass explosions, psychic pressures will more often produce a kind of individual implosion, rushing in to shatter the alienated citizen's lifeline to the political society; those pressures may impel the citizen to seek inner emigration into pseudo-religious and other fantasies. Such individual implosions were not unrelated to the earlier noted event in Guyana, which marred the end of 1978 for Americans. However, the principal casualty of the several deformations in the entire West might well become an authentic political realism. It is a realism that expands its ethical dimension indirectly by concern for public morale, and one that enriches its psychological dimension directly by concessions to political romanticism.

When political imagination has atrophied in the leading power or civilization, what commonly follows is a decline amidst international disorder. Only later will the separated functional orders and the disjoined subjective modes and moods be again refused or viably coordinated. The merger occurs in, and will be effected by, a new leading power and civilization that have been proved capable of relating power to norm and passion to power.

Wealth without nations and the postpolitical man in the West   We just might be living at a turning point in history, reflecting a major division in mankind. Societies that control or merely enjoy wealth are either no longer nations (western Europe) or seem to elude the key characteristics of nationhood most of the time (the United States). Other societies aspire aggressively to possessing wealth and becoming nations. These two models of society operate in different historical time zones with respect to the political dimension. The fact that two evolutionary stages and related mentalities exist side by side need not polarize the parties in conflict, nor has it done so. But, paradoxically, less confrontation may spell greater imbalance in international relations and a greater, because more insidious, internal and external threat to the West as it is presently constituted in scope and dominant sentiment.

Sheer nomenclature conveys the gap felt in the American experience. The overall state, encompassing the several states in the union, is commonly referred to functionally as the federal government and is more exaltedly denoted as the nation. The very fact of mobilizing the connotations of nationhood in order to express a formal-institutional fact intimates the paucity of nationhood as an intensely felt organic reality and presence, outside and independent of specific institutions or regimes. In western Europe, France was the primordial nation and nation-state and has been matched as such by only a few, if any. When the *grande nation* rejected the nationalist Gaullist appeal, it released that appeal for flourishing outside France and western Europe, not least in the third world. The transfer suggested the final drying up of political nationhood at its source and its accelerating diffusion outward.

Political nationhood is at its best and truest when it symbolically reinforces the social precipitate of freely incurred political obligation. In a crisis, the obligation becomes unconditional and dwarfs the indulgences and immunities that rightfully constitute much of democratic normalcy but are not sufficient to sustain an embattled political society. The most intense and active expression of such nationhood has been political nationalism. Nationalism reedited and temporarily perpetuated in Europe the aristocratic values of duty and loyalty, transferred by the rising middle classes from the person of the feudal overlord or divine-right monarch to the institution of the national state. The kinds of dangers and privations to be protected against in return for fealty were changing, and their range widening, even as the sense of obligation and its manifestation in personal prowess were being diluted and reserved for exceptional circumstances. But the essential feeling and phenomenon remained the same, assuring fundamental continuity for the wider compass of related social mores.

A qualitative change has taken place only when the outlook focused on strictly economic transactions was universalized. The basic principle of the new mentality is to discard noncalculating mutuality as the operative ideal and replace it with exactly calculated quid pro quos. The models for social mores and political morality are henceforth the merchant's calculable profit, as a return for investment or reward commensurate with risk, and the journeyman's wage for labor counted by the hour. The norms of capitalistic individualism and working-class collectivism permeate private and public postures at different levels of material well-being; the bourgeois imitation and partial perpetuation of the feudal ethos, first qualified by the mercantile ethos, is gradually submerged in an essentially proletarian mentality.

The mercantile ethos of prudent calculation can usefully contain excesses of political nationalism. But in a progressively democratized mass society, that ethos is likely to degenerate into an all-absorbing pursuit of immediate private satisfactions and either indifference or cynicism about public life and public powers. The degeneration of the mercantile ethos will be relieved, in its immediate public effect, by private *bonhomie* so long as its precipitants in social and physical mobility and expanding affluence endure. But the same palliative signals all the more unmistakably the arrival, hand in hand with the social proletarian as the dominant new type, of the postpolitical man. His arrival coincides with the passing of political nationalism *qua* civism expressed in an uncoerced sense of obligation. His ascent marks a break in millennial political and social history. The break is no less critical for merely counterpointing more conspicuous transformations. The new social type's ascendancy assures the decline and portends the defeat of a civilization rooted in an elitist ethos; it does so no less surely if the decline is clothed in slogans glorifying compassionate humanity.

The West-dominated modern era was fashioned by the confluence of three innovations that were, in part, restorations of previously eroded achievements of antiquity: a strong centralized state, a world-wide economy dominated from one center, and the secularization of faith in the form of political nationalism. The state's growth in strength both fueled and contained the development of an ever more world-wide economy, while political nationalism served differently and unevenly both the narrower political and the larger economic orders. Nationalism unfailingly sustained the individual states, and it imparted specific structures to world economy by filtering through the processes of politics, with mixed results, the operation of any autonomous laws of economics to which the evolution and the operation of the economy might be subject.

All three constituents of the West-centered modern world have been weakened lately, if not subverted. The present era is, in the West, at least as much postpolitical as it is postindustrial when current and classic forms of the two branches of action are compared. The state has ceased to be strong in the West, less because it was no longer able to defend its citizens militarily and more because the reasons and the need for such defense have ceased to be felt. A symmetrical balance of (nuclear) terror has eliminated the quality of fear that was made to man's measure and both stimulated and controlled individual political instincts. The Europe- or West-centered economy has been weakened shortly thereafter, and for similar reasons; it has not ceased to be superior technically, but it ceased to be managed politically from the center and defended politico-militarily at the peripheries. An increasingly asymmetrical relationship of forces between the haves and the have nots has taken shape both within and outside western societies; it has eliminated economic disciplines capable of both stimulating and controlling group interests.

Finally, political nationalism has either waned or failed to mature in the West. It has done so for reasons other than its being replaced by a different and higher faith—be it Europeanism, Atlanticism, or effective humanitarianism. Political nationalism was atrophied by developments of the kind that also weakened the state and undermined the world economy. One concerned transnationality and the statistically plausible degree to which it could be manipulated for shared benefit in material relations among collectives; the other development bore on something akin to self-transcendence and the subjectively bearable degree to which material concerns could become all-absorbing for individuals.

The classic tension which the state system institutionalized between finite terror (the fear of violent death) and metapersonal transcendence (the craving for sublime life) has had one positive consequence. It has produced a viable combination of politically dynamic relations among power aggregates at all times and psychological stability for most individuals most of the time. The present inverse formula is questionably viable: it has combined political statics with agitated psychology. The static condition is implicit in the inability or unwillingness of ostensibly powerful governments to effect major changes by overt acts of statecraft of the traditional (or any other) kind. As for agitation, it is the hallmark of the disoriented or alienated postpolitical man. The new combination came into being when specifically focused fears (finite terror) were replaced by a diffuse, unproductive anxiety (around the balance of terror). Simultaneously gone was a specifically focused political allegiance, expressing the subordination of self; it has given way to aspiration toward a politically uncontaminated economic conduct, expressed in terms of transnationally implemented interdependence. The aspiration is as diffuse as the anxiety; whereas the latter could not be positively routed into anything other than potentially uneven restraint, the former was easy to channel into unreciprocated restraint.

Little help could be expected from nuclear weapons, the poisoned gift of the gods to an affluent civilization that is no longer reliably willing and able to defend itself against physical assault in hand-to-hand and eye-to-eye combat. Nuclear weapons provisionally protect the militarily armed, but they also lastingly aggravate the condition of moral disarmament by eliminating the fear of an attack occurring at the center of the civilization. By the same token, relative affluence has made it possible to distribute material goods more equitably both within and among nations than was or could be the case before. But the newly created margin for setting out to satisfy the less fortunate also eliminated the social disciplines that permit deferral of complete satisfaction and make that redistribution materially productive, politically sustainable, and morally unassailable.

In the relationship of the individual to society, and of different societies to one another, some form of crisis followed necessarily when the new conjunction (off diffuse terror and seemingly boundless material resources) inverted the traditional mix of sharply focused, finite fears and strictly limited material resources. Apprehensions of both governors and the governed centering on specific public predicaments that could be managed at a definable cost were historically the political counterpart of the everyday private fears rooted in the acutely felt scarcity of material resources and rewards. Those private fears underlay the various social disciplines and economically conditioned sense of individual obligations that make up civil existence; they were, in addition, the daily school preparing for the occasionally required feats denoting the acceptance and implementation of political obligation. Fear as stimulus shares with the exercise of power the capacity for guiding man toward his meanest and his noblest acts—noblest when he fears to fail the self-imposed test of virtue or excellence. Being the ultimate stimulus, fear inevitably controls—i.e., inspires, channels, and contains—the *ultima ratio:* the use of force among individuals as well as collectives. And so long as the use of force remains within the psychological and practical ambit of others, a widespread atrophy of specifically focused fear will produce conduct that poses as sophisticated prudence until it is hurried into the opposite of prudence by panic.[4]

Varieties of external threats: strategic and subsidiary

Panic is most likely to take hold when threats have been wrongly identified or poorly managed for too long. How serious any one particular class of threat is depends on how immediate it is and on the urgency of an effective response to it; on its ultimate or worst-case severity; and on how readily it can be managed. Outside threats to the West originate with the Soviet Union and

4. Such panic—the feeling of time running out on moderate remedies and of the outside world closing in—was in variable degrees present behind the ostensibly second or last (and actually the third or fourth) bid of major powers for supremacy: Spain's bid under Philip IV after Philip II, Napoleon's after Louis XIV's, Hitler's after the emperor's Germany, and, up to a point, Britain's late-nineteenth (after her mideighteenth) century imperialism. Late or last bids are typically exacerbated by odds that have been worsened by structural changes both within and in the environment of the affected power. Since bids are invariably subject to repetition on the part of inherently strong states, the ascendancy of the United States that is either still unfolding or already receding before our eyes may come to appear retrospectively has having been but the relatively benign first of its kind (or, actually, second or third, depending on one's assessments and definitions).

the third world. The two share basic structures of both threat and response. The Soviet military-political threat subdivides into a strategic (including nuclear) threat within the central balance and theater, and a purely conventionally (including navally) implemented threat of an amplifying Soviet penetration into the world's peripheral real estate (and sealanes).

The threat from the third world is primarily economic. Its strategic strand is to the central economic system of the West and resides currently in the field of energy supply; subsidiary threats have to do with an unrestricted western access to other raw materials, western absorptive capacity for low-cost manufactures, and generally, the complex of issues involved in third-world insistence on recasting the world economic order. When formulating western response, both threat and response can be alternately abstracted or over-concretized: abstracted into technical dimensions of either military strategics or professional economics; overly concretized into the material dimension of military hardware or economic goods only. The character of both perceived threat and indicated response is substantially depoliticized in either case.

Détente vs. interdependence and degrees in subsidiary threats   The second-named, nonstrategic or lower-level threats in both classes are more subtle or insidious than the first-named or strategic ones. That does not mean that either of them is likely to reach worst-case severity in anything like the near future. They are both in principle manageable (though not necessarily evenly so) by the range of leverages and counteractions still available for use in the West's arsenal, even if they are currently unused. And both kinds of the lower-level or subsidiary threats can be confused even more than the strategic threats by slogans or concepts such as détente (with the Soviet Union) and interdependence (with the third world). Such slogans or concepts raise the issue of how unequally different parties are either sensitive to intellectually catchy cliches or also vulnerable to effective abuses. And the slogans or concepts are themselves vulnerable to either misconception or misrepresentation.

A proponent misrepresents an innovation in policy when he describes it as a wholly positive development, although the policy in fact conceals abdication from a greater degree of self-assertion than he deems currently possible or, under his value system, desirable. The initial overselling of détente made it vulnerable to that charge. Subsequent reaction to the misrepresentation of what détente was has only fueled misconceptions of what détente could mean practically in order to be conditionally viable for both superpowers in both of the two related military-strategic and geo-political realms. The dubious advantage of overselling has been almost simultaneously passed on to economic interdependence. Overemphasis on interdependence can pervert the existing relationship of forces no less than a misguided approach to détente. Both can reduce the side that is effectively stronger to making ineffectual responses to abuses by the more insistent side, bent on catching up. As a result, both interdependence and détente can be deformed into a one-way street in favor of the latecomer. But diplomatic détente is currently more likely than economic interdependence to be seen by the party in possession as a way to freeze the status quo once and for all, notably in the geo-political arena. So to conceive of détente makes it superficially plausible to argue that seizure of unilateral advantages by the Soviets had defeated the effort to implement the most critical aspect of interdependence in the world today: each superpower depending on the other for both strategic stability and politically accented world order. Expectations can easily be too great or appreciations too sanguine in relation to both détente and economic interdependence. They are then apt to run up against a reality that refuses to realize misconstrued possibilities.[5]

It may be more difficult to implement economic interdependence than it is to practice détente to the equal satisfaction and advantage of both or all parties. The parties to economic interdependence are the West or the North on one side and the third world or the South on the other side. They are more asymmetrical than the parties to U.S.-Soviet détente, and economic issues and instruments are even harder to manage than are the politico-military ones. Lately, it has been less fashionable to stress the difficulty of managing economic relationships and using the economic weapon than it has been to dwell on similar disabilities in the military arena. Yet if the use of military force *may* escalate out of control or boomerang, the economic weapon *will* be a two-sided as well as blunt instrument in virtually all situations; few are those who can hurt anyone economically without either hurting also themselves or diverting profit to a third party.

There is another stumbling block. A correct approach to détente involves adopting a well-defined attitude toward parity and the rate of progress toward parity between parties in the separate but interconnected military and geo-political arenas. Interdependence raises the issue of equality and inequality in

---

5. See Introduction (including note 1), chapter 2, and *Quest for Equilibrium* (part II) for observations on détente. The overselling of interdependence has been the monopoly of liberal, and also utopian, world-order advocates, with the unwitting connivance of realistic (or only recidivistic) commentators all taken up by resisting the Soviet politico-military threat. Not the most extreme "neorealist" statements can be found in Robert Conquest, ed., *Defending America* (New York: Basic Books, 1977).

A relatively moderate and studiedly cautious statement of the interdependence thesis is Robert O. Keohane and Joseph S. Nye, *Power and Interdependence* (Boston: Little, Brown, and Co., 1977). But it, too, tries to make too much of a case for the preferred world view by illustrating working interdependence on issues and transactions that have only limited political implications and by projecting the result against the contrasting negative background of political realism (or Realpolitik) reduced by caricature to the use of military instruments. For a critical review of the literature, see James P. O'Leary, "Envisióning Interdependence: Perspectives on Future World Orders," *Orbis,* Fall 1978.

a yet wider range of aspects: who is more and who is less dependent in the interdependent relationship? Who can more effectively withstand the breakdown of such a relationship or more forcefully dominate the limitations it entails? And who is more able to practice blackmail and more likely to submit to it?

When it comes to agreeing on and managing a gradual movement toward parity in superpower access to the geo-political peripheries, a West that is on the defensive may be handicapped relative to Soviet initiatives, and it may be more handicapped than it is relative to strategic-nuclear parity in the central balance. But the West is at a yet clearer disadvantage when economic interdependence with the third world must be managed. Its economic power is great and overwhelming; yet the power is of little use and will not be used because the complexities of western socio-political and economic structures are yet greater.

It is not only that responding to abuses with the economic weapon will also hurt the wielder of that weapon in strictly material terms. In addition, in terms of domestic politics, even a major economic provocation will not be judged worth even a mildly disturbing riposte, liable to upset the ingrained consumption habits of the opulent society. In less than catastrophic conditions, an elective western maker of policy will prove unwilling to cause any discomforts that can be traced to his prior actions. He will thus be at a disadvantage in interactions with mostly autocratic third-world leaders or regimes. The latter will commonly be willing to risk even major economic disruptions for the sake of a political objective, and a primitive economy will survive even drastic curtailments if the bluff happens to fail.

It became habitual in the context of American-Vietnamese military hostilities to stress asymmetries in motivation, political will, and stakes between a global power and a directly concerned local party. The asymmetries were disastrously manifest in the end. They apply, however, with equal weight to situations involving economic interdependence and are apt to favor a wider range of parties, since far fewer third-world regimes are able to match Hanoi's military performance than might be tempted to exploit economic interdependence. Nor will western difficulties be eased if the network of objectively interdependent relationships becomes more complex and confining. On the contrary, more links will at first mean more asymmetry in subjective dispositions either to manipulate relationships or withstand efforts to do so. Radical instability will follow until the utopian end-state has been reached in the form of equalized captivity by all parties to something radically novel: the dominance of economics, embodying henceforth more than speculatively the essence of "high" politics.

There is little to choose between diplomatic-strategic détente and economic interdependence that have both been mishandled or misconceived.

The threat implicit in interdependence is greater on the whole because it is more difficult to monitor—and easier to minimize—shifts in the balance of economic dependence than shifts in the distribution of assured politico-military access or retaliatory weapons systems. An economic risk or danger will appear remote or responsive to technical economic adjustments until a cyclical downturn or an inflationary upswing has proven otherwise. Conversely, anticipatory assessments of worst-case severity tend to be overdrawn in the politico-military sphere. They are readily replaced in the economic realm by anticipatory invocations of best-case solidarity.

Nuclear vs. oil weapons and degrees of strategic threats   Comparative severity is no different for the strategic threat potentials in the central-systemic arena, the nuclear-*cum*-conventional Soviet military threat and the economic threat by major oil producers. The oil threat has already been shown to be more immediate and more urgently in need of a many-sided response than has any Soviet effort at overwhelming militarily either western Europe or the North American continent. The major producers of oil have demonstrated a firmer will and a superior capacity to blackmail the West than the Soviet Politburo has. And, by expert consensus, any one major—or swing—oil supplier with a decisive margin of productive capacity can critically damage the West. It did not require the Iranian revolution in early 1979 to prove that the loss of such a supplier is at all times possible and at some future point likely. Yet so long as there are neither alternative sources of energy nor alternative suppliers of oil, to lose an established one would damage the West sooner and more severely than losing a major non-oil producing third-world country—or even one of the strategically less vital west European countries—to either internal Communist or Soviet control.

It is in some ways also less easy to manage the economic threat than to deal with the strategic politico-military threat; counteraction by equivalent means is not equally available or effective. Military build-up can be opposed to Soviet military build-up without irreversibly disrupting relations while fairly effectively deterring escalation of political objectives. The same is not equally true in all respects if an oil embargo or major price increase by OPEC is met with a quarantine of its economic asset in the West. Similarly, it is both psycho-politically and logistically easier to use western military power in alliance with local forces, not least in the third world. Internal opposition of at least some interests to Soviet penetration will inevitably throw up local elements ready to collaborate with western efforts to contain immoderate Soviet expansion. By contrast, an extortionate or erratic oil policy may well unite an entire population in support of even an unpopular or illegitimate third-world regime, and it may compel the use of western force without any local allies.

The worst-case threat is linked to the vision of a Soviet nuclear blackmail that compels concessions amounting to a change of the political system in the West or, more plausibly, western Europe alone. But a denial or blackmail in the energy field that is motivated politically and rationalized economically can produce social dislocations so severe as to precipitate a no less far-reaching change. The difference may (but need not necessarily) be in the specific kind of ideological orientation that the regime finally installed subscribes to. But in either case, the regime is likely to be more autocratic than the one unable to avert the precipitating crisis. Only a procedural difference is wholly certain: Change in response to a nuclear dictate is apt to be carried out instantly and in an orderly fashion; chaos is apt to intervene before a new order emerges from economic disruption.

Both forms of regime change would mean that western Europe is lost for the United States. It is not clear whether the United States would suffer more from losing access to western Europe or from being cut off from mideastern oil. To raise that question is redundant, however. Although the two aspects of the jeopardy are different in kind and cannot be readily compared, they are circular. Loss of western access to mideastern oil will tend to lose western Europe for America by the economic route, whereas a prior loss of western Europe would tend to ensure America's expulsion from the Middle East by the strategic route. The scenario related to economics is presently the more plausible one of the two. Moreover, it is such not—or not primarily—because the Soviets are capable of cutting off mideastern oil supplies by advances in the Persian Gulf and adjoining areas. That capacity is currently no greater than is the longer-range potential of the Soviets to become the more effective protector of oil supplies for western Europe against interruptions indigenous to the Middle East than the United States sometimes seems to be at present and may easily become in the future.

Advocates of interdependence can downgrade its dangers by combining pragmatic conceit with philosophical or ethical humility. Conceit invokes western economic strength and resilience; humility professes the duty for the North to be sensitive to southern indictments couched in moral terms, and it renders the North vulnerable to the charges in the process. It may be further argued in defense of safe dependence on interdependence that the oil threat alone does not warrant reorienting strategic priorities: it neither creates an aggregate economic threat by itself nor can it be replicated by suppliers of other raw materials. One rider does not make up the apocalypse any more than one swallow makes the spring. Yet, even if the argument were to be granted, and if the oil threat were discounted as the only serious one and the other economic risks dismissed as marginal and liable to be ineffectual, the need for revising the threat hierarchy would not disappear. The same reasoning could then be applied to the Soviet threat. The threat's strategic military side, too, is the only serious one. And its ideological or any other components can be dismissed as marginal even more readily than can be the secondary threats hidden from sight by a reassuring phrase denoting the problematic fact of interdependence.

Determinateness, manageability, and creativity of Soviet and third-world threats
Two reasons have made it attractive to view the Soviet politico-military threat as primary. The quality and the source of the threat are conceptually determinate, and they have become familiar. This is a key difference from the third world and any threat that it engenders. Both are conceptually indeterminate. Moreover, an ever-changing balance of traditional and modern tendencies attaching to both makes them also essentially unfamiliar.

The third-world actors are not states either totally or in the main aspects. Their methods and objectives are, as a result, even less rational and rationally predictable than they would be if they shared structural and other constraints with the more advanced states. It is rarely clear what key third-world parties are and how they ought to be treated: as political entities with corporate identity (i.e., states); as evolving or inert economies; or as haphazard or protean assortments of social, ethnic, tribal, or religious groupings. In either case, their policies will be divergently personalized by strong, if changing, leaders and depersonalized in weak institutions. The presence of some attributes and the absence of others make it intellectually unattractive to assign the inchoate members of the international society a high place in the threat hierarchy, regardless of how relatively serious and manageable the threat they present may be.

All the previously surveyed threats other than the Soviet nuclear threat are intrinsically manageable by restraints and counteractions. The nuclear threat is manageable only theoretically and statically: by conceptually correct, if in fact hypothetical, strategic doctrine and in terms of offsetting capabilities in being. It is impossible to know whether and in what way it would prove possible to control actually released capabilities under any one scenario. The subsidiary Soviet threat, in the geo-political arena, can be managed if suitable western deployments and counteractions become a prime object of determined policy. The corresponding risks reside in the Soviet conventional military, including naval, leverages becoming progressively equal or superior to the American ones, and in the nuclear quality of the escalatory ceiling. How to rank the two kinds of Soviet threat and orchestrate the competing claims on diverse capabilities and policy responses cannot be determined operationally with any confidence. Only political judgment and moral intuition of the highest order can begin to adjust the equation between either threat's severity if it materializes and the probability that it will do so.

No less manageable are both classes of the third-world economic threats, both the strategic (currently oil) and the subsidiary (low-cost manufactures, claims to redistribution, etc.). One condition is that responses are not confined to economic countermeasures. The balance of leverages lies still with the West in the last resort. And the ultimate risk from determined western response is kept relatively low by the escalatory spiral stopping short of being nuclear. What remains is the superior potential of economic grievances or blackmail policies to unite third-world populations behind antiwestern offense or defense. It ought to be possible to deal with that risk by providently choosing the terrain best suited for interventionary actions and electing measures with the widest-ranging demonstration effect.

There is a yet more significant, final difference between the third-world economic threat and the Soviet politico-military threat. It consists not in the degree to which responses to either threat are urgent because the threat is immediate, but in the degree to which both threat and response are or can be creative because their repercussions within western polities are or can be positive over a longer period of time.

The strategic-nuclear threat and responses to it are at best neutral; the best to be hoped for is that they neither galvanize populations into a frenzy nor paralyze them into a state of shock. And neither any likely extent of Soviet penetrations in geo-political peripheries nor any probable responses to them can be expected to raise western publics to new heights of purpose, effort, or sacrifice and remedy their growing shortcomings in those respects. One reason is that Soviet geo-political outreach does not visibly impact on the daily lives of westerners so long as it is perceived as broadly compatible with political balance and does not demonstrably upset vital material needs.

Not only has the scope of Soviet penetration been kept within bounds by Soviet caution or setbacks so far, but the notion of a mortal Soviet threat to the West has been weakened by several combined factors: the cold war became less intense even as the battle fatigue grew from its long prior duration; officially promoted cultural diplomacy and intuitively sensed cultural propinquity influenced both elite and mass publics in favor of things Russian, even if not Soviet, at a time when yet less cognate forces were rising in the world at large.

It is increasingly difficult to represent the Soviet threat as being more than one component in an evolving complex and a changing hierarchy of threats. In its traditional extreme formulation, the threat has ceased being widely credible. As it does so, however, concern with and response to it as prime objects of policy cease to be creative. They are no longer creative internally, by shaping positively the domestic balances between incentives and anxieties. And they are no longer creative internationally, by promoting long-term stability in the world balance of power between receding and insurgent forces for radical or violent change.

The economic threat from the third world is different. It impacts actually and potentially on everyday existence in the West. It is not only real but also credible and increasingly credited. And it is or can be creative, since effective responses to the threat would go far toward remedying critical western weaknesses. Such responses could prompt self-confident assertion of superior western power in the last resort. Or they could restimulate western capacity for temporary self-denial of material gratifications until the end of a confrontation removed the attending economic dislocations.

Ranges of responses to the third world and changes in U.S.-Soviet ground rules   It is not necessary to believe in a constant sum of changing threats as either an objective given, a perceptual propensity, or a psychological need. Nor is it necessary to infer from political dynamics an immutable tendency for the recession of one kind of threat to be compensated automatically by the surfacing of a different threat, the rise of the new threat being both the cause and consequence of the decline of the old one. But even if neither the belief nor the inference are subscribed to, it is still possible to argue in favor of ongoing changes in the hierarchies of either subjectively perceived or empirically demonstrable threats.

The present state of the threat is implicit in the actually or potentially revolutionary arousal of the global peripheries to a largely autonomous politico-economic existence. And it is aggravated by the increasing extent to which the peripheries impinge on the West and its requirements. The threat may be intrinsically manageable, but actual western responses have not therefore been demonstrably more adequate. Each attempt at positive response in the more or less remote past has had a negative corollary. Early in the cold war era, the atempt was to delegate management of still-colonial peripheries to the European imperial powers; any positive potential in that U.S. approach was offset by an ever less doctrinaire and ever more pragmatic or opportunistic anticolonialism of the official U.S. establishment, directed at the Europeans. The related later attempt was to integrate key parts of the third world as allies in anti-Soviet containment strategies; it was negated by a third-world neutralism that became virulent as the attempt got underway and faltered. The climactic effort was to align the third world in a yet more intimate association, one of common belligerency against insurgencies associated (or not) with regional and mostly Communist-managed imperialisms; this effort was thwarted by a resurgent antiimperialism, though one directed this time at the United States itself and from within.

A substitute strategy aimed at disengaging American power from regional involvements would delegate once again the responsibility for regional order, this time to local middle-power surrogates; devolution was defeated by domestic instabilities, including revolution in the (Iranian) paragon of the strategy. And finally, in the changed climate stressing economics, interdependence was offered as the panacea for politico-militarily induced and implemented ills. Mutuality was actually in evidence, but most strikingly in the form of ransom, one side presenting the demands (the oil producers and radical seekers of economic reform) and the other side consenting or expected to consent to extortions in one form or another (both industrial and developing consumers of oil and mainly western suppliers of capital goods and credit).

The persistent failure to find a workable approach to the third world has itself been part of the changing threat. It has also been the source of anxiety. Articulate observers came to fear that America or the West at large would become isolated from the third world politically and morally. The anxiety over isolation was a counterpoint to the hopes reposed in interdependence; prompted by imaginary dangers, anxiety has tended to blanket and smother fear of a real and present danger. Yet being fearfully alive to vulnerability might alone prompt an effort to make the West immune by acts and policies going beyond domestic programs such as the short-lived Project Independence in energy. The West cannot henceforth control most aspects of the development through which the third world assumes, with or without the benefit of authentic revolution, an identifiable shape in the form of viable actors and workable principles of action. There is, therefore, no particular merit to be gained from staying close to the third world across the board and no clear profit to be found in avoiding isolation from the third world *en bloc*. Instead, a strategy for immunizing the West will also have to reflect an awareness of when and how to impose isolation on uncontrollable third-world elements and fields of action, as part of increasing the measure of feasible control in areas where access remains both possible and vital.

The Soviet Union was contained while isolating itself after World War II. Communist China was to be contained but not isolated as both cold and hot war shifted to Asia. Selectively imposing isolation as part of containment in the third world would begin to transfer the defense of the West from an earlier to a later source of international disorder. The shift is parallel with a deeper change, as economic and other abuses of independence join forcible imposition of servile dependence as the evils to be checked. The new task is to draft cumulatively the ground rules to govern North-South relationships and to discipline parties to North-South interdependence. This task is paired with the challenge to rewrite gradually the preexisting rules of the game in superpower relations for the next period, so that it may precede a yet later period of partnership. Such a partnership would implement a nonnuclear negative community of interests, relative to forces in the peripheral zone that neither superpower has been shown able to manage on its own. The new rules would crystallize methods for adding western to other constraints on the rate and location of the Soviet advance toward superpower parity, but those rules would also replace the integral denial of Soviet entitlement to effect or enjoy any alterations in geo-politically manifest power or presence. The released measure of denial would be shifted to delinquent third-world actors. It may have to be so shifted if the West is to have any constraining or controlling impact on socio-political revolution or economic reprisal in the peripheries.

Power gravitation may or may not be attended or propelled by a political or any other revolution. A power or civilization will avoid being set back by either upheaval only when it can still respond effectively to threats from outside or inside. However, a society also declines when it loses the ability to identify correctly the changing configurations and hierarchies of threats. When this happens, the state of not knowing for certain or not discerning correctly what to fear, or fear most, has a way of producing actions designed less to deal with external threats than to still inward anxiety. Such a state of the policy-making will and the public mind is not easily reversed; it is to be feared more than fear itself.

Varieties of internal threats: imported and indigenous

As a maturing political society, America suffered from an unusual experience. Almost without transition, it moved from the virtual absence of warranted fear to the condition of unmanageable anxiety. As a result, the American and his society were not seasoned by one, fear, before being unnerved by the other, anxiety. The anxiety was acute during the Great Depression and was only haltingly overcome; it has been latent and continuing in response to the military-technological revolution in our time. By contrast, western European societies survived many occasions warranting fear. In order to live on, however, they have tended to substitute psychic for physical defenses: they would rather deny the very existence or manageability of threat than to make ready for denying easy satisfaction to the originator of the threat.

Such a situation in the West creates the risk of having the future belong to a different kind of society—a society that stands firm because it accepts the existence and validity of fear; a society that, because it admits to fear, is prepared to use all means, including force, to transfer the weight of that fear onto others; a society that, if there is a choice, would rather embrace definite perils now than yield to panic too late. Neither Europe nor America can henceforth stake all on driving faith and superior force. Both gave the West its dominant position in the world originally, as did the fear of being engulfed from the outside (e.g., by different faces and forces of Islam) and, of course, material greed. But it is no less extreme and would be premature to relinquish the basic incentives and instruments of purposeful action altogether and rely wholly on the acquisitive instinct. Such self-denial is least timely while the elementary world economy is still (or once again) fundamentally a matter of food and fuel, the first being a major western asset and the latter its greatest material weakness.

Invasions from the outside and vulnerabilities within   Empires and civilizations tend to exhaust themselves in contentions with equal powers. But they are more often destroyed in the end by lesser parties that either invade or hold for ransom the physically still stronger power. A kind of invasion from the third world has already begun and has taken many forms. Corruption was imported into the highest political circles in America from the periphery of empire (e.g., the so-called Koreagate scandal). The exposure of the political establishment to material attractions from a reactionary source was of a piece with the ideological identification of antiestablishment forces with a revolutionary force: the Vietcong rebels against the empire during the Vietnam war. From much the same (Korean) source came a politically motivated, pseudo-religious grass-roots movement (that of the Reverend Sun Myung Moon). This was only the most conspicuous, because the best organized, example of the influx of Oriental religious sectarianism into a western culture faced with a single-minded religious resurgence in key parts of the third world.

The periphery invades the West at its moral core most subtly when it imposes its own interpretation of the costs and benefits, the merits and demerits, of imperial colonization in the past and of its sequelae. One result of the intangible assaults is western man's loss of faith in himself and his cause. On the material side, only the future can tell whether the rising volume and widening range of lower-cost manufactures that invade the West from the developing countries will be, on balance, beneficial or harmful. Will it or will it not jeopardize economic prosperity, social peace anchored in both full and productive employment, and security contingent on an irreducible minimum of productive self-dependence? Will or will not the West, like the world of the proverbial French bourgeois investor in foreign securities or the upper-class British remittance man of yesteryear, increasingly become a rentier society living off the patents and the *placements* orginating in a more productive era? Both visible and invisible invasions are less readily noticed than the ransom imposed by the oil embargo and collected through the price hikes of OPEC. The ransom may or may not be replicable by other raw material producers; however, its one instance is as significant symbolically and effective psychologically as it has been damaging materially and divisive politically—despite the alleged marvels of petrodollar recycling.

The military-political threat from the Soviet Union is not nil. But it is at its most dangerous when it obscures the more insidious threats to the West from its inner self and the outer peripheries. Fixation on Soviet military means and geo-political goals blocks out salutary fear of either the wholly invisible or merely economic or material threats from elsewhere—and of the lack of defensive reaction to them. A one-sided preoccupation lest Soviet armaments make the United States number two militarily risks transforming diffuse anxiety into something close to panic; a sense of unassailable economic superiority and psychological immunity to corrupting or enervating influences nullifies the requisite dose of fear and deflects long-suffering moderation into the exercise of what may be only deceptively superior prudence.

Unlike the modern European empires—notably the British—the American empire has not declined for primarily economic reasons. However, the spectrum of sources and symptoms of decline and dissolution is nearly identical for most or all empires of history. On the economic side, those sources are exorbitant taxation, domestic inflation, and imbalance in external payments; on the institutional side, excessive and ineffectual bureaucracy and centralization; and on the social side, inordinate economic pretensions by the lower classes and retreat from political commitments by elites, along with various forms of upper- and lower-class cultural perversions. The European colonial empires—and Europe as a state system— collapsed under the consequences of massive military engagements that speeded up the unfolding of latent social and economic maladjustments, both within and outside the imperial polities, to nearly everybody's detriment. The more broadly based industrial American economy was first created and more than once revitalized by war, from civil war to the Second World War; it is unlikely to suffer fatally from the costs of competitive peacetime armaments. On the contrary, the capacity of the economy to challenge the Soviet Union to an intensified arms race, and to win it, is the ultimate safeguard against excessive (and a check on inordinately effective) Soviet geo-political adventurism.

The renewed western European economies themselves may survive, in the short run, the shock of spiraling fuel prices at a bearable cost in inflation and unemployment. In the longer run, western Europe may even avoid the historically recurrent pitfall of overdepending for material prosperity on a favorable export balance and for political immunity on a favorable external balance—favorable because it is a stalemated balance among military powers or lends itself to an active policy of playing off such powers against one another. If she does avoid that pitfall, a more or less united western Europe will be better able to maintain, in the twenty-first century, some of her late economic reflowering and its political dividends. She would then avoid the economic and political distress that brought low a disunited northern and central Italy in the seventeenth century and the spuriously united Netherlands provinces in the eighteenth. But the odds are about even.

So long as economic strength and resilience continue, psychological intangibles will be the most potent cause and manifestation of the West's graying. They derive less from the failure of economic productivity and technological innovation, as they had for past empires and civilizations, and more from the paucity of political and moral safeguards against the decomposing effects of an affluence that has grown out of the hypertrophy of both. The graying of western Europe has been the normal, and may be the incurable, evidence of old age; there has been too much of history. In the age of the welfare state, nations come to resemble individuals and may win the right to retire to the benefits of social security under the nuclear umbrella.

Conversely, America's premature graying may be only a metaphor for a confused state of the group mind in search of both valid history and validating direction. That is why it is possible, if only tentatively, to view the immediate American problem in terms less of irreversible decline than of a tempting reversion. The attempted return has been to earlier patterns of foreign policy bounded by deceptive idealism (i.e., moralism) and all-to-real materialism (i.e., economism). The reversion itself may be reversible. But it has already done harm by distorting the view of what is henceforth possible and sufficient. Neither America nor the world is the same for the intervening experience. One cannot preach convincingly when he has visibly sinned, and it is not as easy to purchase peace or restraint all around as it was to buy Alaska. Since America's graying is so much a matter of mood, it is not misplaced to emphasize deficiencies in the intangibles of faith and fear; it is so least of all at a time when the United States faces, with weakened brute power and less brutal will, countries and civilizations that are replete with the immaterial attributes and a superpower displaying a growing amount of tangible instruments.[6]

Problematic remedies and continuing misperceptions   It is not certain that American interests are best served by combining static (or minimally deterrent) military defense with inflexible denial in geo-politics relative to the Soviet Union, and by combining, in relations with the third world, a high

6. Apolitical economism cannot but deepen the psycho-political disequilibrium between North and South. Thus, at the very moment when third-world spokesmen claim access to western technology as a good constituting the common heritage of mankind, technical criteria of substitution and replacement costs monopolize western assessments of a fair price of oil. (See, e.g., Alan L. Madian's "Oil Is Still Too Cheap" in *Foreign Policy* [Summer 1979].) Western technology is the product of individual ingeniousness brought to fruition at major social sacrifice; the oil was developed by western enterprise and would be worthless without western technology creating a use for it. Which is, then, more properly humanity's common good held in trust? The western economist would further play down OPEC's part in the West's economic distress by impugning the previously too-low price of petroleum. So to argue is like smothering questions about present and future effects of interracial school busing on the intellectual performance of the nation by invoking the history of Ku Klux Klan lynchings in America's South. Disguising foreign-policy paralysis by academically respectable economism improves little on the legalism of the 1930s.

degree of flexibility or adaptability in economic and political matters with abdicaton of any and all military instruments that are not easy to display or profitable to sell. Such strategies may be prudent, and the approach to the third world may also be mature and based on justified self-confidence. Or the flexible approach to the third world may be insufficiently fearful, while the inflexible one toward the Soviets in the peripheries springs from timidity due to a lack of self-assurance. Only a long series of actions and results can supply final evidence; it may come too late to help deal with the dilemmas of contemporary strategy.

The present time lacks once more sufficiently stable and determinate structures of power that would themselves suggest an optimum diplomatic-political strategy over even the "medium" term. Everything is only uncertainly in the making when it comes to the other great power or powers and to the key third-world states: the middle powers labeled most recently the new influentials. One or both of the great powers are unpredictable as to longer-term external orientation; at least one of them and the middle powers all are also internally unstable. It is a necessary task of speculative clarification to discuss contemporary international politics academically in terms of alternatives and pulls: between empire-type hegemony and balance of power globally, and between great- and lesser-power responsibilities for order regionally. The necessary task is also in a sense a heroic, because knowingly self-sacrificial, exercise. The so-called facts supporting both premises and conclusions are both unripe and highly perishable. To speak instead of the goal of American foreign policy as one of achieving "a diverse and stable community of independent states" is to give the goal and the road to it little or no precise meaning; to add that the United States is in the process of *creating* such a state is to exceed the bounds of currently available means and feasible strategy.[7]

If this is so, it is not altogether wasteful to spend some of the waiting time on viewing the world—and the West— from two outer boundaries of the strategic problem, one made up of psycho-cultural dispositions, the other of long-range historical trends and vision. An operative strategy is intermediate between the two; it is conditioned by existing dispositions, but it may also be deliberately inflected to correct for their biases. And the strategy can be only marginally shaped by a future-oriented historical vision, but in incorporating it may also be raised to a new height.

---

7. The quoted phrases, and the reference to the optimistic vs. pessimistic view of history as the issue underlying the supposedly emerging foreign policy debate in the United States, are from an address of 15 January 1979 by presidential adviser Zbigniew Brzezinski. In a parallel address, Secretary of State Cyrus Vance spoke of a "stable system of independent nations" in Asia, and presumably elsewhere, as the American objective. See the *New York Times*, 16 January 1979, p. A 11 for excerpts. The architectural improvements over the "structures of peace" of the preceding administration are less than self-evident.

It is one controversial part of such a vision that the western powers mismanaged over a period of half a century the integration into the global system of a Germany rising in the East. It is another related and widely accepted part that the European state system collapsed in a chain of essentially civil wars to the advantage of previously peripheral powers. The two interrelated events are only the most recent reminders of a wider and older phenomenon. The underlying secular tendency is for the more west-lying power or powers to view the day's main east-lying land power as one that draws on a more-than-actually powerful base for hatching mysterious schemes in support of more-than-life-size expansion. So perceived in otherwise changing conditions were, in succession, the Ottoman empire before its decline, expanding tsarist Russia and unified Germany, and lately the Soviet Union and (for a time) China. Each of the eastern powers felt itself in turn (and not always mistakenly) put upon by more-than-normally self-seeking and self-righteous maritime powers in the West. The easterners saw themselves as systematically encircled over land and debarred from legiti-mate outlets into the seas: the Ottomans by the Portuguese and the Spaniards in different bodies of water; the Russians and the Germans alternately by Europe's westernmost offshore island power (first the English and later the Americans, intermittently aided by allies farther east). France occupied an intermediate as well as double-faced position along both the geographic and functional divides; western perceptions grew more suspicious and the threats more ominous as the target power moved eastward.

Applying confinement to the east-lying land power from the outside was never easy. If erosion and decay were significantly speeded up at all, they were so only over either centuries or (more recently) decades of see-sawing contest at the frontiers of confinement. The price to pay was to see the receding power replaced by a like-minded successor, and one either bigger or fresher than its predecessor (not only France by Germany in central Europe but, yet more to the point, the Ottomans by Russia in eastern Europe). In the meantime, outside checks did anything but promote an essentially free association of the states or societies within the zone of confinement. The imputations and the denials merely made worse the instinct of the frustrated, artificially bottled-up land power to repress others within the narrowed orbit of its sway. Its thrusts outward while it was rising *or* declining helped disintegrate the central system. They also reserved reconstellation of the system for interference or imposition by previously peripheral or extraneous powers.[8]

8. The repressive effect of external confinement differs from the potentially positive effects on free association by action aimed at confinement from within. Regarding this point, and the point of disintegration and reintegration of the system, see the outline of a possible unification strategy in note 6, chapter 1 and the subsequent discussion.

Postscript 4.   Historical Vision, Strategic Nostrums, and Optical Illusion

The most fateful interactions of modern international history can be only analytically divided into struggles between western and eastern powers and between maritime and continental powers. And they can be only ideologically reduced to an antithesis between democratic and autocratic regimes. The complexity was fused in the real world when detonating ever vaster and more violent conflicts. The crescendo has lately faltered before reciprocal nuclear-strategic deterrents, aiding and aided by either benign or paralyzing social evolutions. The underlying pattern was not nullified, however. Organic unity and historical continuity are rooted in fundamental western and eastern psycho-cultural dispositions, fostering and fostered by inertial awareness of situational disparities. The main changes are largely technical and inspire only normatively supported restraints.

Weighing continuity and change against one another suggests rhetorical queries as a background, rather than dogmatic assertions as a guide, in the search for a realistic response to the day's challenges. Has it become possible to start breaking out of the secular policy mold and try the alternative way of voluntarily releasing the eastern land power into a free-wheeling competition over world-wide continental-maritime equilibrium? To do so would mean reevaluating the immediate risks and costs of a deliberate decompression of, and diversion from, Soviet retrenchment in eastern Europe against the long-term costs of ineffectual containment. And has it become not only possible but mandatory to diminish the advantage outlying powers or peripheral forces gained traditionally from a central contest, at a time when the Europe-derived former wing powers can converge for either reciprocal frustration or for common shelter in the so-far still privileged eye of what may well be a rising world-wide storm?

Historically rooted vision can match normative aspiration as a futile shortcut to utopia. Yet, if properly assessing what risks are necessary, it can impart a vital impetus to the discernment of what is desirable, because alternative pitfalls are probable and may become unavoidable. Inbred professional deformation of the foreign-policy specialist will frustrate or provoke, we have noted earlier, the layman given to normatively inspired shortcuts; the different barrier to be broken down in behalf of the historical vision is too literal an observance of directives summarized for quick studies in manuals on diplomatic statecraft.

Counteracting Soviet expansionism by reinforcing China is the obvious strategic nostrum in mechanistic terms. Either the breakdown of interethnic hierarchy within the Soviet Union or a preemptive Soviet breakout eastward risks then seriously unsettling world politics. Or, a different derangement, if China has been strengthened only enough to make her fit for reconciliation with the Soviets, America risks having to compete with such a China over directions in Soviet policy instead of both Communist great powers continuing to court the United States. China remains a factor in the converse approach to equilibrium, by way of gradually reapportioning American and Soviet global presence, but only as a secondary regulator: her remaining options set limits to what the Soviets can reasonably aspire to and what the Americans can safely concede, without either antagonizing or alienating the Middle Kingdom beyond endurance or repair. Whereas the first strategy artificially anticipates China's countervailing military strength, the second stakes much on the third world eventually becoming an economic threat to both superpowers. Anticipation is part of any long-term strategy. But only if it is buttressed by historically evidenced structures and laws of power does present policy become an organic link between past and future. Only then is policy genuinely conservative without ceasing to be enlightened.

The western powers are still—or shall I say already?—engaged in the stage of mutually manipulative relations with the eastern superpower. Fundamentally misconceived strategies toward the outside will henceforth only compound any internal failing in material supports or supporting morale. External action and internal assets and attitudes are readily interwined, as cause and effect, in an accelerating process of either growing or declining strength and vitality within a power or political civilization. As this happens, the perceived external rival may imperceptibly become nothing more and nothing less than the external crystallization of self-doubt; the lingering perception of a receding threat will be kept in the forefront by either habit or self-deception; and optical illusion will be interposed between the self and the real—if voiceless—enemy, to be looked for and fought within.

Part Three
THE STRATEGY.
Multiple Revolutions
and the Two World Systems

V

RESTORATION OF
THE OLD REGIME
OR FLIGHT INTO UTOPIA?

The world is aging but also ever straining to renew itself; man is dominated by the past but would coerce the future by denying its antecedents. The revolt against history implies that cyclical reversions to little-modified earlier states of being can be broken by revolutions that invert causal or social, determinative or deferential, hierarchies and, through such reversals, effect radical change. The revolt further implies that, even if we must define the present by reference to the past, because the present is but an instant turning point in transition to an unknown future, projections from the past neither constitute nor aid a valid prognosis. On the contrary, the mere rejection of the past as henceforth irrelevant is held up as a merit that will earn for the rebel the realization of utopia.

Varieties of social change and stabilization:
revolutionary and evolutionary

Defined by the immediate past, the present could be viewed as post-Gaullist in western Europe, tentatively postimperial in America, and, when compared with pristine or perverse antecedents, post-Communist for the great powers of Eurasia and Asia. Western Europe has lingered in the grip of pragmatic opportunism that was labeled Cartierism not so long ago. America has been more recently sliding into an impolitic or opportunistic moralism, currently identifiable as Carterism. Totalitarian Communism was mostly silently and gradually—and for that reason all the more convincingly—undergoing a change in post-Stalinist Russia even before puritanical Communism began to pass vocally and dramatically from the scene in post-Maoist China. It is hard to say whether the world center is progressing by disparate routes toward more freedom for the many. It may be only shifting gears toward greater license for a new category of the few. And less constraint of the several kinds may only mean more corruption of different kinds in its capitalist and socialist segments.

Meanwhile, the forms that were either only renounced or also denounced in the main seats of power have migrated to the third-world peripheries. Among them was not only Gaullism as the intensified affirmation of nationalist independence, but also imperialism as regionally asserted dominance (Vietnam's in Indochina) or equally delimited policemanship (Pahlavi Iran's in the Persian Gulf). And Communism also has migrated from place to place (rather than being exported from one place) as an ever more exalted radicalism and a thinly ideologized second best for consumer materialism. It is likewise uncertain whether the migration of ideologies and impulses to the peripheries will produce there a successful repetition or a prolonged regression: will it repeat the modes and paths of development that were either exemplified or only intimated in the several zones of the world core? Or will faulty timing in the diffusion of ideas and institutions augment the effect of differing conditions and once more—as before between western and eastern Europe—turn surface convergence into in-depth divergence?

The record of East-West currents inside Europe prompts doubt that the periphery can or will converge with the center over any but a very long time, despite accelerating rates of change. Whether it does and under what auspices will depend not least on the path global developments take from the turning point apparently reached in the center's most advanced and western segment: whether the erosion of the territorial state and its support in political nationalism will be reversed in the West or will spread to the peripheries after only a brief and ineffectual reactionary spasm; and whether the world economy will or will not be reconsolidated around a single center or compatible centers. The path can be either one of genuine revolution or only falsely revolutionary innovation, presumed to consummate a long-term evolution.

Revolutionary cycles and utopian reversals   The most recent grand-political revolution has reached its climax and has begun to be resorbed in a late stage of its international manifestation. The revolution's key domestic constituents were politico-economic claims expressed through secular ideologies. Its setting was defined by a whole range of successively impacting functional revolutions, among them the military-technological (from gunpowder to nuclear weaponry), the economic (from the thirteenth-century commercial to and past the eighteenth-century industrial), and the administrative (reducible to bureaucratic) revolution. And constituents and setting came together prominently in the conflict-ridden interstate arena. The revolutionary drive was repeatedly channeled into bids for parity or preeminence by ascendant powers, only to be gradually also contained as part of such bids and the resistance to them. The most recent challengers constituted a third generation in the chronology of state types that either dominated or at least set the tone in the era ushered in by the dissolution of the Roman empire. Originally dominant had been the sacral monarchies: holy Roman imperial, Roman-papal, and incipiently national northern; with the aid of, and by the end of, the first major modern revolution (associated with religious reformation), the one way or another theocratic powers were superseded as the ascendant type by secularized mercantile powers, headed by the maritime states of Europe's Northwest. In a progressively globalized arena, both before and after reinforcement by the United States, the latest international aristocracy was challenged for either equal status or effective succession by the tardily consolidated autocratic land powers of central and eastern Europe.[1]

The first internationalized revolution was originally religio-political and the second was politico-economic in origins. Both were focused, though in a different way, on a world beyond the known and limiting one. And both were subject to a concentric pull and a sequential loss of momentum. The initially escalating ideological effervescence within states was constrained and pulled back toward a middle-of-the road, or moderate, position by gradually reasserted pragmatic, reason-of-state politics among states. Related to the pull, and in part resulting from it, was a sequence of steps in interstate as well as intrastate politics. The steps led from intense violence or contention (terror), through reactive compromise and accommodation (Thermidor), to modified reconstitution of prerevolutionary conventional politics (restoration).

In the still ongoing international revolution, the momentum was progressively radicalized in our time as the First World War passed into the Second and the latter into the cold war; the revolutionary bid in the international arena was simultaneously passed on by imperial to Nazi Germany and by the

---

1. The first generation's sacral character made it analogous to the first estate of the clergy in the French revolutionary context. The second generation of leading powers was, by the same token, equivalent to the second estate of the nobility, despite a mercantile orientation and the increasingly middle-class character of its oligarchies. The third-generation powers constituted the *tiers état* in the second grand-political revolution. They recalled the third estate despite the aristo-dynastic trappings in both Germany and Russia before World War I and collectivist trends · in Russia after the war, not only by way of analogy but also by virtue of the initial internal sources of the drives underlying the quest for maritime-mercantile parity.

latter to Soviet Russia. Key characteristics of the thermidorian transition have begun to emerge only in the phase of U.S.-Soviet détente since the several attempts at accommodation with Germany not only failed in themselves but, more importantly, could not appease the revolution while the Russian problem remained in abeyance. The international thermidor developed *pari passu* with the Soviet Union becoming ever less the first and foremost socio-revolutionary force and ever more the latest key continental-eastern European party to the land-sea power schism and the East-West dialectic. Whereas Russia substituted for the failure of social revolution in Germany in the first capacity, she succeeded to Germany in the second (schismatic) context. Situated yet farther eastward "behind" Russia is China. She is part of the same geo-strategic and structural matrix, while belonging less certainly to the same Europe-centered, revolutionary series.

Critics of détente have feared lest a false thermidor yield to a more real military dictatorship by the Soviet Union. Brezhnev then would not be a more successful Barras of the Soviet revolution but only the armorer for a Soviet Bonapartism reaching outside Russia as well as beyond revolution. It is at least as essential to ponder the effect of the concurrent, and only beginning, revolutionary phenomenon in the third world on the scope and substance of any ultimate restoration at the center of the international system. Will the key third-world countries enlarge the field of forces open to action by the Communist great powers? If they do, they could make the enlarged arena susceptible to domination by the Soviet Union as the currently representative third-generation power. Or they could help China succeed to the same or comparable position, in either the initial phase of a new revolutionary cycle or in a temporarily recidivist phase of a continuing revolution of the familiar type.

Or will key third-world countries relate themselves to the West as it were directly? They might then be gradually co-opted into the restored international system emerging out of a termination of the Europe-centered revolution, or they might grow out of their issueless status of noisemakers at the half-marginal and half-extremist fringes of a maturing revolution and become the carriers of a new, successor revolutionary movement challenging the postrevolutionary order established at the world's center. Much will depend in the latter case on whether the potential or would-be third-world revolutionaries acquire either the unity of purpose or the unifying leadership of a major power. Such a power is the more likely one to guide a revolution through successive phases as the power itself changes in and through interplays with other major powers. It could thus save the updated expression of initial revolutionary terror from degenerating into anarchy inviting suppression by the forces of conservation or reaction. But, in affecting the prior or ultimate choice between co-optation and revolution, even more will depend on the principal defenders of the restored-and-renovated order of essentially the western type. Will they or will they not prove able to oppose an effectively countervailing mentality to a more than ever antiwestern revolutionary movement? While the peripheral revolution would be in one sense proletarian,[2] the opposing mentality must not continue being such in a different sense. That is, it must not be dominated by petty materialist drives and non- or antipolitical dispositions.

A bona fide revolution tends to vindicate its name even as it betrays its stated objectives. It does so by ending in a reversion to a prerevolutionary condition that was only partially revised by adaptations to the disturbances produced in the environment by the revolution's passing through its several phases. Since the finally realized social change and redistribution of power are limited, it commonly takes several successive or interlocking cyclical revolutions to create the impression of a linear movement toward substantial transformation. This very limitation of revolutions consigns to frustration any hope for lastingly radical change replacing discontinuous evolution.

In practice, dissatisfaction with revolutions that end up in only gradual revision will more often give rise to utopias. The utopian is not satisfied with merely revising that which is, because the revision is possible without causing injury to essential security and stability. He would reverse prior hierarchies into an order that ideally ought to be, because the reversal seems necessary for some kind of salvation. Thus the basis of a new, transnational order has come to be looked for in world-wide material interdependence, while the order's only fragile normative superstructure is variably defined in terms of peace, human rights, or something like planetary humanism. The attempted move beyond state-centered particularism to transnational relationships is also a return to prenational universalism, reversing the hierarchy of the medieval antecedent. Whereas the foundation of the new order is material, the basis of the Christian order was normative; if the immaterial superstructure is still fragile and can be actually disruptive, so was the material plane in the medieval conditions of only primitive interdependence within narrow orbits of sustenance.

Evolutionary sequences and psycho-political barriers to world order   To posit the emergence of a transnational world order is to look for new horizons while heading for an impasse. The conceptual impasse is no less for the effort aiming to extend the sequence of tested principles of order into a new, at once

---

2. "Proletarian" is true not only by historical analogy when compared with the quasi-bourgeois (or third-estate) revolution by the third-generation powers, but also in terms of its own socio-economic foundations and demands. These were essentially underprivileged even while being carried along by "bourgeois-nationalist" political values and mentalities. For proletarian mentality in the West, see chapter 4, p. 86.

open-ended and "final" order of being and doing. It is only the social arena to which the nomenclature is applied that determines whether the postulated sequence is one from status to contract and beyond or one from empire to the balance of power and beyond. The stage that lies beyond the one to be left behind may be called welfare within a political society and world order among states; it connotes socio-economic solidarity in both instances. Status hierarchy buttresses order within society and empire creates it among societies by conjoining unequal responsibility with unequal power; reliance on contract and on balance of power (implemented by internation alliance treaties) would erect order on a species of reciprocity aimed at containing the arbitrary exercise of unequal power. In the third stage, reducible to solidarity, responsibility and reciprocity are both expected to give way to responsiveness to the needs of weak parties occupying a strong position: those endowed with inferior positive power but superior in either moral claim or capacity for causing material disruption.

Always in the ideal—and often in the real—world, political rationality predominates in the exercise of power over economic rationality, while the latter generates the supporting resources necessary for dealing with stresses and crises. The limitation of such resources is one major constraint on politics. The essential core of politics consists of efforts to control, counteract, or coordinate either forces or functions. It is subject, next to material limitations, to checks from norms and to pulls of passion. The normative checks can be effective (or are effective only?) in conditions of less-than-normal stress; the pulls of passion work disruptively (always or mainly?) in conditions of more-than-normal stress. The normal condition is a combination of material and immaterial, structural and subjective, constraints on the exercise of power; the combination tends to make empire impossible and the balance of power insufficient as an indefinitely lasting and stable principle of order.

The hierarchically structured control that is institutionalized in empire is itself rationalized by the normative principles of peace and order. The empire formula tends either to fall short of sufficiently effective normative restraints on or stimulants of ascendant power or, more commonly in the long run, to fall victim to the lack of sufficient material supports for centralized communication (of control-related devices) and widely distributed compensations (for induced conformity).

The balance of power institutionalizes the containment of overwhelming or the reduction of merely superior power. It breaks down when countervailing intent in the first case, or incidental outcome of competing drives in the second, fail to overcome the absence of a shared normative framework or the ability to make unequivocally rational calculations and decisions—i.e., fail to substitute automatic response or result for contrived requisites.

Since the two principles of order are lastingly inadequate, they tend to alternate. But they do alternate because they are the only ones with a solid foundation in political instincts. One such instinct prompts deference to control in return for protection by superior power; another underlies conflictually implemented opposition to a threatening hostile or oppressive power. Therefore, both empire and equilibrium can in principle relate viably to both the normative and the passional, as well as to the material (or economic) dimensions, while mediating between them and keeping them apart as needed.

The same is not true for "world order." It may be normatively imposed by morality demanding equality or justice. And it may be materially enforced by economic rationality implementing the requirements of national survival through the potentialities of interdependence. But it will lack the vital political midterm or center between the polar extremes that confers and ensures viability. It is easy to invent a sustaining political rationale for an international order realizing solidarity. The need for peace will serve as well as the costs of conflict. But the political rationality called upon to initiate and implement the framework for such an order is apt to lack psychological (that is, instinctual) foundations. For what and against whom is such an order to be created, and what power configuration or concentration is, as a result, to sustain it?

One possible and popular answer points to the need for a more rational control over the environment and for safeguards against disruption or destruction of that environment. The intended control is then over self in the last resort. And the conflict to win by countervailing action is with one's own drives that promote or produce such disruption or destruction. Accordingly, the central politics is that of self-control and self-containment. As such, it is unlikely to link effectively and to mediate between the normative realm, as the seat of ethical imperatives, and the material realm, as the arena of practical compulsions and potentialities. Nor, for the same psychological reasons, is an alternately threatening and inviting impersonal environment a sufficient substitute for flesh-and-blood actors: the commanding power and the conditionally conforming dependent in the context of empire, the threatening adversary and the contingent ally in the context of the balance of power.

Varieties of politics and civilizations:
traditional and New World

It is not surprising that so utopian a new international politics has been most insistently professed from the New World—i.e., America—in behalf of the interests of the newest world. Nor is it astonishing that the proposed advance to a new frontier in internationalism and beyond has gained strength from the recoil from an old-type imperial frontier. Whereas the intellectual utopian would revert to medieval universalism with a difference internationally, the American political psyche has groped for a return to a more recent national past of world-embracing moralism. The parallel gains strength from the medieval ideal being in part as fictional as is the idealized national past. Nor would it, finally, warrant amazement if actual practice of the new international politics failed in any attempt to relate its precepts to old civilizations—be it Chinese, Islamic, Indian, or any other—that have been reemerging to a full part in international relations.

Latitudes and limitations in the American approach to politics   The characteristically American approach to international politics has one trait in common with the latest world-order model: it too is weak on the political midterm between the poles of moralism and materialism. The American political tradition is rich on the normative side: that side has been represented by doctrinal reverence for law (including international law) and enlightened public opinion and, more recently, by variously formulated versions of humanism or humanitarianism. As actually operative, American politics is, either in conformity or in contrast with the political tradition, no stranger to the material or materialistic side of things: the latter has been represented by economically defined geographic sections before the Civil War and pressure groups after the civil conflict, and more recently in the stress on either economic growth races or interdependent relationships internationally. The constant effort has been to reduce the normative side to specific rules of conduct, and to politicize the materialistic side by relating stakes to specific rules of the game. No necessary conflict is postulated between the two kinds of rules; a possible one can and will be reduced by, and the reduced amount be managed within, the latitudes provided by material plenty. Only vague or flexible precepts have insured a corresponding latitude in the moral sphere. The two latitudes have made it possible to see and practice politics as a close but limited competition for instant payoffs, as a compelling but low-pressure incentive for continuously keeping the score of individual gains and losses while only rarely settling scores in overt group conflict.

The view of politics as a matter of who gets what and when has been thin on the historical perspective. Individuals could move up and down on the social and economic ladder once or several times in one generation, and families could return to "shirt sleeves" in three generations, while America as a nation would keep growing and rising all the time. But just as there was little inclination to see the domestic fluctuations in terms of specific and rival social classes or ethnic groupings, so neither experience nor imagination was sufficient to transfer the perception and acceptance of fluctuation to the international arena. It came even harder to discern in others, behind the ebb and flow of power, the legitimacy of seeking prominence by virtue of an entitlement founded in organic rather than moral factors, spurred by a sense of historic injustice rather than the ability to dispense selfless justice, and encompassing both old and new nations and continents.

Circulation and assimilation of rising elites worked nearly effortlessly in the successively pioneering, prosaic, and prosperous American existence. But American political and historical vision did not assimilate either phenomenon as the main challenge of real (as contrasted with imaginary) social evolution among states. If, as a result of this, the dominant view of politics was ahistorical, invoking the canons of private morality was impolitic when ignoring the effect on public morale of alternative courses of action in the world at large. Thus intelligence about politics was curtailed in the depths that harbor the socio-psychological dimension of policy, as well as in the historical dimension that bears on the length of the temporal sweep that is treated as relevant for policy.

The New World approach and old-style frontiers The sometimes chaotic operation of the business cycle notwithstanding, the latitude created by the norm of economic plenty supplied the scope for exercising minimal morality at a tolerable level of either overt compromise with material interests or unconscious hypocrisy, concealing infraction of the group ideal. Salient tests of self-knowledge were rare, and were conspicuous mainly in connection with the North-South issue within America well before the issue's globalization. The political hustle could go on freely most of the time within a community that was even less constrained from without than overcrowded within.

The turning point came, and optimism veered toward pessimism, when the orbit of action and expectations was suddenly contracted. The material latitude was foreshortened with the appearance of apparently long-term limits on ever-expanding plenty; public morale was undercut by the seeming impossibility of going on effortlessly harmonizing the rules of conduct with the rules of the game at the previously ever-receding—first continental and then imperial—frontier. It was the American side of the imperial war in Asia that came to accuse itself of violating the moral rules of conduct; it was the Vietnamese side that refused to obey the rules of the game as understood by the Americans. Both kinds of rules and both attitudes were even more complexly related to the various tactical and strategic rules for an effective conduct of military operations. But fundamentally, American morale crumbled as the New World politics of solving problems with materially specific content at little cost in moral capital, and with instantly discernible as well as divisible payoffs, ran up against a fundamentally different view of politics: a view with a longer historical span and greater psychological depth, one of an old civilization that may have been updated, but was not uprooted, by the techniques and the morality peculiar to a radical social ideology.

The retreat from the farthest point of imperial advance was the consequence of particular weaknesses. But, as is often or aways the case, the retreat itself became a sufficient cause to continue inner shrinkage and debilitation. The shock from the recoil was potentially greater, and its aftermath more prolonged, because the retreat was due to accepting limits that were more psychological than material. It minimized only the immediate effect of the shock to define the reversion to an antecedent policy posture as a recovery of values.

Historically, an expanding overseas frontier in the New World stimulated European enterprise, though it was not as decisive and wholly beneficial as is sometimes averred. Also historically, Americans managed to adapt creatively to the closing of their continental frontier. The stimulus to inventiveness became for a time at least a blow to self-confidence when the constricting frontier was located overseas in areas abutting on the Old World: in Asia or the Middle East as well as previously in eastern Europe. The attempt to revert to the values of a continentalism antedating world empire was not tantamount to resuming the strategy of isolationism in national policy. But like the attempted reversion to premodern universalism in schemes for world order, the attempt entailed a reversal: not the reversal of a spiritual into a material foundation as the determinant of solidarity, but one of physical frontiers (as a challenge) into psychological limits (on response) as determinants of the degree of self-affirmation. It was that reversal which mattered, not the rhetorically highlighted one of material (or self-interested) into moral (or altruistic) motives and responses.

Falling back on traditional American notions of politics under the guise of new international politics was likely to fail in dealings with old civilizations. Especially when undertaken from a posture of diminished national self-confidence, such an effort was likely to prove as utopian as the intellectually overconfident designs for a world order are illusory. The main attraction of such designs has been an unadmitted potential for concealing the fact, and minimizing the consequences, of American demoralization. But morality as remedy for demoralization could not but wear off fast so long as national tradition and global utopia were equally devoid of sustaining political instincts, at all times abroad and in the long run also at home.

Varieties of strategic responses to threats: central-systemic and peripheral

While the socio-political ideologies and related strategies and instrumentalities of Gaullism, imperialism, and Communism were being simultaneously diffused and deformed as they migrated from the world's center to its peripheries, they encircled the globe without imparting to it a noticeable unity. Thus affected, diffusion defers anything approaching concord to the completion of a hypothetical evolutionary sequence—from status (or empire) via contract (or a balance-of-power and alliance system) to solidarity (expressed in materially interdependent world order). Such evolution and its terminal state are, however, easier postulated by savants than promoted by policy-making strategists. It may be more promising to intensify efforts to shape and direct an ongoing revolution (initiated by the third-generation great powers) and a possibly emerging next-in-line revolution (mobilizing the third-world lesser states). To that end, the operative concern is not how to midwife the natural birth of the last stage in a three-part sequence. It is, rather, how to manage alignments or splits within each of the three segments of the contemporary political universe: the Atlantic West, eastern Europe or Eurasia, and the third world (including China)—each of which has a role in the three-sided (military or economic external and psychological internal) threat to the West.

Actual cleavages and alternative scopes of possible convergence   Within the Atlantic-Pacific West, comprising western Europe and the United States (and Japan), the main—if latent—cleavage is generationally conditioned; in the Eurasian segment comprising the Soviet Union and the lesser eastern European states, it is geo-politically determined; within the third-world periphery several, if not all, of the potential splits are functionally defined. If Japan is only tentatively part of the western center, China is in the same position relative to the loosely speaking eastern periphery.

The generational split in the West is between European old age and American middle age, between too much and too little history. It has been manifested in differences between structural regression and largely senti-mental reversion (as western Europe came to resemble earlier and smaller declining subsystems, such as northern and central Italy and the north-western Netherlands in earlier eras and settings, and as Americans lapsed back into moods preceding their ascent to world power), and between settling for social security and clinging to status seniority (as the western Europeans withdrew into guaranteed minimum prosperity and Americans fretted about military and other challenges to their first-rank status as a condition of physical security).

In contrast with the Euratlantic area, the geo-politically conditioned cleavage within Eurasia reflects the natural recoil of smaller powers from a regionally preponderant big power. That split has been contained by ultimately forcible controls. It is aggravated not only by differences ingrained in national cultures, as between the Soviet Union and the lesser countries, but also by continuing diversity in social class patterns and economic standards of living. The geo-politically conditioned and culturally intensified recoil of non-Russian east Europeans has only been reinforced by economic attractions from the West. But the centrifugal impulse is also contained by whatever complementary economic structures evolve from regional coordination and whatever similiarities of historical and cultural experiences relative to the West survive coercion within Eurasia. Therefore, the more spectacular cleavage through eastern Europe might, in a test, prove less deep than is the more subtle one within the West; it might give rise to fewer fundamental political dealignments and realignments than on the other side of the East-West divide in Europe—if and when spontaneous reorientations have again become possible on both sides.

No single split or reason to split is clearly the main one within the third-world segment. The several lines of actual or possible divisions include (in addition to the obvious one between the larger and potentially imperialist and the weaker and potentially victimized states in a region) the functionally defined differences between states with economies that are or are not capable of sustained development, and between the chiefly economically and mainly militarily strong states. Moreover, functional divisions coexist with cultural, racial, and other diversities expressed in historical enmities that have been reviving as the parties involved are released from the constraints of colonial empire and shed the quietism of colonial dependence. Just as no cleavage has yet replaced the waning one between colonial masters and helots, so the diversity of the various cleavages is likely to yield to a new simplicity only if relations among the great powers are not only repolarized but are polarized over issues that find an echo in the third-world countries' own needs and predispositions.

Two different basic responses to the various external and internal threats can either surface or submerge the latent fission between western Europe and the United States. One possible response leads to a European or "small" solution, another to a "large" or western solution. The first involves East-West fusion within Europe only. That particular process would get underway (1) if the economic threat to western Europe from the third-world peripheries were to exceed the physical and ideological threat located in eastern Europe; (2) if the new balance of threats could be ascribed to the United States reacting to outside economic pressures in a manner more divisive than defensively effective (one that would accentuate the self-induced states of mind that constitute the internal threat to western civilization); and (3) if the military power of an internally evolving Soviet Russia underwent a parallel meta-morphosis and from a potential threat became a possible alternative protector of western Europe against peripheral abuses and exactions within a modified threat hierarchy.

A different, "large" or western solution would result from a U.S.-Soviet convergence. It would implement the confluence of previously disparate and disparately experienced threats: a tangible one from China to the Soviet Union and a less tangible one from the third world to the United States, either directly or by way of its effect on western unity. Such a confluence was most likely to get underway as both China and the Soviet Union were further industrialized, augmenting China's capacity to step up politico-military pressure on the Soviet territorial periphery in Asia and on western interests in the global periphery while increasing Soviet economic sensitivity or vulnerability to some third-world countries, along with China's attraction for other third-world countries.

U.S.-Soviet accommodation would express in policy a logical if, as always, provisional adaptation to developments along the two principal pathways of preeminent power gravitation: the world-wide transoceanic one in the northwestern direction and the Eurasian-continental one in the eastern direction. If, instead, reciprocal hostility continued first to distract and gradually to erode the two superpowers, preeminent power would either bypass the Soviet Union while prematurely leaving the United States and definitively downgrading the West, or the Soviets would be reduced to reacting forcibly to the West's implied complicity with China or a Sino-Japanese complex as the geographic end-station of both of the ultimately converging power trajectories. Yet a gradual American-Soviet accommodation is not only possible, but it is made likely by two additional historical processes. One of these processes concerns the setbacks that eastern Europe incurred in the past as a result of the uneven diffusion of technological and institutional innovations. The defects have been in part corrected and in part offset by the debilities the West incurred over time from conflicts among unevenly amphibious and expansive land and sea powers. Another process is the normal one of reciprocal assimilation between near-equal powers caught up in a protracted competition and unable to reach a prompt or decisive resolution in favor of either.

It would not surprise if the combination of lessened defects in eastern Europe and incompletely compensated debilities in the West has set the stage for such a convergence in U.S.-Soviet relations. The convergence is provisionally impeded by residua of the land-vs.-sea power schism that still affect superpower relationships. But it is also promoted over time by one change and one constant. Shortening time lags in transmission and greater similarity in receptivity make it less likely for West-East diffusion of both techniques and institutions actually to widen the East-West gap in Europe. In addition, the latitudes for recovery from temporary setbacks and for long-term regeneration of unevenly setback parties continue to characterize the interregional interplay in the larger theater.[3]

3. See chapter 3 for background to these observations.

Continuing options in the peripheries and domestic effects of systematic inaction   The prime mission of strategy has become that of managing both the potentialities and the risks that inhere in the several cleavages and latent splits within all three segments of the world system, and to manage them in such a way as to render disruptive combinations less likely and stabilizing convergences more likely, while both perceived and actual threats move up and down in the threat hierarchy. The critical quandary for strategy can be stated by way of interlocking and increasingly specific queries. How best can western state-craft exploit progress toward restoration in the maturing revolution at the center of the international system without exacerbating the drives and interests that would set off the system's periphery on the road to another revolution? How best can it proceed to fuse the Euratlantic and Eurasian core segments rather than adversely realign the subdivisions within them (e.g., western Europe toward Soviet Russia or Soviet Russia toward China), while avoiding a polarization along racial lines in relation to the peripheral segment? What must western statecraft do to keep Japan from being driven into the orbit of China (e.g., by U.S.-Soviet complicity or U.S. retreat in Asia), without allowing the extension of the West into the Pacific arena to impede its enlargement on the European continent? And how can it avoid driving China into radicalized leadership of third-world would-be revolutionaries, without allowing continued divisions within the larger West (including Russia) to prevent a western-style systemic restoration and project China prematurely into the lead of an East-centered era of world history?

The most fundamental prescription is for the West to cultivate one kind of circle and resist another kind. A virtuous circle results when faith in self is rooted in the belief in a cause and self-centeredness then becomes one with metapersonal transcendence. The cause may still validly be the West's continued leadership, if the concept of both West and leadership is enlarged in scope and contents. The vicious circle results when the suppression of specifically focused fears merely augments diffuse anxieties. The fear to retain is that of falling below a level of self-confidence and self-assertion at which any use of force either comes too late or has to be unlimited because prudence has given way to panic.

The most likely arena for forceful self-assertion will continue to be in the global peripheries. Such self-assertion will have to observe the economy of force. This does not mean, however, that it will be lastingly sufficient to employ force only in politically or logistically easy situations against flimsy opponents. Commendable in itself, an example of such a situation was the 1978 intervention by the French and Belgian paratroopers, with logistical U.S. support, in behalf of Zaïre's weak and willing Mobutu regime, beset by rebel inroads from Angolan bases. Nor will it suffice to employ force in easy forms only. In this category are U.S. naval demonstrations combined with arm supplies; the latest in a series took place in early 1979 in support of the Saudi-backed North Yemeni against inroads from South Yemen.

Systematically choosing only the "easy ones" will in the long run confirm the impression of inability or unwillingness to take on the "tough ones." Such action may end up being inferior to a posture of calculated, even if not masterful, inactivity. Nor is it compellingly persuasive to represent naval deployments or arms supplies to victimized protégés as adequate deterrence or, still less, punishment of delinquents. Worthwhile punishment must attach a substantial price tag to disapproved conduct. It may then constitute, if it is repeated or applied consistently, a kind of cumulative deterrence of comparable delinquencies over a period of time, even when failing to defend a particular victim successfully. The sanction may consequently have to entail acts of apparently purposeless or even irrational destruction. One such act of calculated terror was China's punishing assault on North Vietnam in the spring of 1979. Because such an action does not establish a visible relationship to a specific objective (e.g., the withdrawal of the Vietnamese from their simultaneous takeover of Cambodia), it may be all the more impressive in and to certain cultures. However, the same kind of seemingly purposeless use of force is apt to be very difficult for an open society to undertake and sustain. It will outdo in awkwardness a more extensive and costly intervention undertaken for a stated specific purpose, such as preserving self-determination for the South Vietnamese or economic life lines for the West. Yet is it wise to let difficulty be seen as disability?

The merits and demerits of western actions and western inaction will continue to be assessed in terms of the openings that alternative approaches create for Soviet geo-political progress. Any prescription to reduce such openings by reducing local instabilities side-steps related questions. In order to promote stability, is the West to be neutral and abstain from interference between parties to local disorders (e.g., in Iran at the turn of 1978 into 1979)? Should it align western policies on the preferences of presumably moderate or conditionally prowestern indigenous parties (e.g., the front-line states in southern Africa)? Or should the West engage in unarmed, but in all other respects officious, mediation (e.g., the Middle East)? Or else does having a part in stabilizing the world require, at least from time to time, acts both intended and sufficient to demonstrate the will to be an effective, as well as independently motivated, party to shaping the patterns and procedures of socio-political change?

Western and, specifically, American abstinence or conformism will favor prolonged turmoil in the peripheries, sometimes facilitating and sometimes legitimizing Soviet involvement, especially when the latter is adjusted to local taboos (e.g., sanctity of territorial frontiers in Africa). Risk-taking interventions will make similar results possible: the Soviets will be able either to exploit the consequences of an abortive western intervention or to claim the right to counterintervention, by virtue of specific instruments (e.g., a half-forgotten Soviet-Iranian treaty from way back) or general principles of international law or politics. Moreover, inaction in any one case will often be vindicated by local parties rebounding westward from a temporarily successful Soviet entrenchment or Soviet-favored indigenous regime—or even from the mere prospect of either. The rebound will express preference for either independence or dependence on the materially better endowed and politically more permissive West. Examples of such a recoil have already been legion.

Since both action and inaction can create opportunities for the Soviets, and passivity may gain a dividend for the West, the basis for choice must lie in larger considerations. One of them is that systematic inaction will reduce over time western (or American) attractiveness in the peripheries, as well as western power to bargain with the rival superpower. The situation is similar internally. Both action and inaction can, and on occasion will, have adverse repercussions in the domestic arena. Action is more dangerous for office holders than for the society itself. Setbacks traceable to a prior initiative are more damaging for decision makers than reversals that can be charged to uncontrollable local events or worldwide currents. The opposite is true for the body politic, the political system, and public morale. A setback attributable to governmental action can be redeemed by punishing the responsible administration at the next election. Or it can be turned into a stimulus for facing up to a previously only latent or ineffectually affirmed crisis, such as the energy shortage. The issue-resolving larger consideration is that systematic inaction will be punctuated by nerve-wracking ups and downs, as accidental or partial recuperations alternate with expulsions from positions and the two average out into gradual slippage. Such slippage is more likely than occasionally abortive action to generate a sense of helplessness and irrelevance for the national community as a whole; it will foster either final abdication or more or less timely and drastic reactions.

Containment vs. ground rules for postrevolutionary system restoration   A predominant tendency to inaction will be especially trying at any one time and demoralizing over time if there is no explicit strategic mandate for inaction as well as action as a matter of deliberate and motivated preference. The false choice has continued to be between a strategy labeled containment and one labeled détente. Both are meaningful only in relation to existing structures of power. Unlike containment, however, détente *qua* relaxation of tensions is not a strategy but is only the possible outcome of a strategy. And, if it is to persist, détente must also reflect an appropriate spirit pervading the policy-making systems and motivating the policies of rival powers.

In the period of U.S. ascendancy, global structures of power and American strategies were comparable to those of traditional empires. Similarly,

America receded from paramountcy amid structures that were broadly analogous to those causing or attending the declines of earlier power aggregations. The similarities left it to a peculiar balance to decide the issue of how authentic the empire was and how final its decline. On one side of the balance are the relatively new or newly intense forces of internal and external resistance to one-power ascendancy, and on the other is the unprecedented material capacity of a major power to recover from symptoms of decline. The changing balance is thus between resistance and resilience. It is apt to be swayed one way or the other, and traditional patterns are apt to be confirmed, qualified, or invalidated, by the less changeable intangible factors of political nature reducible to "spirit". It is that fact which justifies placing such intangibles (including faith and fear) at the center of both diagnosis and cure.

American-Soviet relations have unfolded more recently in the midst of some diffusion of power among great powers globally and lesser ones regionally. More or less related to the diffusion has been a certain erosion of the instruments and the initiatives that made up the world-wide U.S. system of access, influence, and—on rare occasions—control; intensified Soviet initiatives have aggravated the erosion, but they have also (ironically or functionally?) compensated for its consequences. American action after World War II was spirited by the perception of a two-power conflict more than by any acknowledgment of a one-power empire held in trust. The spirit has weakened conjointly with changes in the underlying structures, and changes in both spirit and structures have now made necessary a revision of strategy. In view of the misfortune that befell the term détente, the name for the strategy is less important that is the related revision of the rules of the game.[4]

The new ground rules must continue respect for the spheres or domains that each of the superpowers had effectively reserved for itself and has effectively upheld since. They will furthermore have to redefine strictly what constitutes vital interests in regard to specific positions and what are legitimate uses of a position, either held or in the process of being acquired by one of the superpowers. Both redefinitions will be interdependent with the more fundamental one of the two superpowers' entitlement to projecting power and influence abroad. Just as the Soviet policy makers must learn in non-Soviet eastern Europe, so the American policy makers must learn in the global peripheries to define their vital interests narrowly and to distinguish

---

4. In the Introduction I spoke of decompression (inside the Soviet Union and bloc)-*cum*-diversion (of Soviet drives and pressures) as compared to containment, to be implemented by reapportionment of geo-politically significant positions overseas. I first raised the related issue of the rules of the game to be changed accordingly in *Quest for Equilibrium* (Baltimore: Johns Hopkins University Press, 1977), chapter 10, especially pp. 169-70. For a later and more factual discussion, see three articles published under the topical heading "America and Russia: The Rules of the Game" in *Foreign Affairs,* Spring 1979.

them more carefully than before from nonvital and expendable interests in regard to external security, internal stability, or comparative status.

The United States may choose to initiate this trend, as an extension of its at least partial abdication from the role of maintaining global order. Any effort at graduating interests as more or less vital was largely impractical in the imperial context and was subordinate to the expediential requirements of sustaining that role. Thus the American action in Vietnam was directed at a rival regional imperialism that inhibited American access and was accordingly justified regardless of any immediate bearing thereof on American national security. Renouncing the exacting role has undermined the sweeping derivation of rights, or legitimate interests, from the assertion of disinterested responsibilities. Such derivation continues to be tempting in the postimperial, balance-of-power setting. But it is practically as well as conceptually incompatible with the requirements of a viable approach to a global equilibrium among several powers of equal status.

It is implausible in terms of either national or western security to treat henceforth as equally vital and inalienable the American interests in all the positions either lost or endangered: Angola (relative to the South Atlantic), Ethiopia or South Yemen (relative to the Red Sea), and Afghanistan (relative to either Iran or Pakistan and, ultimately, the Persian Gulf and the Indian Ocean). Any rights the United States has acquired and any interests it has precariously vested in itself since World War II must be henceforth more finely calibrated in regard to either sea communications in general or access to oil routes in particular, in regard to either the intrinsic importance of particular countries or their potential for unleashing or perpetuating the once-ridiculed falling-domino effect. Redefining American rights to a continuing presence or access is the increasingly necessary counterpart to working out in practice the legitimate modes, scope, location, purposes, etc., of Soviet outreach and consequent penetration in the third world.

Western positions and interests will be unavoidably more vulnerable than before as geo-political access and presence are reapportioned. The greater the new vulnerability, the more important it is to evolve rules to govern also the uses of the reapportioned geo-political positions that are permissible because they are consistent with a new equilibrium. Conceding acquisition of strategic nuclear parity by the Soviet Union has created a presumption in favor of condoing Soviet employment of the enhanced capability as a background for graduated ascension to a matching world-power status in the geo-political arena as well. But, by the same token, condoning the *employment* of resources depends on a tolerable Soviet *use* of the expanded overseas presence. What constitutes a tolerable use cannot be deduced from an apolitical notion of a functionally dovetailing structure of an equitable world order. Such use must be compatible instead with a historically grounded, long-range vision of an evolving great-power configuration that would underpin and constrain such an order and justify a fundamental revision of American strategy. Both the vision and the revision are insuperably barred by the persistence of a mind-set identified with containment, however modified.

The American use of positions in the third world created the spectre of encirclement and the fact of surveillance for the Soviets. Any reversal of trends pointing to America's countercontainment awakens western fears of Soviet capacity to strangulate the western allies by interdicting their access to resources vital in peace and to one another in war. Redistributing overseas possessions promotes an abstract symmetry between the West and the East, in that it supplies both the U.S. and the Soviet Union with pressure points and bargaining chips and creates a formal equality in status.

Rules of the game that would look beyond abstract symmetry toward material parity must take into account differences between the two systems: the western oceanic system, with exterior lines and scattered resources, and the Soviet continental system, with interior lines and greater self-sufficiency in raw materials. The asymmetry is probably favorable to the Soviet Union when no more than bare survival is the criterion; the advantage is offset for purposes of strategic superiority by the oceanic system's greater potential for technologically promoted mobility and economically fostered political attractiveness. Nor can any serious effort to strike a rough balance of assets and liabilities between the two systems ignore their being susceptible—although in different ways—to decomposition under external pressures.

Any evaluation of which uses of outside positions are permissible and which are illegitimate is of necessity complex and controversial. So too will be any process of bargaining, whether explicit or tacit, verbal or by deeds, over what the new rules are to be and how they are to be applied—even if such a process is undertaken in the best of faiths on both sides. Yet, undertaking such evaluations and evolving such understandings within a radically changed framework of reference is a need that follows from two considerations. One consideration is policy specific: the Soviets must have some extra-regional territorial assets if they are to support or even tolerate the resulting world order and if the Americans, when bargaining with the Soviet Union over the shape of such an order, are to dispose of usable pressure points on the Soviets. The targets of a pressure that can be routinely applied must be extraneous to the orbit of truly vital Soviet security concerns if American counteractions are not to be immediately provocative in the highest degree.

There are thus operational reasons for reversing the present American posture. Since the posture is one of undifferentiated, but mostly only rhetorical, denial of any Soviet right to geo-political gains, its opposite is to police effectively and to constrain a Soviet progress toward world-power status that has been conceded in principle. The operational rationale for the strategic inversion is reinforced by a consideration that amounts to a philosophico-historical rationale.

It will be possible to reevaluate and reapportion assets by common consent only when the U.S.-Soviet relationship has been stripped of an ideological cast that has little to do with the opposition between communism and capitalism and not much with that between freedom and oppression. Viewing the contest in terms of Soviet expansionist aggression against American defense of world order has been the most recent heir to viewing it in terms of the defense of the free world. The new mandate continues to invoke a normatively based providential entitlement as both superior and fatal to any entitlement deriving from an empirically traceable historical process.

The United States inherited the providential entitlement to rule the waves and regulate the tides of power from Great Britain. And Britain herself had been only the latest in a line of insular or quasi-insular mercantile-maritime powers that were, and behaved like, the *beati possidentes* of world-wide positions. These positions were won by virtue of more up-to-date socio-economic structures and dynamics at home, along with more efficient instruments for projecting the quest for wealth and power abroad; continuing possession was vindicated by the real or alleged vulnerability of the gains flowing from the initial advantage and the real or alleged utility of the resulting performance for other states. Furthermore, the possessing powers, being more efficacious, could claim to be also more moral than was or could be the preeminent land-bound power of the day. They certainly could rely on less oppressive means of control. By virtue of their position, the land powers acted on more intensely centrifugal forces and were exposed to more powerful proximate counterpressures than was the lot of the liberal maritime power. Faced with conditions and presumptions favorable to the rival, the land power could assert any countervailing entitlement to overseas expansion only in ever more forcible or broadly based challenges from increasingly autocratic to totalitarian regimes (from tsarist to Soviet Russia, from imperial to Nazi Germany). The result was a crescendo in the international analogue of revolutionary terror.

In a nuclear setting, the historically rooted entitlement of Russia to world power may have to be both asserted and heeded differently. The more and sooner this is done, the better served will also be the tendency of the interstate aspects of revolutionary upheavals to find a conclusion in the restoration of an orderly system. Such a restoration involves a mixture of redistribution of power and conciliation of principles between initial antagonists—a redistribution that both implements and mutes the gravitation of power. The dominant norm or model of a major international actor to emerge from opposition between a primarily land- and a primarily sea-based and oriented power was most likely to be a continentwide amphibious state, proficient both militarily and navally. Redistribution of power and conciliation of principles points toward an equilibrium among such states. And the equilibrium is an alternative to the amphibians destroying one another to the sole benefit of third parties in conflicts resulting from the efforts of one principal party to force the other back into the land-bound pattern of national power—a pattern that is, on balance, inferior.

It has been necessary to fit a yet wholly land-bound China into a triangular balance as one factor among several for graduating or regulating the Soviet ascension to the status of an amphibious continentwide state. The triangular approach need not, however, be rounded off into an encirclement strategy in either fact or appearance. One reason is that the Soviet ascension is, in the longer run, both desirable and necessary for an evolution that would provisionally terminate in a balanced concert of several amphibious world powers—a concert including and restraining a China newly powerful and enterprising on both land and sea. A balance and a concert that are properly understood for what they can be and do make up the only known configuration of forces and attitudes to undergird anything approaching a stable international order independent of a hegemonic power. They are best suited to consolidate the results of a prolonged revolutionary wave and to preclude or, if they fail therein, to contain an either socio-economically or racially inspired successor wave of revolutionary terror along geographically expanded East-West—or reoriented South-North—lines.

A revolutionary reprise was, among other things, most likely to take place if the U.S.-Soviet relations and the related U.S.-Soviet-Chinese triangle were mismanaged, and if the mismanagement first accentuated and then helped maintain a long-range trend. The trend is for each of the successive land powers with overseas ambitions, located ever farther east of the French prototype, increasingly to qualify its culturally neutral, functional character as a navally aspiring land power by way of its culturally or racially defined character as an eastern power. In the case of China, this trend would tend to subordinate completely the functional cleavage to the cultural and racial cleavage. Whereas the former has become increasingly manageable in an enlarged global context among equally continentwide states, the latter is less than ever manageable in a shrinking world of many-sided varieties.

Transient socio-economic orders and enduring values   Without a change in basic vision, from a moralizing normative or opportunistic utilitarian perspective to a philosophizing historical one, any change in operative strategy will be lacking in depth and direction. It will lend itself to the range of misconceptions and misrepresentations that have beset and helped discredit U.S.-Soviet détente most recently. Lodged in a yet farther background, or at a yet deeper level of motivation, is the issue of what values to defend, by whom, and, if necessary, against whom.

The West does not stand for any one of the historically changing socio-economic systems, and no historically realized order is final. Not being such, it is neither designated for irreversible triumph nor does it compel costly efforts to speed up its elimination. Similarly, the exact measure of individual freedom and its particular expression realized at any one time are but provisional outcomes of a historical process that is fueled, among other things, by interactions between powers more or less ready and able first to institute and then to institutionalize freedom or freedoms. The oppressors of yesterday not only may be, but are likely to be, tomorrow's bulwarks of feasible liberty; any contest between powers that implement in their peculiar ways different kinds or degrees of freedom is more likely to enhance the power of outside parties than to expand the total sum and area of freedom in the world.

Even more peculiarly western than the cultivation of individual freedom has been the indomitable instinct for safeguarding the autonomy of the group that men in any one era viewed as essential for enhancing life. That instinct was in modern times expressed either in a dispassionate Reason of State or in what often only seemed to be an irrational and purposeless nationalism. Under both auspices, the instinct promoted a discernible evolution in that it kept alive and shaped the struggle upholding a balance of power against one-power hegemony. The western pattern contrasts favorably with the opposite model that may or may not be fairly described as more typical for the East. That model can be schematically reduced to essentially sterile, because unevolving, cycles alternating despotic empires with interregna of chaos, as concentrations of power rise and fall without a discernible pattern and engage in mutual exploitation, warring predation, or submissive parasitism.

Though central to western politics, the preservation of group autonomy was in the last resort but a proximate end related to larger ends. Though variable, the larger ends always tended to reflect a dualistic conception of both man and the matrix of man's actions. It was the multiple and partially changing dualisms that, occasioning conflicts, have secreted the ultimately creative tensions. Accepting the ordeal of such tensions as an occasion for resolution defined western civilization as inimical to stultifying monism, including the ascription of monopoly on political virtue to any one power or type of power. It also defined western man himself, as one who would rather live with conflictually enacted revolutions in history than to seek release and repose from the revolving wheel of fortune outside history.

Constantly reviewing the hierarchy of threats to the West on the plane of values cannot, therefore, avoid a crucial determination. Which definition of the threat hierarchy, in what kind of vision of the future, is more likely to maintain the West in a state of creative tension or restore it to such a state? One critical tension to keep alive is henceforth between faith in self and the fear of losing that faith and with it the capacity both to experience and inspire the socially requisite minimum of fear. Another is between the temptations of resignation and the will to renovation. The threatening resignation is related to mere survival amidst reawakened political societies and cultures, organized around the recourse to force while lacking any proven capacity for systemic, if no other, creation; the renovation is related to, and may be contingent upon, a new form and direction of expansion. For the West to renew itself will almost certainly require henceforth an enlargement that is neither conquest nor colonization and one that does not amount to one-sided conversion. The West can be so enlarged only if it includes at long last the cognate polities that have been kept outside the western family by either accidents of the recent past or the injustices and grievances of millennial history. If the injustices are more elusive and the grievances less vocal than other and more commonly dramatized ones, they also go farther back in time and weigh more heavily on a more immediate future. They point unequivocally to Europe's East. They cannot be dealt with to anyone's lasting advantage by failing to heed the entitlement felt by the presently foremost third-generation power of European history to a role in the third world.

Postscript 5. Unrealized Prescriptions and the Necessary Hope

If the foregoing identifications of the turning point and of external and internal threats are even remotely correct, and the third world retraces western developments with a time lag rather than taking a short-cut toward the West's new directions and destinations, then world history has begun to move past one stage to another. The traversed stage was dramatized by the East-West confrontation known as the cold war; the next stage is distinguished by the overt struggle over the conditions of coexistence between the West and the third world, tied up with a hidden contest between them over the alignment of the Eurasian core of the "second world" as a valuable ally that has failed in its ambition to become the deciding arbiter.

It can be argued that de Gaulle's surrender to *political* third-worldism in Algeria was justified only if the latitude thus won for a European policy was used to bind France firmly to the military nucleus of a west European polity (and made the latter helpful in fulfilling the expectations attached to decolonized Algeria). So judged, the surrender has not yet proved justified; its continuing cost to France has been no less, if different, than the cost of the opposite policy would have been. Similarly, any western concessions to *economic* or otherwise motivated assertive third worldism are justified only if they do not thwart strategies for preserving the West's immaterial attributes alongside its internal stability (while augmenting the probability of benign developments in such areas as economic moderation, politico-military surrogation, and the socio-political co-optation of key third-world parties).

If policies need be justified, so do modes of writing about them. How can one justify writing about weighty affairs in a loosely speculative manner deriving a warrant for license from the absence of responsibility? Writing in a mode that combines analysis of past events with an attempt to inspire future acts entails risks that are obvious and has merits that are less so. Even if the analysis is only half correct, failure to heed it at all will reduce the effort to an exercise in futility at the author's expense. Yet the aftermath of the failure can be turned into an indictment of the actors, warranting a verdict. The writing, proven inefficient in affecting policy, takes its place in intellectual history. We have still not improved materially upon contemporaneous explications of the causes of decay and decline of once-mighty Spain. The writing's more enduring value is then the writer's revenge on the doers whose activism resolved itself into immobility or worse.

Supposing this to be true, is it justified to extol political man and rationality while construing the attribute "political" as one that embraces fear and faith while comprising acts of force as an indispensable component? Is such a view not a throwback to the doctrines of Fascism, even as the policy argument looks forward to pragmatic changes in Soviet Communism? Only the most simplistic of liberals could return an unqualifiedly affirmative and accusatory answer. If Fascism was first shaped and then defeated by its too backward-looking vision (Italian toward conquering Rome and scheming Renaissance and German toward the Middle Ages with their thirst for faith—any faith—and their addiciton to crusades, including corrupt crusades); if it was exacerbated by its too great disharmony with the tendencies of the time and finally perverted by too great a disparity between the core idea and the quality of the implementing pseudo-elite, when all this and more is said and admitted, Fascism did spring nonetheless from a certain premonition of the kind of future it instinctively strained to delay and actually precipitated into becoming. Not necessarily for the last time in a continent teeming with frustrated aspiration and underemployed intelligence, and not necessarily in an unchangeable manner, unworthy agents externalized the unresolved tension between reasonableness and will, freedom and constraint, accommodation and defiance. Their abuses were made easier by contrary excesses, immune to strictures by the high-minded.

Even when worshipping false gods, the political man, as conceived here, was for a time the only surviving genuinely religious man. He was the one most likely to find serenity—the *inner* peace—at a level where the pursuit of private happiness is tempered by the self-imposition of public duty. The first may be a right under the American Constitution; the second is a key constituent of the degree of contentment attainable by man as naturally constituted. One being tempered by the other will best serve ends that need not be flawless to be deserving and may be pursued by means that can be forceful without being either futile or damning.

To put forward such propositions is not to offer yet another "exhortation from exile,"[5] but only to give expression to an intuitive conviction. If drift continues, the time may come—and in justice ought to come—when the rediscovery of pride in being a European man would nourish the renascence and impel the reascent of the political man, in his original habitat, without much regard for the stimulant's ideological source, the resulting lines of power, and any sacrifice of affinities that had proven, in the crunch, sterile.

5. See *Europe Ascendant,* p. 167, echoing Machiavelli in regard to the unification of Italy.

VI
STRATEGIC CHOICES
AND THE LAWS OF POWER
IN HISTORY

It goes—or ought to go—without saying that the laws manifested in history are no more than variably determinate tendencies operating within recurrent functional relationships and within a limited range of possible structures of power. Yet, even so downgraded and diluted, such tendencies constrain feasible strategies and ought to influence strategic choices if these are to rise above the plane of day-to-day tactics and remain this side of utopias.

Varieties of revolutionary power migration: interstate triangles and domestic transformations

A key law—or set of tendencies—of moment for major strategic choices of the present links the migration or gravitation of preeminent power to schism-centered triangular interplays, with implications for intrastate social orders as well as interstate political relationships.

In the early period of the Euroglobal system, marked by the schism between spiritual and secular powers, the gravitation unfolded along a North-South path, between the emperors in Germany and the popes in Italy. An indecisive fluctuation of preeminence between the two poles had repercussions in the East-West dimension, affecting alternate third powers: the emergent French or Spanish realm in the West and the declining Byzantine or initially ascendant Ottoman empire in the East. By the time preeminent power seemed to have finally settled in the North, with pope-centered Italy subject to a briefly triumphant universal emperor (Charles V), the North-South path was already being superseded by the East-West pathway. As part of the change, religio-political issues were yielding primacy to politico-economic ones; a Germany torn by religious reform was losing salience to proto-capitalist sectors in what was about to become the independent Netherlands.

Whereas preeminent power had moved several times up and down the North-South path, it moved almost concurrently in both directions on the two separate East-West planes. First, preeminence reflecting primarily economic (commercial, financial, and, in due course, industrial) aptitudes moved westward, or northwestward, from northern Italy (Venice, Genoa) via southern Germany to northwestern Europe (Antwerp, Amsterdam, London). At the same time, the disturbing and stimulating detour to the Iberian peninsula initiated the eventual trans-Atlantic and Pacific extensions of the trajectory. Second, preeminence reflecting primarily military (feudal and rural) values and aptitudes moved eastward across the continent, from Spain via France to northern Germany and on to Russia. Just as the North-South power fluctuations had ramified into subsidiary effects in East and West, so the latter pathway, when it became dominant, was slanted in the alternative direction when the eastward trajectory of preeminent military power was inflected northward (from Spain via France and northern Germany to Russia) and the arenas of schismatic conflict between mercantile and military powers moved southward, from the Baltic and North Atlantic toward the Indian Ocean.

The sliding knot of conflict and the "terminal" triangle   These two (transoceanic and transcontinental) East-West trajectories were intertwined operationally in a succession of three-power interplays or geo-politico-economic triangles. These spanned the spectrum from the primarily maritime-mercantile to the incipiently amphibious (navally ambitious land-focused) and on to the most strictly military-continental power. In the midseventeenth century, the first triangle contentiously related the independent Netherlands, Cromwellian and Restoration England, and, at first, declining Spain and then reascending France. In the eighteenth century, England, having moved up by way of ambivalent relations with Spain and Holland, was locked in conflict with France, while French mercantile-colonial ambitions had begun to be conditioned by the concerns over German resurgence that reached their peak during the late nineteenth-century spell of Anglo-French colonial rivalry.

By the end of the nineteenth and beginning of the twentieth century, the second German empire took France's place as the aspiring amphibious middle power in the triangle, while Russia replaced pre- and immediately postunification Germany as the conditioning continental third party and Britain only began to recede from her sea-dominant position. By the end of the twentieth century, the triangle was being reconstituted, with the United States, Soviet Russia, and China spanning the spectrum in what were by then classic interactions.

At first only loosely intertwining the two East-West trajectories, the triangles were repeatedly tightened into knots of hegemonical conflict by the dynamic of two-sided schisms opposing the navally ambitious land to the dominant sea power, and vice versa. Only intimated at first in the contention of the maritime Dutch with the more land-rich Spain and England in succession, the schism assumed its perfect form in the Anglo-French and Anglo-German conflicts and has residually survived in the U.S.-Soviet contention. To an ever fuller extent as the pattern materialized, the normal intensity of power rivalries was aggravated by the structural asymmetries between the two parties, impeding both the extension of a continental into an oceanic equilibrium and the combination of continental with maritime empire in one power. The conflict was made more absolute by rival socio-political ideologies, embedded in the both different and overlapping characteristics of the two main types of power. And the schism was brought to its active climax by a third, so far most strictly continental, party either only endangering the incipiently amphibious power on land or also developing the capacity to displace it as the prime challenger of the maritime empire—unless the would-be amphibian had in time managed to overtake the oceanic overlord. Yet, since it proved repeatedly impossible to cut the knot of contention for good by entrenching one party to the schism in the results of a final and decisive military victory, the knot could be only untied (as one or both parties dropped out of the competition) in order to be retied and retightened among successors to the superseded parties. The triangular interplay was by then being shifted along one or both of the East-West trajectories to parties operating from a bigger territorial and a better coordinated resource base than their predecessors.

Thus, the heterogeneous Iberian (Castilian-Portuguese) hegemon, having partly displaced and partly co-opted the Italian initiators of the commercial-*cum*-navigational revolution, was replaced by France; insular England supplanted semi-insular Dutch as the dominant mercantile-maritime power; and, while England was able to hold her own for some time longer, Germany superseded France as the amphibious challenger and Russia replaced Germany—first as the background continental power (with effects for the causes of World War I) and, as a consequence of World War II, also as the challenging amphibious power. By that time, the United States had taken the place of Britain, even before China began to emerge as Russia's replacement in the role of the conditioning continental-background party.

As the powers changed roles and were successively braced and broken by the competition, the European or Eurocentric system of states was superseded by a global one. And, beginning with the initiating Spanish-Dutch interaction, by the end of which maritime power became defender as much as aggressor, a *grosso modo* feudal-mercantilist-authoritarian socio-political system within states was being superseded by a bourgeois-capitalist-liberal one. Whereas the latter increasingly marked the maritime powers as they gained in predominance, the successive seekers of amphibious status also had to move beyond an economy and a socio-political order that either perpetuated or merely updated (while functionally equating) the feudal order, if they were to qualify for an effective oceanic outreach.

This seemingly self-perpetuating pattern prompts questions for contemporary strategists. Can the newest triangle be prevented from being tightened into a knot of hegemonical conflict? Can parties to it escape both the lure of cutting through the knot by major military efforts and the liability of being displaced along the power trajectories, to the benefit of successor powers? Yet, if the military resolution was always inconclusive, further geo-political displacement appears newly difficult, if not impossible. The new given is that the emergent parties to the updated triangle are also the terminal ones on their respective trajectories: there is no manifestly eligible successor power beyond Russia and China on either the continental-Eurasian or the trans-Atlantic-Pacific overseas trajectory. Both trajectories intersect in one or both of these two powers, one of them problematically western and European, the other manifestly eastern and Asian.

As the material elements of major power scaled the Urals and spread toward the Pacific—abortively at first via Japan and lately more organically across and beyond the North American continent—the Europe-originated pattern could continue past its apparent end station only under certain circumstances. It could do so if, in function of reciprocally but unevenly destructive conflicts and resulting role shifts among parties to the "terminal" triangle, a nuclear and naval Japan were to replicate Britain as the insular mercantile-maritime power in a Japano-Russian-Chinese or Japano-Sino-X power triangle. Any such triangle would largely or fully Asianize the center of world politics, possibly pending its worldwide reexpansion when major southern powers (an India, Australia, or Brazil, alongside China) have qualified for roles in continuing triangular land-sea power interplays.

A positive dénouement of a receding intra- and interstate politico-economic revolution, we have noted,[1] would be for the apparently terminal U.S.-Russian-Chinese triangle to evolve into a military-political framework of world order, via balance of power-*cum*-concert of land-*and*-sea powers.

1. See chapter 5, p. 129.

Barring such systemic restoration, and as an alternative to the traditional pattern of conflict shifting to Asia, the main path of power gravitation might move back from the East-West to the North-South direction prevalent at the origins of the European system. In such a case, the materially more developed northern powers would interact with the less developed continental or insular powers of the South. They could do so in a unified global theater or within initially separate western and eastern hemispheres, and the interactions might very well reintroduce—as a function of divergent, culturally conditioned, belief systems—religio-political motifs into politico-economic motives and stakes reshaped to fit the intervening change in the make-ups and identities of the aspiring have-nots.

If, as is likely, the East-West gravitational pathway remains provisionally determining, the historically manifest transfers of primacy from one territorial power to another are likely to be indefinitely, if not necessarily definitively, muted. They are apt to be muted not only in deference to new military-technological and economic-organizational givens, but also in recognition of the impasse implicit in the configuration of politically organized space and the latitudes created by the fact that major power only began to be diffused, be it southward (a fact important for North-South relations) or in favor of China (a fact important for Russo-Chinese and, through them, U.S.-Soviet, relations). A more constraining military-technological setting might combine with the currently prevailing distribution of power across the maritime-continental spectrum, and with the possibly increased managerial efficiency in all of the greater powers, to extend the timetables for bringing the conflict to a "decisive" confrontation between any two critical parties to the triangle.

The doctrinal cost of globalism and two continental ideologies   Both because of and despite relaxed pressures, the dominant values and principles of social organization are unlikely to remain frozen for either type of power. A shift away from the residually feudal, incoherently mercantilist, and unevenly effective authoritarian regime to an incipiently bourgeois-capitalist-liberal social order was historically manifest in those land-oriented powers that were not wholly frustrated in their aspirations to overseas self-affirmation. One example, complete with an increasingly bureaucratic and state-capitalist transition, is premaritime Tudor and recidivist Stuart England before her seventeenth-century revolutions. Other examples (within the limits of a liberalization that sought expression against traditional patterns exacerbated by inertia and opposition) are France at different points of transition from the *ancien régime* and pre-World War I imperial Germany in the earlier stages of her *Weltpolitik*.

The trend for the external role change to be reflected internally is unlikely to stop completely. In the Soviet Union, the probability has consequences for its quasi-feudal party-state relationship, its mercantilist state capitalism, and its tentatively posttotalitarian authoritarianism. Probability comes close to being certainty so long as the Soviet regime remains unprepared to reenact for Russia a portentous precedent—that is, to have a military overseas empire coincide with covert dependence in the economic sphere on western multinational corporations, merely updating the Genoese managers and the Anglo-Dutch exploiters of Castile's extension into New Spain overseas.

The frustrations of tsarist Russia's outreach to the oceans, backed by the British even when implemented in their behalf by the Japanese, opened a breach for the internal socio-revolutionary challenge to a traditional land-power political system engaged in the initial throes of economic growth. Conversely, the Marxist doctrine that gave intellectual structure to the revolution was, at its root, a reaction to the practical shortcomings of the liberal-economic doctrines and practices peculiar to the Anglo-Saxon sea power itself. The shortcomings in Britain's private sector were tolerated, if not fostered, by a state power bent upon maximizing and prolonging the international advantages that an earlier liberation of productive economic forces gave both the British state and the British economy. The shortcomings were so tolerated, and only marginally adjusted, despite the changing interclass balance of power controlling state power, so long as Britain was in a position to contest the successive continental challengers effectively. The challengers themselves were in turn engaged in often clumsy, and on balance abortive, efforts to manage the release of economic forces from traditional modes, while denying the domestic socio-political implications of that particular method of seeking more power for the state in the world at large.

Thus, a land-vs.-sea power schism, producing a strategic stalemate and promoting ideological absolutism, has proven throughout to be a partially autonomous, codetermining external factor in conditioning internal socio-economic change in a particular direction. The schism has affected the rhythm of social conflict even as it invariably intensified the competition of the differently endowed and situated states over ultimately identical stakes of power in the form of parity or preeminence. If the process is allowed sufficient latitude to unfold in contemporary conditions, unusually relaxed in some respects and constrained in others, Russia's continentalism is unlikely to be globally transcended in the longer term without matching changes in the Soviet system interrelating domestic with thermidorlike intersuperpower détente and moderate system restoration. However, it also follows from the interplay between international and domestic system dynamics that the land-vs.-sea power schism is equally unlikely to be transcended in the future without the liberal-capitalist order and values becoming only one term or component in revised social organization and attitudes—if, that is, the West is to be equipped for effectively coexisting with symmetrically endowed (i.e., navalized-globalized) Soviet and, eventually, Chinese power and is to display more widely attractive and assimilable characteristics than would be increasingly the case otherwise.

As an alternative to mutually injurious conflict between the West and Russia, revisions in socio-political orders will or must occur on both sides. Their extent and direction are apt to be influenced by the possibility of moderating or (if the delimitation of West from East is displaced further eastward) suspending the operation of traditional interplays in relations between the West and Russia. Those interplays kept the western and eastern parts of historic Europe apart by associating one-sided value conversion (of the East) with conquest (from the West). And, when the need was to blunt the international side effects of the diffusion of ideas or institutions turning into cultural divergence, the two parts of Europe had nothing more fundamental to fall back upon than a temporary strategic diversion of representative western and eastern powers in opposing directions.[2]

Such divisive interplays and interacting divisions, which initially paralleled and increasingly exacerbated the maritime-continental cleavage, may or may not be containable by the regenerative potential of both sides until such time as they have given way to a degree of effective convergence within a consequently enlarged West. Whether they can be contained will be conditioned also by the extent to which a North-South path of power gravitation can rival the East-West pathway effectively. That extent is, in turn, likely to be contingent upon whether the point of gravity in the so-far dominant interplay either shifts definitively eastward or stabilizes at the geostrategic center of the "terminal" (U.S.-Soviet-Chinese) triangle, only ramifying southward while revising the role of the South from passive arena to active influencer.

Where the point of gravity does stabilize in the next phase of world politics will depend on western recovery of the capacity for self-assertion. It also will hinge on the West's resultant capacity and disposition to meet imaginatively and constructively (rather than with stubborn and ineffectual denial) the Soviet ambition to expand globally the scope of factors relevant not only to the security and standing of the Russian state but also to the long-term relationship of forces within the multiracial Soviet land empire. These forces include the U.S.S.R.'s potentially western (or European) and so-far dominant element and the essentially southern or eastern ethnic components, which are demographically and otherwise expanding. It may not be too rash or

2. See chapter 3, p. 59 for the discussion of East-West interactions in Europe.

premature to speculate that, as in the case of any ruling elite, success of the more western element in foreign policy will increase its internal prestige and, consequently, its capacity to influence in a generally westernizing direction the long-term strategic choice between a defensive recoil from Asia and a conformist or opportunist alignment with South or East. The choice will be hard to avoid indefinitely should a theoretically posited, and preferred, Eurasian or otherwise neutral orientation once again prove to be a non-existent and therefore unrealizable third way.[3]

Whereas the dominant western doctrine, intellectually controlled by the Anglo-American tradition of equating land-power insurgency for parity with an aggressive bid for hegemony, ignores the qualitative cleavage within the international system, official Soviet doctrine merely demonstrates a continuing deficiency in international relations theory. This doctrine was formulated decades ago on the narrow issue of imperialism in a foreshortened late-nineteenth-century perspective: it confines the interstate aspect of social change to a one-directional projection of the alleged internal contradictions in capitalism onto a crisis-prone, world-capitalistic system.[4] It just might be that the trend of thought initiated by an expatriate German, as he drew on the example of early capitalist Britain's treatment of under-privileged factory labor, can be usefully expanded—and balanced off—by taking up again the major theme in the turn-of-century orthodox-academic and official German critique of late-imperial Britain's foreign policy attitude toward an underprivileged military land power. The German doctrine merely echoed the older French viewpoint, perpetuated from the eighteenth century to the present in de Gaulle's approach to integration of the European community and the "two (Soviet *and* American) hegemonies."

Both critiques of the Anglo-Saxon system from the vantage point of implicity or explicitly continental values stress that system's tendency to monopoly: one in regard to capitalistic structures, the other in regard to overseas dynamics. Combining and mutually offsetting the two critiques

3. See the Introduction on *westernization* as contrasted with *Europeanization* in relation to Russia.

4. I have implicitly addressed the Marxist-Leninist theory of imperialism in *Career of Empire* (Baltimore: Johns Hopkins University Press, 1978), specifically so when delineating the hypothesis of "economism as a late state of imperialism" (chapters 3 and 8)—in contradistinction with the view of imperialism as the late stage of monopoly capitalism. More generally, the theory of imperialism is at issue in the book as a whole, when I expand the analysis of imperial expansion into its inter- and intrastate political dimensions as being in part extraneous to economic determinants and in part mediating and processing these in terms of power and security-related competitions. The international (both structural and strategic) aspects of the land-vs.-sea power schism, manifest both historically and presently, are extensively discussed in *Quest for Equilibrium* (Baltimore: Johns Hopkins University Press, 1977), and the discussion there ought to be referred to for elaboration on or clarification of points more summarily made in this essay.

promotes a more satisfactory integration of socio-economic issues into the
analysis of change and stability in both international and domestic politics
than is being provided by either contemporary liberal economism or the
most updated of Leninist excursus into theory making for international
relations. Only a new synthesis may provide a constructive theoretical basis
for a positive strategy in East-West and, specifically, U.S.-Soviet relations.[5]

Historically manifest tendencies and the policy cost of ahistoricism   It is the long-
term patterns of gravitation, configuration, and contention affecting the two
major types of national power (demonstrable in some parts and plausible in
others) that policy making in the West (and the East) will have to relate to long-
term strategy, keeping in view the operationally subordinate laws that can be
more or less reliably inferred from the historical record of the European past.
These laws cover diverse but interconnected phenomena. Foremost among
them is the tendency for parties to irresoluble, protracted conflicts to
converge in key attributes, and the tendency for ideas to migrate and for
techniques and institutions to be diffused in advance of effective power
displacement, conjointly with the rise and decline of powers and empires.

Also important are (1) the tendency for relatively more primitive political
cultures to have advantages over more sophisticated ones in both competition and amalgamation that cannot be reduced to brute power; (2) the
tendency for the tension between hegemonical and balance-of-power modes
to remain unresolved in favor of either, any more than in favor of both empire

5. A different use of historical analogy, replacing socio-economic issues and ideologies with
religious or quasi-religious ones, and abstracting ideologically neutral power politics from
both, would profitably serve to analyze East-West and U.S.-Soviet relations with reference to a
different triangle, constituted by Sunni Ottoman empire and Shi'a Persia (beginning with 1500)
within the Moslem "camp" and the Habsburg monarchy as leader in the Christian "camp." The
continuing propulsion of Ottoman power overland, in the Middle East and the Balkans, and
seaward, in North Africa and the Mediterranean, in a preemptive move against an aggressive
Shi'a heresy, thus is equivalent to continued Soviet expansion insofar as intended to preempt
and neutralize the Maoist heresy in the third world.
Similarly critical for eventual system restoration, in strictly power-political terms, are events
attending upon and following an East-West stalemate: it was reached as a result of Ottoman
inability to conquer Vienna (equivalent to West Berlin?) on land and Malta (yet to be equated?)
on sea. The traditionalist and bureaucratic rigidities inherent in the Ottoman system—its
incapacity to renew itself and adapt to the requirements of protracted competition with an
ostensibly disunited, but inherently dynamic and vitally innovating, West—would have in such a
scheme of comparison ample contemporary counterparts in critiques of the Soviet system and
vindications of the western system. These views may offer useful correctives to the biases shown
in the pattern of interpretation adopted in this book. (On the Ottoman-Persian-Habsburg
triangle etc., see Paul Coles, *The Ottoman Impact on Europe* [London: Thames and Hudson, 1968]. I
can cite no single comparable source in support of my preferred model, given the cavalier use I
made of the data and interpretations enshrined in the excellent historical works consulted on the
critical sixteenth and seventeenth centuries in particular. Failure to cite does not imply failure to
acknowledge a debt the scope and limits of which will be clear to anyone familiar with the vast,
and growing, relevant literature.)

and equilibrium being lastingly replaced by principles of action and order independent of either form of asserting power; (3) the tendency for the resort to force to be perpetuated in the state system either on different levels or in different forms of violence—or by way of late-coming new powers entering, or resurgent ones reentering, the system in an enlarged and activated role; (4) the tendency for the link between economic proficiency and politico-military capability to be loosened or severed only provisionally, and for the leadership role in setting the framework for both arenas to be repeatedly fused; and (5) the related tendency for the relationship of external expansion to either concentration of authority or diffusion of both economic and political power within states to be complex and to depend, among other things, on the balance of leeway and constraint offered to expansion from the outside.

Other policy-relevant laws can be inferred from events unfolding on a somewhat different and higher plane. One such law covers a tendency for the international manifestations of socio-political revolutions to termine in systemic restoration. Whereas such revolutions can be—and the latest series was—fired by the slowdown of movement beyond the so-called feudal stage on the part of powers frustrated in their oceanic outreach, the fact of eventual system restoration reduces the extent of sustainable evolution even as its revolutionary antecedents militate against peaceful linear progress.

Over an even longer cycle than is covered by either the empire-equilibrium, the bipolarity-multipolarity, or the revolution-restoration alternations, there is also the tendency for universalist or trans-"national" structures and thought patterns to alternate with particularist ones. Then the likelihood is that ideally defined or motivated values, priorities, and actions will be reversed in favor of materialistic ones—not least on the part of declining defensive civilizations. Such a reversal will alter and may derange the relationship between politics on one side and either transcendental (religious or quasi-religious) commitments or transactional (mainly economic) utilities on the other side. Both commitments and utilities are closely related to the tendency for successive schisms to exceed and encompass routine conflicts. The schisms themselves are subject to reciprocal subversion of parties incapable of being separated before one or both have been eroded and superseded, to polarization of policy-relevant attitudes within parties, and to interactive absolutizing of their ideological value systems and institutions. The exacerbation will serve in turn as an incentive to reactively pragmatic (whether institutional or strategic) correctives, often as part of a protracted two-power contest becoming triangular or yet more extensively multilateral.

Finally, an especially important phenomenon to note at the present juncture, and to incorporate into one's strategy, is the tendency for exceptions from, or suspensions of, the range of historically manifest laws to be only apparent, and only apparently to permit apolitical—either moralizing or strictly materialistic—approaches. Such interludes are likely to be no more than short-term manifestations of a temporary lowering of politico-military crisis consequent on exhaustion or deadlock, and the sources of such lull periods will themselves be the seedbeds of the next crisis cycle.

For purposes of strategy, even only tentative laws of this kind become directly pertinent when they illuminate the hierarchy of threats confronting a power or a civilization. The issue encompasses variations in the degree of threat, time lags in the different threats becoming active and being perceived, and the role of surfacing "new" threats in reducing the salience or restoring to a more realistic perception the intensity of receding "old" threats. If next-in-line threats looming in the future have to be exaggerated so that the previously all-absorbing menace may be reduced to its proper size, trends must be extrapolated from the past if those responsible for framing strategies for the future are to avoid two opposite excesses: one, concentrating on short-term tactics nourished by preoccupation with, and ostensibly dignified by expertise in, instrumental technics; another, indulging in utopian perceptions of the present and formulation of goals deduced from normatively neutral, material givens or propelled by empirically unfounded aspirations.

The first of these excesses has increasingly informed and deformed the conception of international relations by the latest generation of intellectualized foreign policy bureaucrats in the West, and in the United States especially. The second has again inspired of late much of academic efforts in delineatng systems and devising scenarios. The two biases have been known to predominate in one and the same individual as his role shifted between the theoretical and the practical spheres of activity.

In a historically informed strategy, the source and identity of alternative key threats will be identified in the proper context, locating existing structures and ongoing revolutions within a longer evolutionary process and situating actors within larger fields of power distribution *and* gravitation than are instantly noticeable or readily noticed. Furthermore, strategic response will be liberated from aspirations and attitudes that are rooted in misperceiving both the identity and the context of threats. Illusory aspirations will impede advance toward a minimal strategic goal that may be usefully traditional before its achievement can serve as a point of departure for the pursuit of melioristic goals.

The effort to relate goals not only to currently available instrumental means but also to historically evidenced laws is the only way to limit or soften the negative impact of such tendencies on parties pitted against one another by, or doomed to suffering from, the continuing incidence of such laws. It is the only way not just to relax (if not suspend) the operation of those laws but also to exploit the positive and creative potential inherent in them—in their ambiguities both individually and together. To adopt instead an arrogant belief in complete freedom of strategic choice is to take a major step toward making out of contingent tendencies the constituents of inescapable necessities.

Varieties of gravitational revolutions: derived and direct attraction

A philosophically conservative view of the relation of trends in history to formulating strategy—and empirical propositions about the trends themselves—has made it possible to view the future course of a more idealized than investigated Russia as the key to world order. A currently still weak and confused third world has been at the same time highlighted—and, if anything, pilloried—as one of the two main prospective threats, and the principal external one, to the West as that order's still vitally requisite sustaining core. And the two interdependent feats have been performed in a set of fragmentary glimpses of pertinent events and issues without either presenting an exactly true-to-life depiction of current happenings or (it is hoped) radically misrepresenting contemporary reality in its essentials.

At a yet farther remove from events and issues than the so-far offered explicit propositions, but in the last resort underlying these and either reinforcing or discrediting the policy argument, are the laws of pure power politics and the axioms about primary motion in the international system. Such laws or axioms are the hard core of, and encompass the hidden propellents behind, the tendencies inferable from the historical record of observable events. They constitute the physics of politics—a body of suitably adjusted (including inverted) principles of Newtonian mechanics. The adaptation incorporates Aristotelian and Cartesian antecedents when taking into account the fact that bodies politic have animate properties, including dispositions and purposes even if not affections; that such bodies must be in direct or indirect contact in order to undergo attraction-repulsion and make up a system in consequence; and that the political universe does abhor a vacuum.

The physics of politics and its manifestation in history   The first law of the physics of politics agglomerates the denial of indefinitely continuing vacuum and the affirmation of inertial motion. It holds that, once activated by the attraction of a power vacuum (i.e., inferior power), superior power will keep moving, i.e., expanding, until it has encountered a blocking or deflecting milieu or resistance—for example, intra-actor group conflict or culture-induced inhibition as milieu, and counterforce or system-generated constraint as resistance. That same power will resume motion (i.e., expansion) or recover direction only when invested with a new impetus, such as expansionist compensation for intergroup domestic struggle or for material deficiency in a dynamic universe.

If the above is law number one, law number two postulates that if a vacuum of inferior power attracts, superior power repels that inferior power. The superior power is a threat to the basic law of the inferior power's nature, its tendency to seek corporate autonomy—that is, freely to accept subjection only to the laws of power or politics and not to the dictates of another body politic or power.

In pure power politics, there are no secret sympathies or magnetic attractions between either cognate or complementary ("male and female") powers *qua* part-moral and part-inanimate entities that would either prompt the quest for reunion or impel the weaker party to court domination by the stronger party. Typical instead is repulsion between identical (both positive or both negative) magnetic poles, in the guise of two either autonomy- or ascendancy-seeking powers. Any phenomenal appearance of magnetic attraction (by a stronger power for a weaker, in search of protection, constituting alliance) is only the second-step, visible manifestation of antigravity: as the smaller power recoils from a power located in close proximity and invested with superior or overwhelming mass in the direction of a remoter, and thus less threatening, power with a mass potentially countervailing to the proximate one. The smaller, threatened, power will gravitate toward the remoter, larger power, and may even come to revolve around it as its satellite, as part of and in recognition of the impossibility of continuing indefinitely along the path of its centrifugal tendency, away from the proximate threat—the impossibility, that is, of flying off in a straight line into a vacuum of superior power and threat, and of thus opting out of the system of differentially greater and lesser powers.

Summing up, there are two basic kinds of motion and related laws. One kind of motion is toward a power vacuum or inferior power and is inertial; it responds to the only reliably operative attraction, one exercised by a smaller mass on a larger one. Subsidiary to it is the apparently reciprocal attraction of near-equally strong and dynamic powers converging into virtually unavoidable conflict over a complete or partial power vacuum, one of them moving or appearing to move forward first and thus attracting countervailing power, the other appearing to supply countermovement and counterpoise. The other kind of motion is expressed in recoil or flight away from greater power, constituting counterattraction or antigravity. The two kinds of motion occur in two different conditions that can be described in terms of a vacuum: partially present in the form of inferior power, wholly absent if vacuum means nonexistence of a threatening power or a system comprising no superior-threatening power.

The two related laws of attraction and counterattraction acting together account for the gravitation of bodies politic. They condition the resulting constellations within a geo-centric cosmos, centered upon the territorial state in principle and upon the interactions of such states in practice rather than upon the planet earth itself (*qua* world community). It is possible to postulate additional laws, relating to constant sums—for example, of conflict or of political energy either present in a system or required for its maintenance over definite periods of time. The object is then to account for other phenomena, such as the expansion of the system and shifts in centers of gravity within the system.

Such elementary dynamics, and the laws of attraction and repulsion governing it, operate, as do the economic, cultural, or coercive modifiers thereof, in one way within both the American and the Soviet orbits, in both the western hemisphere or western Europe and in eastern Europe (as well as, incipiently, in China's orbit); they operate in another way in the intermediate arenas of intersuperpower (or triangular) contention. The two fundamental laws can be illustrated, freed of contemporary implications, on the land-vs.-sea power triangle in evidence from the sixteenth through the seventeenth century. In the earliest phase of that period the Dutch were recoiling from submission to the Crown of Spain and gravitated for support toward both England and France, either interchangeably or simultaneously. When gradual progression toward assured independence had first reduced and eventually nullified the recoil from Spain, the United Provinces (of the Netherlands) were attracted to either Britain or Frances alternately, depending on which was more threatening at the time. They turned to Britain if France threatened more overland in terms of physical-military security and to France if Britain was the greater threat in terms of naval-commercial power and competition.

The gravitation could produce only a straight movement toward one of the bigger powers. Or it amounted to satellite-type revolutions around it, conditioned by the concurrent domestic power struggle between divergently oriented (Orangist and oligarchical) ruling-group alternatives. Throughout, the gravitation was constrained by territorial Holland's inability to give way fully to the merchant community's innate tendency to fly off into the oceanic vacuum free of territorial conflict, in pursuit of assets for politically neutral mercantile-maritime activities. At any one time, the thus conditioned gravitational movement of the Netherlands as a body politic in a system of such bodies was an active agent in the changing constellations shaping the northwestern-European subfield of forces. Within the total system, that subfield was more or less closely interrelated with other partial constellations resulting from comparable dynamics, such as the repulsion and derived attraction experienced by declining Spain in relation to the French and the Anglo-Imperialist power complexes.

The provisionally "final" outcomes were the fitful revolutions of the United Provinces as a reluctant satellite around England, following their defeat in the Anglo-Dutch maritime-mercantile contest. The revolutions were only intermittently and incompletely distorted by deviant, commercially motivated Dutch movements toward neutrality in eighteenth-century Anglo-French conflicts. While operative, the satellite-like revolutions were only redundantly consolidated, legitimized, or rationalized by ideological or confessional—i.e., libertarian and Protestant—affinities or (in Aristotelian terms) mutual sympathies. The same cultural factors had, if anything, intensified the Anglo-Dutch conflict at its peak, while it was still unresolved in terms of culture-free trade competition and power politics.

The political economy of power gravitation and its matrix in geography   Radically different from the gravitation experienced by bodies politic *qua* powers is the gravitation of preeminent power *qua* attribute—the first relative to one another, the second across space. Power as a prime matter permeates the system; it is variably clustered within successive bodies politic, imparting to them specific mass and, with that mass, the capacity to repel or (as a function of repulsion) to attract in consequent relationships. The differential power attribute can be seen neutrally as moving or migrating along a path from one place or incumbent to another. The path's direction can be inferred from observable events in history and, if the path and its direction add up to a meaningful pattern, they can be seen as illustrating a historical law. But for such movement to warrant the term gravitation, responding to a law of motion, it is necessary to identify some kind of direct or derived attraction.

One previously noted gravitation consists in the northwestward, or transoceanic, movement of what was originally economic preeminence from the Mediterranean to the Atlantic and beyond to the Pacific basin. The direct attraction accounting for that gravitation can be seen as residing in (1) the increasing potential implicit in the ever-expanding bodies of water and surrounding land masses and (2) the successively optimal conditions enabling individual trade and financial centers—Venice, Antwerp, Amsterdam, London, New York, and points west—to exploit that potential. Assisted by real or apparent historical accidents, the potential and the capacity to actualize it come together, and produce the commercial, industrial, and related or derived politico-military primacy of corresponding territorial powers. The resulting displacement of preeminent power will commonly institutionalize some kind of functional revolution and will incarnate a cause-effect interplay, as politico-military preeminence perpetuates for a time the economic preeminence that underlay it at an earlier stage. Dynamically supplementing—or operationalizing —the direct attraction exerted on gravitating power by higher material or organizational potential were the recoils and the derived attractions at work between any two of the unevenly maritime-mercantile parties to a land-sea power triangle. The interstate movements promoted or only conditioned the migration of preeminent power and influenced the timing of actual power transfers.

The other, eastward, power gravitation on the Eurasian continent in the modern era occurred comparably, in response to the attractive pull of the vaster potential implicit in successive territorial units: Castile, France, Germany, and Russia so far. Given the expanding shape of the Eurasian peninsula as it stretches eastward, the potential was actualized in ever vaster clusters of national power. Each successive cluster was slower to organize than the preceding one but was more powerful when finally formed. At first, the next-eastern major political space was organized only enough to get preeminent power moving; in the second phase, prepared by the initial displacement, its speed increased as the operationalizing motions—recoil from the previously, if decreasingly, superior contiguous power to the west ending in reciprocated attraction into conflict with it—compelled the rising power to coordinate decisively its so-far only latent resources.

So long, finally, as preeminent power gravitated in early Europe up and down the vertical South-North pathway, the variably attractive magnet resided in the alternative efficacy of the spiritual and the temporal weapons of the two corresponding types of powers, papal and imperial or monarchical. Mediated by recoils from either as a threat, the two kinds of weapons imparted momentary superiority to one or the other power in function of changing secular opportunities or the belief systems of third parties, which conditioned their allegiance and the principal rivals' legitimacy.

Laws and choices: system dynamics and détente strategy

For the time being, more critical than the spiritual has been the secular realm, dominated by the surviving residuum of the land-vs.-sea power schism—as implemented by the triangular interplays of a maritime, a would-be amphibious, and, compared with the two former, a more strictly continental power. The interplays can be reduced to both kinds of attraction—direct and derived from repulsion. And they bring into the open both kinds of gravitation, involving power as an attribute and powers *qua* bodies politic.

Triangular structures and laws of motion   The aspiring amphibious (i.e., navally ambitious land-focused) power is commonly attracted by and to seapower as the key component or outright source of preeminence. In the would-be amphibian's perception, the attraction will convert the dominant maritime state, or sea power, into a target exemplifying the productive value of seapower as attribute and asset; that same attraction will reinforce the would-be amphibian's revulsion from the more strictly continental, contiguous land power, perceived as the source of principal overland threat and the agent of possible preemption in the bid for oceanic outreach. The attraction and the recoil will combine in fueling what either amounts to, or is readily viewed as, the would-be amphibian's drive for world hegemony.

In a thus activated field of forces and gravitational movements, three main additional movements will occur: one, the maritime state (embodying attractive seapower) will gravitate toward alliance with the most strictly continental state, thus implementing their joint (if differently motivated) recoil from the would-be amphibian; two, the aspiring amphibian and the more strictly continental power will be drawn into overland hegemonical conflict, also as a result of the blockage imposed by the maritime state on centrifugal escape from confrontation by one or both overseas. And finally, the incipiently amphibious and the maritime state, the former recoiling from total conflict and the latter from total alliance with the most narrowly continental (and farthest eastern) state, will be drawn together into a quest for negotiated accommodation.

To succeed, such a quest would require two complementary adjustments. The aspiring amphibian would have to withstand the full force of the *subjectively felt* attraction exerted by overseas assets; the maritime state would have to resist the full impact of the *objectively given* structural inhibitions on the reapportionment of continental and maritime assets, implicit in the would-be amphibian's bigger land base and/or vaster economic potential. Attempts to negotiate outright union or only alliance took place between the Dutch and the English, the English and the French, and the English and the Germans in periods before respective wars: the Anglo-Dutch, over Spanish succession, and the first modern global. They all aborted, also because they were not aided by a parallel evolution that resolved both socio-political and functional or technological revolutions by promoting convergence between the two types of powers within an international system perceived as expanding in scope, and within critical timespans recognized as extending.

The basic laws conditioning interplays within the successive power triangles remain in force. The successively expanding arena, and the growing distance between either the parties themselves or the decision-making centers within them were offset by the growing mass of the successive incumbents of the three interlocking positions and roles. Nor did growth of distance necessarily entail loss of contiguity, critical for the primary impulse-imparting recoil movement.

Contiguity was lost least of all between the aspiring amphibian and the more strictly continental power. Where necessary, contiguity was established in time by the elimination of interstitial powers, thus of Poland between Germany and Russia (and different actual or potential buffer areas between Russia and China). It was, consequently, in the decisive period either not necessary or not vital for impulses between physically noncontiguous great powers to be communicated by way of revulsion-attraction movements among power units interposed between the major actors. The situation could be different while the next-in-line triangle was in the making. Thus in the stage preparatory to the Anglo-German-Russian interplay, it had been the intermediate so-called northern powers that pulled Muscovy into the central (or all-European)system, as the Muscovites reacted against Polish-Lithuanian or Swedish expansion into a Russian power vacuum (e.g., the Time of Troubles). Subsequently, it was Russia herself who extended her sway into contiguity with the two major German powers (Austria and Prussia), in response to the gravity-exerting vortex effect created for the three adjoining partition powers by the variably turbulent decline of Poland-Lithuania.

In the contemporary phase, U.S.-Soviet relations thus far can accordingly be decomposed into the operation of interlocking laws of political physics and historical processes. The cold war in Europe implemented the law of attraction by power vacuum on vacuum-adjoining superior powers. Both acted in that period as essentially identical territorial powers, only secondarily conditioned by the second-level (regional land-vs.-global sea power) differentiation or the third-level (socio-ideological) differentiation. The resulting deadlock at the center of the system, provisionally legalized in due course by accords averting or deferring a decisive confrontation, occasioned a deflection of the contest into peripheral competition.

Further stimulating the deflection, and amplifying it, was the attraction that the prestige and the perquisites of naval power and overseas entrenchment came to exert on the Soviets. That attraction was in turn compounded by the increasingly amphibian Soviets' preemptive recoil from China as the (so-far) strictly continental power. American-Soviet détente represented an attempt to counteract, through accommodation, the differently negative or onerous implications of alternative courses for both superpowers: for the Soviets, the risk of integrally yielding to the *direct* attraction of seapower, entailing captivity to third-world radicals as well as heightened conflict with America; for the United States, the risk of losing control over the *derived* attraction exerted on and by the strictly continental power—a loss of control entailing captivity to China's irredentist revanchism vis-à-vis the Soviets.

Laws of motion and preservation vs. static strategies   The costs of failure were thus not confined to the nuclear-strategic sphere. Nor was success anything like assured. The laws governing motion and motivation of the key actors pointing to détente were counteracted by failures to adjust strategies to other kinds of laws which, affecting the system as a whole, have continued to stimulate the conflict over the third world. The laws at issue relate to the preservation over time of constant sums of violence, conflict, or exercised energy in the system. According to such laws, just as reduction in high-level violence or conflict is offset by increase in low-level activities of the forcible kind, lessened energy in one (American) power, producing or attending its disengagement, will be offset by an increase in the energy of another (Soviet) power effecting its penetration; by the same token, the regression of original or established parties will be compensated for by the activation of new parties entering laterally into an evolving system, as it were.

It is the most forward of the third-world states that, moving into the void created by the various constrictions incurred by the longer-established western powers, have come to constitute, in the wake of unified Germany in the nineteenth and Japan as well as America and *Soviet* Russia in the twentieth century, the most recent lateral entrants into the international system. As is usual, they have expanded the scope of the system and perpetuated its rigors while setting back its tone.

The success of American-Soviet détente has come to hinge on the ability of both sides to overcome, by taking into account intervening transformations, the historically evidenced, structural inhibitions on mutually agreeable reapportionment of assets between so-far primarily land- and sea-oriented powers. At issue are interdependent sets of ability and disposition. Thus both powers would have to allow for an eventual identity of interests in unimpeded overseas access for economic purposes; both would have to acknowledge the reduced practical utility of competitively sought political access and influence under contemporary conditions. American policy makers would have to replace the strategy of regional containment with that of controlled decompression of Soviet power globally. Their Russian counterparts would have to adopt a timetable and a method for a global outreach, tending to geopolitical parity, that are flexible enough to permit one kind of decompression to mesh, with a minimum of time-lag, with another kind of relaxation—of domestically and regionally practiced coercion, traceable to psycho-political complexes and socio-economic backwardness.

At a yet deeper level, success will depend on adjusting the two parties' will-to-power to the ways of power, as historically manifested in laws of social dynamics and political physics. These include the laws governing the gravitation of preeminent power and the evolution of politically biased revolutions, both intra- and internationally, within a systemic context created by another kind of revolutions. They are revolutions obeying, in the last resort, the laws of motion underlying pure power politics among socio-ideologically and culturally neutral bodies politic. They prompt foreign policy strategies and result in diplomatic constellations that can be only partially deflected with impunity, and will be so deflected in fact only transiently, by modifying peculiarities of a cultural, ideological, or any other kind.

Postscript 6.   The Crime of Galileo and *La trahison des clercs*[6]

With questionable influence on real affairs and actual strategies, but also as if weary of sterile quarrels over method and nostalgic for the excitement of the post-World War II realist-idealist debate, international relations scholars of the post-cold war era reenact—like so many medieval scholastics and early-modern scientists—the contest over rival cosmologies. At issue is not, as in the sixteenth and seventeenth centuries, the choice between the Aristotelian (*cum* Ptolemaic) earth-centered or geo-centric, and the Copernican (*cum* Galilean-Keplerian-Newtonian) sun-centered or helio-centric, models for the universe. The choice is, instead, between two types of geo-centric orders for the earthly cosmos: the traditional one, focused on the territorial state in isolation and interaction, and a revisionist one, focused on the planet earth as the shared habitat of a world community.

As in the earlier controversy, at stake is ultimately the relation of the different orders to man as the center of concern (i.e., their anthropocentricity). Just as the Copernican system, by displacing man along with earth from the center of the universe, seemed at first to have more drastic consequences for man's self-esteem (as well as self-abasement before his Maker) that it was to have actually, so the world-community proponents set out today with more emphasis than insight to reelevate man in the secular order of things by liberating him from subjection to the state; they would place the individual in free and unmediated relationship with the new order's co-equal, universal, focus.

So-called planetary humanism unites mankind in a fraternity that the opposing, state-centered political realism expects confidently only from interplanetary warfare; the reversal of medieval universalism from its spiritual to a materialistic foundation is matched—and materialism re-

6. The title refers to, and the text draws upon, Giorgio de Santillana, *The Crime of Galileo* (London: Mercury Books, 1961) and Julien Benda, *La trahison des clercs* (Paris: B. Grasset, 1927). The most suggestive source for the competing cosmologies and related questions I know of is Herbert Butterfield, *The Origins of Modern Science 1300–1800* (rev. ed., New York: Free Press, 1965). I owe my late introduction to this subject to the inspiration, the bibliographical guidance, and the substantive knowledge of my son.
The preceding and subsequent points about the evolution of the international system are more extensively treated in the final section of this book (the Coda).

deemed—by the individual's restoration to the center stage in international, following upon democratic national, politics. In a but partially sobered mood, individualism is again fitted into the scheme of rediscovered harmonies; lest he fail to recover paradise lost, man is ejected from his tribal cocoon to face either himself alone or his numberless kin. A sovereign man may presumably cease being the political man without cost; the state may go, without its departure producing the trauma of statelessness.

Yet the news of the demise of the territorial state has by now been acknowledged, by the earliest (post-World War II) soothsayers themselves, to have been premature. So is the report of the emergence of a world community with the capacity to rival, if not dispossess, the territorial state as the prime object of attention and analysis, if not the subject of action. The absolute state grew out of the excesses attending the religious wars, themselves a reaction to the premature secularization of life by the Renaissance; the modern totalitarian state has signaled a reaction to the premature liberalizing of the absolute state wrought by the night-watchman state. Both kinds of emancipation—secularization and liberalization—were premature in terms of man's capacity to deal with new freedoms in the absence of socially contrived substitutes for old constraints. It is not certain that first the welfare state and, soon thereafter, its merging into an expanding world community will prove to be the ultimate correctives to the antipodal excesses of nineteenth-century liberalism and twentieth-century totalitarianism. Not least when proclaimed obsolete, the territorial state has a way of showing itself absolute, as a value or shield for values even when not as a framework of coercion.

The issue is of some importance for both the theory and practice of international politics, for the perception of the global system and its translation into grand strategy. The main difficulty with the world-community model is that it lacks convincing laws of motion. Such laws, if they are to encompass both the physics and the *praxis* of politics, must denote the merger of the most visceral instincts with the highest sense of obligation in one single, psychological foundation of individual and collective responses to other bodies politic, threatening or protecting, adversary or allied. Neither the imperatives of self-control by the individual anxious henceforth to preserve his physical habitat on planet earth nor the converging imperatives of individual utility and mutual solidarity between economically interdependent collectives will do; neither one nor the other has the intellectually compelling or the normatively sustaining quality that would make individuals or groups move in a new kind of revolutions and bring them into a new kind of constellation in relation to one another.

The finally decisive advantage of the (helio-centric) Copernican over the (geo-centric) Ptolemaic mathematical model of the cosmos was the former's greater parsimony. It could reduce the number of the so-called epicycles necessary to account graphically for the visually irregular or deviant movements of the planets in the sky. Continuing to subsume increasingly but intermittent or apparently deviant movements of territorial states under the classic model of incessant interstate revolutions actuated by pure power politics—small states revolving around great powers in search of protection and great ones around one another in search of each's vulnerability—has doubtless come to require a growing number of qualifications and reservations, tantamount to the ancient cosmologist's epicycles. How long will it take the political realist, it may be asked, to discover that just as the circle is not the perfect and only possible form of motion for celestial bodies, neither is conflict originally determinative for all motions of the earthly ones?

If epicycles were necessary to account for a planet seemingly stopping in its course in the sky, is it either sufficient or necessary to postulate periodic postcrisis lulls or interpower deadlocks to explain, as an exception, temporary reductions of conflict? And if epicycles were necessary to account for a planet apparently turning back in its course, why is it necessary to rely on a regressive tendency within socio-political revolutions in a national system, or on the regressive effect of new entrants into the interstate system, in order to vindicate the periodic resurgence of variably conflictual pure power politics?

If, finally, epicycles were necessary to account for the apparently altered speed of an individual planet, is it sufficient or necessary to put forward functional or technological revolutions to explain accelerations in systemic evolution? And what about falling back on the notion of functional equivalence (e.g., between medieval papal and contemporary U.N.- or latest U.S.-type mediation), and on the effects of diffusion and assimilation of functional innovations, in order to show that (or why) any such acceleration was finally less than had been initially apparent? How much of interpretative subtlety or just sleight of hand is permissable in an effort to make facts fit theory, to (in the ancients' and the schoolmen's words) save the phenomena?

The answer would be easy, and the verdict on power-political realism damning, if a more parsimonious world community (or any other) model were equally or more convincing. Yet, where the traditionalist would finesse deviations from his model (e.g., by postulating the growth of lower-type to make up for less of higher-type violence at any one time), the proponent of world community/interdependence tends to suppress the deviations from his model. For example, he will discount or deny the recourse to force. Where the traditionalist seeks to integrate novelties (by way of the device of functional substitutes and equivalents) and to differentiate real innovations from only apparent ones (e.g., the periodic recurrence from an irreversible rise of economic issues and motivations in international politics), the futurist would blow up all that differs from the day before and treat it as unprecedented. Ignoring even the relatively recent past, the novelty seeker is condemned to reverse the remote antecedent (e.g., the hierarchy of moral and material factors in the medieval universalist order).

When finally compelled to deal with Galileo's indiscreet propagation of the Copernican system, the eternal Church fell back on the distinction between a mathematical hypothesis and a pretended description of reality, the first having no implications for faith and the second very significant ones. Galileo's work on the two rival world systems was placed on the Church's index of forbidden books as falling into the second category and thus constituting error; the fatal extent of Galileo's crime was having tampered, contrary to prior warnings and understandings, with issues of theology.

Any index on which to place either scholarly or strategy-related ideas is presently under the control of the intellectual avant-garde; recantation is no longer obligatory, even during an inquisitorial spell in the actual making of foreign policy. Therefore, from a traditionalist viewpoint, it can be said only by analogy that the community-*cum*-interdependence world system is unimpeachable so long as it is propounded as a hypothesis; as such, it is an intellectual stimulant for the present and reserve for the future. The same model is conceptually questionable when it is put forward as a true-to-life description. And it would be socially dangerous if successful as a prescription, i.e., if it were to mold attitudes and policies in advance of its time, dealing thus a terminal blow to one kind of faith before sufficient numbers elsewhere in the world were prepared to adopt the other set of beliefs and loyalties.

Even while writing, soon after World War I, against the extreme nationalism and power politics born of prewar revanchism in some of France's greatest scribes—and rooted in other impulses in like-minded thinkers elsewhere in Europe—the author of *La trahison des clercs* made sure to stop short of endorsing unrealistic illusionism. Could it be that using the concept of the international "system," while voiding it of meaningful dynamics and outpacing its organic evolution, is our time's treason of the scribes? It is, again, the self-conscious shapers of socially accepted truths, interchangeably this- or other-worldly as they enjoy or merely await their brief hour of social power or only function, who betray their calling when they give way to revulsion from one kind of excess in preaching another kind. They mislead their natural wards when they react against the excesses of nationalism in the West's recent past and give way to the preference of a precipitately matured civilization for the easy over the good life; when they think and write as if the world, before becoming a community, did not have to contain as well as conciliate a new revanchism—one more widely spread and less readily appeasable by only material compensations than the ardent French Lorrainer's longing for the blue line of the Vosges had been at its peak.

CONCLUSION. *Continuing Challenges and Problematic Change*

Three kinds of revolution condition, and in essence constitute, international relations: socio-political, originating in upheavals within states and ramifying into relations among them; functional (including technological and organizational) giving rise to innovations first applied within states and diminishing in unilateral advantage as they are diffused and assimilated in interactions among states; and mechanical or gravitational, set off by impulsion among bodies politic and reacting back upon their internal orders.

The dynamics of the international system tend to break down into sets of more or less salient and determining triangular relationships. For each party to consider two more parties is commonly the smallest relevant, and the greatest manageable, number to encompass in tactical and strategic calculations on any major issue. Such triangular interplays will commonly activate both narrower and wider, both bipolar and quadripolar or pentagonal, structures of materially or militarily major power.

The evolution of the international system is unequally due to changes in three areas. Change is most marked in the internal make-up of actors, both individual as to mentalities and collective as to organization; less in the patterns of configurations and resulting interactions among states, also because new and relatively unevolved actors constantly move into the active system; and least in the modes and mechanisms of system change itself.

However, there is no reliable indication of there being three evolutionary phases, from status (empire) to contract (balance of power and alliances) and on to solidarity (interdependence in community). Nor is there on record any world order that is not dependent on either controlling or countervailing, hegemonical or balanced, power. At least from the ancient Greeks on, the political intelligence of man knew that the alternative to hierarchy and equipoise is unregulated strife and chaos.

The pattern of system change is so continuous as to reduce dramatic changes to the status of appearances. The system evolves as individual members and their configurations are structured by a limited number of successive, centrally dominant, major conflicts and regional so-called questions; as ever new members are socialized into technically more refined, but basically little-changing, rules of the game and locally conditioned foreign-policy traditions; as the effective system's scope alternately expands through integration of so-far peripheral subgroupings or lateral entrants, and shrinks with the decline and withdrawal into passivity of previously assertive states or political civilizations. Finally, the velocity of systemic activity rises with individual bids for supremacy and falls with interactor stalemates; it fluctuates also as the several socio-political and functional revolutions pass through their rhythm of initial turbulence and progressive absorption into but marginal effective change, itself absorbed as a stage into gradual and cumulative overall change.

The general validity of the policy argument presented earlier depends on the validity of the just-sketched outline of system dynamics and evolution. More specifically, the premise adopted for the argument (and outlined in the Introduction) may remain constant if international politics is essentially continuous across the system as a whole, in regard to both goals and means, regardless of local readiness or desire for radical change.

The contemporary configuration of major power, decisive for the issue of world order, has been the result of not unprecedented events. The rise of unified Germany drew the United States in two stages into permanent participation in world politics, while Marxist revolution and Stalinist industrialization positioned—and German invasions activated—Russia as the next-in-line challenger of the status quo, with help from the soon-following decline of political energies in the West and the coincident rise of China in Russia's eastern rear. One concrete test of the essential continuity or discontinuity in international politics is offered by the possibility of seeing the antecedent modern European order as arising out of comparable developments and configurations. As part of these, unified Spain (standing for Germany) drew England (standing for the United States) into steady continual involvement, while France (anticipating Soviet Russia) went through political and economic upheaval and reconstruction preparatory to her Great Century, and Germany-to-be (like modern China) began her decisive internal crystallization, with help from competition among the earlier-established major powers. Europe's so-called northern system of states (including early Russia and comparable to today's global South) concurrently went through the turmoil of determining the identity of its middle and great powers.

Significant questions arise about particular differences in size, scope, and sequence between recent and remote dramas, and about the different identities and degrees of prominence of conspicuous human agents of change. Are these differences significant enough to reduce pattern continuity to the status of irrelevant historical accident as far as policy is concerned, and parallels to the condition of merely curious historical analogy from the viewpoint of theory? Or else is it proper to hold that there would have been real change in the pattern of interstate relations only if Germany remained divided, the United States isolated and isolationist, Russia backward economically and organizationally, and China either in a world of her own or partitioned into spheres of influence by outsiders?

If the balance of judgment favors continuity up to the present, does this or does it not prejudge the issue for the immediate future? As here presented, the issue rests on the continuing relevance of the great-power triangle as it spans the continuum of land-sea power types and conditions the strategies of parties to the related schism. Is there or is there not a meaningful continuity in type and role between unified Netherlands, the United Kingdom, and the United States (as maritime powers); between pre-Cromwell England, and post-Colbert and Richelieu France, post-Bismarck Germany, and post-Stalin Russia (as navally aspiring, land-focused powers); between not yet centralized France, barely unified Germany, and preindustrial Russia and China (as by comparison strictly land-bound powers)? Are all these comparable as parties to several successive triangles (Dutch-English-French, Anglo-French-German, Anglo-German-Russian, and U.S.-Soviet-Chinese)?

And, even if they are comparable, is there not a basic difference, and one that will tend to critically reduce or intensify incentives to conflict, between a triangular interplay that occurs within a total system of more than three great powers and one that gets underway while there are only two authentic great powers in being? What is on balance and at what stage more destabilizing: the fact that, in the first case, the parties to the triangle are entangled in *structurally* secondary great-power conflicts with independent capacity to trigger system-wide conflict (e.g., Franco-German and Austro-Russian contentions in the Anglo-German Russian triangular setting) or the fact that, in the second case (closely approximated in the contemporary, residually bipolar setting), the triangular interplay is both isolated from distracting issues involving other near-equal great powers and cut off from potentially delaying or compensating transactions, the immediate *strategic* significance of which is comparable to the land-vs.-sea power interplay itself? Or do the different pluses and minuses cancel out into an indeterminate effect of the overall structural setting?

The distances and masses have changed: America differs less in space and resources from Russia than Britain did from Germany; China is less immediate a threat to Russia than Russia was to Germany. Also changed, to a degree, are internal socio-political and governmental structures and, more importantly, the technologies for making war and for acquiring or maintaining productivity, as well as (due to the latter) the time spans available for peaceable adjustments. But the pattern also continues to be tied up with the East-West cleavage between states, with only uncertainly converging, different or rival, socio-economic orders and ideologies within states, and with dovetailing attractions, recoils, and attempts at accommodation among the differently situated bodies politic. The continuities make it possible to go on regarding the geo-political issue as a major axis of international politics, at least equal in importance to its military-technological and related strategic axis, which is currently nuclear; they do not make it impossible to key attempts at resolving the geo-political side of conflict to a recognition that the inhibitions built into asymmetrical geographic structures have been provisionally relaxed, while, in deterring or waging military conflict, the dilemmas engendered by both geo-political and technological asymmetries are newly rigorous.

The main evolutionary changes, it has been noted, take place in the make-up of representative powers and, relatedly, of provisionally tone-setting political mentalities. Yet if these changes have presently pointed in the West to a kind of crisis of state (not least as the kernel of empire abroad and seat of imperium within), even that crisis is not unprecedented and confirms rather than disconfirms essential continuity systemwide.

The premodern western state in the making, as typified but not exhausted by the Carolingian empire, went down in a ninth-century crisis highlighted by invasions from North and East. The postmodern western states are exposed to invasions of a different kind, but not wholly different in threat, from South to East. Beginning with the sixteenth century, the next crisis of empire, due to religious, ethnic, and economic disruptions, affected mainly the continental Habsburg conglomerate; it eventuated in the revolt of the Catalans against that conglomerate's innermost—and by then nearly post-imperial—Castilian core. Almost simultaneously exposed to crisis were the overseas empires of the Mediterranean city-states, typified by but not confined to Venice.

The second crisis era for (post-Roman) empire may or may not be comparable to the contemporary crisis period. The third prolonged crisis has likewise extended from continental empires (in eastern Europe) to overseas empires and from there to the threat of ethnic decomposition of the postempire nation-states. Its causes are again both cultural and economic, although economic ambitions and alternatives (local assets and alternative frameworks such as the United Nations, European Economic Community) have replaced, as the key material motives of most of the separatists, fiscal and other exactions by the center. It remains to be seen, and may not be in the joint interest to see, whether ethnic decomposition overtakes first the oldest states of the West or the Soviet power in the East.

Be it as it may, the earlier—sixteenth to seventeenth century—crisis of empire carried over into a general crisis of political authority within states and of incipient world economy among them, conjointly with the more deep-seated revolts against traditional religion and an accelerated advance toward a new cosmology. Whether or not authentically general (the point is disputed among historians),[1] the crisis—or set of crises—cleared the decks for the rise of a number of medium-sized territorial nation-states, fit to engage in quasi-Newtonian power-political revolutions and to expand successively and competitively into overseas empire making globally. Both of the initially interstimulating two activities were not evenly open to all of the updated state actors. They diverged and took a course toward systemic crisis as the quasi-Newtonian revolutions, making up the earthly cosmos, came to be increasingly impeded in regard to the New World by policy rigidities and structural asymmetries peculiar to the land-vs.-sea power schism. The tension between the simple (interterritorial) and the dualistic (continental-overseas or bi-elemental) power politics proved to be more disruptive for the European state system than were any cultural or institutional modifiers unrelated to the schism.

The crisis, culminating in World War I and surviving into World War II, again cleared the decks for a next stage. Its constituents have grown out of the momentum of the global conflict and of the U.S.-Soviet cold war and, most recently, out of the merger of yet another crisis of empire, the American, with a national one. Having midwifed a continuing evolution, the interrelated actual or potential catastrophes engendered the wherewithals of a world system constellated around symmetrically maritime and continental great-power amphibians globally, and largely indigenous leaders in interrelated balance-of-power systems regionally. Only from such bases in conflictually ordered power, combining elements of hegemony and balance, was likely to emerge in due course an order anchored in authentic regional and global communities.

The prospect of such a beneficent evolution may easily prove to have been but a false dawn, however, comparable to western Europe's eighth century and undone by events comparable to her ninth's. There is little advantage to be derived for the international system as a whole, and yet less for its western segment, if conflictually ordered interactions among viable powers expand at

1. For the debate about the economic and/or general political crisis, see Trevor Aston, ed., *Crisis in Europe, 1560–1660* (London: Routledge and Kegan Paul, 1965) and part I of A. D. Lublinskaya, *French Absolutism: The Crucial Phase 1620-1629,* translated from the Russian by Brian Pearce (Cambridge: At the University Press, 1968).

what were once the peripheries, while their psycho-political foundations atrophy at what was the center; if new entries only replace weary withdrawals, and the sum of energy actuating the system is relocated rather than being more evenly diffused.

The contemporary crisis of the state in the West, whether manifest in ethnic separatism or generalized civic apathy, in materialism or moralism, is reducible to issues of over- and underprotection and over- and underperformance. Nuclear-type overprotection by the push-button state against one (military) kind of strategic threat has been matched, in ultimately demoralizing effect, by its conventional underprotection against another (economic) kind of strategic—and subsidiary—threats; functional overperformance by the welfare state has fostered a growing appetite, with escalating expectations fostering competing attractions: those of supranationally expanded welfare functions on some and, on others, of nationally reasserted authority and power in protecting access to the external sources of social and physical mobility within the postindustrial societies.

For the territorial state to continue holding the center of the world stage is not the same as for any of its internal regimes to be unchanging. As a matter of fact, changes in political structures and related capacity to manage and project power have been the internally and externally, morally and materially, ramifying hard core in the evolution of the international system itself. The central issue throughout has been the search for the time's most effective reconciliation of man's desire for a modicum of private and public virtue, as part of the good life, and his and society's need for a saving dose of *virtus*, as a condition of minimally assured life. Only lately, and in part disastrously, has the call for the easy life been injected into the critical political equation. In the Roman form of *virtus* or the Machiavellian of *virtu*, the safeguarding quality stands for the moral quality, not less than physical display, of manliness. The aspiration is not culture-bound: the Arab language, for example, has one word for honor and manhood.

The issue of manliness has been symbolically raised by the increasing incidence of she-leaders as the "real men" in western or western-style democratic governments. Before dismissing the phenomenon as one more commendable feature of the modern woman's rise to functional equality with man, or as one more manifestation of a currently pervasive deadlock—in this case between male politicians in parliamentary contentions void of great issues or overt dangers and thus intolerant of great men—it is worth remembering that a similar phenomenon attended the maturity and decline of the preceding, monarchical political order. The parallel suggests, without proving, that the political and moral crisis of western European parliamentary democracies in the period between the two world wars has reemerged in the West and has been generalized world-wide into a crisis of representative institutions as such.[2]

Symbols and symptoms, suggestive or not, must yield pride of place to underlying substance. The substantial lack, or need, confronting the West is symmetrical with that facing Soviet Russia. The critical issue for both is one of conservatism: what key values to conserve and against what kind and source of most pressing or primary threat. Beyond this common denominator, requirements differ in kind while potentially converging as process. Russia's need and capacity for meaningful westernization, as a means to consolidate internal and external gains, is matched by the West's need—and questionable capacity—for a measure of rebarbarization within, as a safeguard against both internal and external threats.

What passes for the spirit of Russia has been treated here as the last reservoir of the primordial human qualities and drives open to the West, to draw upon and make again its own. In the process, the image of Russia and the Russians was romanticized in defiance of all contrary evidence. Simultaneously, non-Soviet eastern Europe has been presented as the last remaining reservoir of political idealism in search of means and framework for realization. This, too, may be a vanishing potential asset and a fading quality. If so, the two sections of Europe's East would have to stand as mere code-names: one for recovered forcefulness, the other for restored faith, both recoveries direly needed by a West lacking the moral courage to bring into the open, and face, its intimate fear or fears.

There is no dearth of decline-of-the-West forebodings in word or print. Nor was there at any time lack of doomsday prophets in any mature, overrefined, or overindulgent political civilization. Pessimistic musings and predictions are likewise habitually met with intellectually superior optimism by the sophisticated. They can be so met, at only the alarmist's expense, until reality has replaced condescension with uselessly mounting despair, and raised eyebrows have given way to sinking hearts. The choice between optimism and pessimism about the future is, in the last resort, a matter of mood as much as of thought; of being or not being at ease only with the

---

2. Among such "real men" belong without question Indira Gandhi in India and Golda Meir in Israel as well as potentially, at the time of this writing, Margaret Thatcher in Great Britain—all preceded or also followed by relatively unimpressive male politicans. Some might include in this class also a Bella Abzug or a Barbara Jordan in the United States, where the presidential system is less receptive to a similar breakthrough. Following the more strictly feminine roles of even an Eleanor of Aquitaine or an Empress Mathilda in the medieval monarchical culture, the ascendant curve of effective female rulership coincident with first the climax and then the decline of the monarchical institution displays such names as Isabella in Spain, first Elizabeth and eventually Victoria in England, and Maria Theresa in Austria—not to mention the Medici women in the late Valois and early Bourbon phase of the French monarchy.

present or also with the projectable past; of viewing the role of statecraft as one to moderate supreme evils or one to bring about individual and social bliss. The future is uncertain; the supreme evil is to let it be determined by future alone.

Coda

THE SYSTEM.

Patterns of Persistence and

Revolutions within Evolution[1]

Plus ça change . . . The disabused Frenchman's dictum about politics and institutions has two merits: it concerns political processes, which are also our concern, and it corrects the variously motivated intellectual restlessness that leads to seeing change all the time in all corners of the political landscape. Each age is an age of transition, if only from the past to the future. But not all ages—or most ages—have the dearly paid-for right to view themselves as eras of revolution, especially if revolution connotes a break in continuity rather than a partial return to its starting point. It is revolutions that are part break and part recurrence which make up evolution, and the degree and direction of change are more surely seen in the mental quiet of retrospective contemplation than in a fever of contingent anticipation.

Attitudes to change vs. *the scope of effective change*

There are many reasons why modern western man in general, and contemporary international relations scholars in particular, claim to perceive

1. This essay summarizes and expands highlights relating to the evolution of the international system and scattered through the main body of this book. It was written under the auspices of the Lady Davis Foundation and presented as a paper at the 1979 annual conference of the Leonard Davis Institute for International Relations of the Hebrew University in Jerusalem, a conference dealing with changing patterns in international relations. The essay continues the effort begun in "Continuity and Change in International Systems," *World Politics* (October 1963) and carried on in chapter 2 ("Evolution toward Regional Systems: The Lesser and Less-Developed Powers") of the author's *States in Evolution* (Baltimore: The Johns Hopkins University Press, 1973).

—and having perceived, acclaim—radical changes in the patterns that make up the political process and concern man in society, the state in the system, and the system of states. One reason is the tendency to draw logical inferences from material innovations, including technological and organizational ones. Since novelties such as nuclear weapons or multinational corporations ought logically to entail new international politics, the leap is easily made to concluding that they actually have revolutionized relations among states.

Another tendency is to psychological or normative compensations, when individuals, societies, or civilizations feel uncomfortable or inadequate in the face of traditional predicaments and ways of doing things. This is especially true when the predicaments are confronted or the ways continued with zest by others. An aspirational leap into postulating new and better ways will then be tempting, and the temptation may be irresistible. A modern western (or any other) culture enamored of techniques and tangibles is especially vulnerable to that mechanism when it finds itself on the defensive against rash claimants to the old prizes and rewards of resolute power and stern will. If the defensively motivated or inferentially posited new image helps consolidate gains secured by traditional politics in the past—unless, of course, positing the new way helps appease the sense of guilt over the procedures that effected such earlier gains—then why not? And all the better!

It only remains to add to the brew the ingredient of academic culture— in the social sciences generally and in international relations specifically—that is ever straining toward new frontiers. The combination then becomes explosive, even if at first (or for longer) it is mainly destructive of the reputation, as distinct from the validity, of traditional patterns. How much more intellectually exciting and profesionally rewarding it is to forage in advance of the slower moving train of actual politics for new food for thought, for trends-in-the-making, rather than to scrape the bottoms of old barrels and marginally refine or update one's understanding of existing, inherited trends! Who will object if, in order to establish both the novelty and the superiority of the new, yesterday's patterns of thought are transmuted into so many men of straw and past images or initiatives into so many caricatures? The new will appear yet newer and the good yet better when it is projected against the distorted and distorting foil.

Such harsh words can themselves be impugned as hyperbolic distortion. There is little prospect that the war of caricatures across the continuity-vs.-change divide will soon subside and end on the triumphant note of mutually acceptable synthesis of the traditional and the innovative. It even ought not to, because the utopian voyagers into outer-spatial "world order" can be as worthy of their keep as the practitioners of the ancient magic and the repetitors of the hoary myths associated with "international anarchy." Each forces the other to do somewhat better than he would in the absence of the other, as he self-consciously either restates or repudiates what was done, said, and believed to be noble, useful, or just plain necessary before.

How to isolate and identify the actual margin of effective change is, of course, the real question and the real difficulty. It matters whether one starts from the postulate of novelty because new shapes or magnitudes are, or appear to be, unmistakable by the naked eye and unbiased mind, or whether one is prepared to concede as hypothetical or provisional novelty—until further notice—only that which cannot be accounted for as something that continues preexistent functions and replicates earlier structures, even if it differs in outward form and presents a different semblance. In outlining one possible approach to the sphinx, resulting in a tentative assessment of the margin of effective change, I shall start with three static portraits. I shall then try to relate them by way of a dynamic evolutionary process, and shall aim to conclude with observations that first imply and finally also state my view of the net degree of change and its locations.

Static portraits of diverse international systems

To be portrayed first here is the central norm of international politics, that of essentially the European or Europe-derived international system, encompassing the triad of state, interstate system, and social individual. From that norm—something that approximately existed at the climax or maturity stage of the aforesaid international system—will then be distinguished the prenorm (the early or initial stage) and the postnorm (the lately surfacing or contemporary stage, manifest among the most advanced members of that system). In the interest of economy, the portraits will be cast in terms of three polarities: universal vs. particular identities or perspectives; means vs. ends; and internal vs. external functions of government.

The central norm was closest to actuality in the late eighteenth and the nineteenth centuries. The state was by then sufficiently consolidated to relate enhanced means to circumscribed ends, with some aid from institutionalized national bureaucracies and foreign policy traditions acting as counterweights to the personal idiosyncrasies of individual decision makers. The reduced imbalance between means and ends was also due to another progressively evened-out imbalance: one between a previously weak governmental capacity to perform socially useful functions at home and the capacity or compensating inclination to project power abroad as a means to all kinds of satisfaction. The result of the improved combination of efficacy and self-limitation on the part of a finite number of major, or representative, states was an essentially particularistic international system, revolving around states as "empires within their own realms." The universalist element survived in balance-of-power (or equilibrium) outcomes of competition, only rarely combined with concert-type procedures. Moreover, in such a system, the coherent major amalgams of many-factored national power and economy will at least begin to ramify into, and add up to, a world economy. Yet the latter is anchored in one leadership economy as much as the balance of power or a concert of powers is anchored in one politically or diplomatically preeminent state.

The corresponding social type and supporting mentality are those of the quintessentially political man: largely secularized but residually religious, and religious in the sense of embracing the practice of statecraft or of state-related patriotism as a religion-substitutive faith traveling in easy tandem with institutionalized rituals and observances of an older and deeper spirituality. The political man of the norm is insistent with increasing effect, and on a widening social and functional front, on his rights in regard to the internal functions and powers of government. But he is no less firmly wedded to his sense of obligation to the state as a power in its external involvements. This balance of rights and duties, of satisfactions and sacrifice, is upheld by the tension between terror (relating to physical insecurity) and transcendence (of the material self); it is itself the source of a psychic balance that corresponds to, and ultimately sustains, the other equilibria: between ends and means, between domestic and external functions in relation to both surpluses and deficiencies, and between national particularisms and the practical measure of system-wide universalism.

Just as the norm is a blend of theoretical construct and historical reality, so is the prenorm, closely resembling the medieval European pattern. Its prime actor is not yet a state in the modern sense, but a neutrally denoted "power." Whether secular or spiritual, such power lacks a continuously stabilized and stabilizing central authority. And mundane powers in particular are alternately torn to pieces (their component fragments) and pieced together into variously sacral, near- or pseudo-universal, aggregations. One reason is a chronic misfit between ends and means; another is a radical imbalance between feasible domestic functions and the external initiatives actually undertaken. The ends of statecraft are typically vast in scope and lofty in conception, and reach well beyond the available material and procedural means. Equally marked is the paucity of feasible internal functions, extraneous and additional to minimal resource mobilization for action abroad; this kind of functional scarcity leaves ample room (in terms of policy attention) for, and creates ample incentive to, concentrating on external affairs. Action turned outward is the chief potential supplier of always needed goods and sometimes deficient legitimacy; it offers the most convenient (or only available) way of reducing unwanted surpluses of internally disruptive energy, as well as offsetting unbearable material deficiencies.

The two imbalances—between ends and means, internal and external functions—translate into extreme fluidity in an inchoate system. Aggregations of power rise and fall abruptly and unpredictably, less in response to effectively implemented collective thrust or balancing counterpoise, and more as the product of exceptional individual achievement, of unique if invariably transient asset, or of individually manifested accident (in Europe in the Middle Ages especially biological accident, in the form of monarchical longevity or procreativity). Power concentrations fall in the same manner, subject to a similarly encompassed tendency for the accidental aggregates to disintegrate. That tendency is the inchoate multipower system's ultimate safeguard against forcible unification.

The very weakness and instability of slowly crystallizing particular entities shield them from the initially potent universalist ideal being realized by any single power. Universalism is thus less an operative pole or a practical alternative for the multipower system than it is a variably real threat for all powers but one or two at any one time. It is, most of all, a pervasively potent myth for the socially and politically conscious man and his mentality. When that mentality is not wholly religious, turned past and beyond the City of Man to the City of God, it is inextricably religio-political: it seeks both to approximate the cosmic order on earth and to augment earthly power for that order's human agents, with the aid of the arts and crafts of pragmatic or cynical statecraft. But it also sees in an austere and brutish actuality no more than a dark passageway to an ultimately all-justifying, redemptive utopia.

The postnorm stage is closest to the contemporary western. It inorganically blends elements of both norm and prenorm, while the prenorm elements tend to appear in an inverted hierarchy or relationship. The principal actor is no longer fully a state in terms of the norm, subject as it is to divisive or subversive neofeudal challenges and postnationalist fissions; nor is it eliminated, however, as the provider of ultimate security and daily sustenance in conditions of apparently lessened outward threat and enhanced inner efficacy. The misfit between ends and means and domestic and foreign governmental functions reappears, inverted: the strictly material means that are in principle available for use in both of the arenas—interstate (e.g., nuclear weapons) and intrastate (theoretically mobilizable material resources)—exceed the politically feasible and actually proposed goals; the theoretically infinite and practically expanding range of plausible and seemingly feasible internal functions of government distracts either public commitments or popular support from external functions that are not directly and visibly related to domestic welfare.

More far-reaching or less conspicuously compelling foreign objectives are, again, typically left over to leadership initiatives largely isolated from collective effort. They are undertaken when the modern prince, yielding to personal predilection or systemic pressure, reaches out to the international arena for ways and means of effectively insulating internal dynamics from external inhibitions—and enhancing individual prestige or regime legitimacy in the process. "National power" reverts, likewise partially, to the prenorm stage. It becomes, again, less an organizationally contrived and rationally managed concentration of multifactor resources, and more a matter of personal risk taking (with disintegration-prone results), of specific assets (liable to overuse), or of accidents (reflecting a fickle public mood).

The extreme outcome is erosion of the power balances existing as near-static states globally and near-chaotic states regionally, combined with the ultimate dependence on either by particular actors. Universalism is reascendant in institutional, functional, or normative dimensions (via inter- or transnational organizations). But it is reappearing ineffectually, since its positive potentialities continue to be exploited and its solvent potency resisted by particularist actors and interests. One reason is that the universal factor is inverted when compared with the prenorm stage. It is now seen as lodged in the material dimension of economic interdependence rather than in the ideal layer of secular and spiritual unity. It is, furthermore, turned upside down with questionable efficacy, since a not-yet consolidated politico-military equilibrium (or one not capable of consolidation) tends to coexist with a likewise situated world economy. Both of them lack a sufficient range of internally cohesive parts interacting dynamically and a consistently regulating moderate center.

The corresponding dominant mentality is, fittingly, that of the essentially economic man. No longer political in the sense of subjecting himself freely to obligations turned outward; overinsistent on materially manifest rights within the body social; and no longer sustained in mental health by the tensions peculiar to the norm stage, the postpolitical man oscillates between petty hedonism and compensating socio-political utopianism. He is not yet quite able to be fulfilled by consumerism and is no longer fit for detached stoicism. In a disintegrating polity, he will readily founder into a sectarian pseudo-religiosity that is politicized only negatively (via rejection of the "system," its injustices within and at large) or naively (by embracing compassionate solidarity). When even that recourse fails, he graduates from individual anomie into collective hysteria.

The postindustrial man is the postpolitical man in the classic meaning of the earlier type. He is thus also the essentially postreligious man in both the historical meanings and any intrinsically valid meaning of religiosity. His connecting link with the man of the prenorm stage is escapism, manifested on the mass level in superstitions and on the intellectual-elite level in world-embracing utopianism. There are differences between the stages. But they are mainly or solely in the quality of the anxieties and incantations against anxieties on the part of the many, and in the nature of the terminal states and procedural remedies visualized by the few.

The dynamics of transition between systems or phases

Two great successive revolutions, one religio-political and the other politico-economic, related the three statically portrayed system phases dynamically; helped form the territorial state and its sustaining material base, organizational framework, and public sentiment; and were instrumental in crystallizing the relations of states in a political system and their relation to a world economy. The revolutions themselves arose out of and climaxed two major divides or schisms: between secular/temporal and spiritual powers, and between essentially land-oriented military and essentially sea-oriented mercantile states. Neither schism accounts for all conflicts or explains everything about resulting structures: the papal-vs.-imperial cleavage in the Middle Ages was paralleled by major contentions among secular powers, pitting France against England and the Holy Roman Empire in the West and pitting both western and eastern Europe against successive Islamic powers. Land-vs.-sea power conflicts were paralleled, and sometimes dramatically overshadowed, by conflicts among comparably constituted powers, e.g., Spain vs. the Ottoman Empire at the beginning of the modern era, and France vs. Germany and Germany vs. Russia toward the end. But such conflicts also merely adjusted the setting within which the primarily system-formative, schismatic conflicts and related revolutions unfolded.

Just as the medieval secular-spiritual contention climaxed in the early-modern religious wars, so the land-vs.-sea power contention climaxed in the late-modern socio-ideological conflicts. And in each case a preliminary build-up of rival forces and tensions culminated in a climactic confrontation (the terror stage), followed by the fragmentation of contending forces and, in reaction to their sectarian excesses, the reassertion of political, Reason-of-State, pragmatism as a thermidorian prelude and precondition to the restoration of a viable, because relatively moderate, political system.

The creatively destructive process had two main aspects, one structural and one ideological. In regard to structure, the successive parties to the schisms tended to erode and destroy one another to third-party advantage, as each tried to match or outbid the other in its natural sphere. The popes and the emperors gave way as prime actors to secularized "national" monarchies even before the end of the religio-political revolution; both the leading maritime and the preeminent continental contenders were repeatedly superseded by larger-based or better mobilized successors within a not yet reliably terminated politico-economic revolution: the Dutch by the British and the latter by America on one side, Spain by France, France by Germany, and two successive German Reichs by Soviet (taking over from tsarist) Russia on the other side of the land-vs.-sea power divide.

In regard to ideology, both schisms had directly or reactively absolutizing effects on beliefs and institutions. The waging of the medieval secular-spiritual schism helped absolutize the religious issue directly. It discredited the spiritual power and increased the appetites of secular powers. The result was to polarize totalitarian reformist (Calvinist) and counterreformist (Jesuit Catholic-reformist) ideologies and movements. Thus stalemated, the religious ferment helped absolutize the secular state indirectly. It did so by provoking a reaction to disorder-producing religious differences, which served as incentives or pretexts for resisting emergent centralizing power within states. Among states, the religious differences stimulated or were used to justify the new habit of counterposing trans-"national" confessional alignments to routine power-political interests and conflicts. Both aberrations were forcibly contained in due course.

The *politique* resolution of the crisis favored rationally economizing state power. It was fostered by the ultimately moderating interplay of rival extremes, was supported by emergent nationalism, and was allied with the ascent of the middle classes. Having thus consolidated the spread of secular "sovereignties" initiated by the anterior (temporal-vs.-spiritual power) schism, the final resolution itself overlapped with the beginnings of the next-in-line (land-vs.-sea power) schism and (politico-economic) revolution. The latter made world-wide the diffusion of economic activities and began a trend toward rediffusing political power within post-"feudal" states, although once again turbulently and unevenly.

The second multigenerational revolution was wholly secular. Its course was determined by the frustrations of land powers denied a free oceanic—mercantile and colonizing—outreach by the paramount maritime state. This denial absolutized the traditional values and institutions of continental statecraft into an escalating authoritarianism, which only culminated in Germany's totalitarian fascism. Economic and social dislocations also attended the inadequate implementation of the contrary stated values and formal institutions by the liberal Anglo-Saxon sea power. This malfunction set off a likewise absolutist reaction, in the guise of an ideological radicalism culminating in a theoretically anti-*étatiste* Marxism. The latter was metamorphosed into practically statist Soviet totalitarianism, with help from the land power-type limitations, frustrations, and reactions besetting the tsarist regime and hoisting the Soviets into power before becoming their lot. It mattered more in the politico-economic context than in the religio-political context that the schism was caught up in the tensions peculiar to the East-West interplay and division within Europe. Superficial convergence and in-depth divergence between the two parts, asymmetrically operative conversion and conquest, came into play as ever more markedly eastern powers replaced Spain and France in the role of preeminent rivals and challengers of the maritime-mercantile insular West.

As a result, a geo-culturally induced intensification of the schism reinforced the latter's inherent tendency to ideological escalation. Only when the combined effect began to wear off in relations between the newly central American and Soviet parties, have these reached the zone of possible moderation in a thermidorian (détente) prelude to system restoration. Once again, the ground for moderation was prepared by the clash of ideological absolutes. Only now it was Maoist China's challenge to flagging Soviet radicalism that has replayed the role of the Calvinist challenge to Lutheran reformism in opposition to a correspondingly intensified reaction from the conservative right. The *politique* resolution itself has been initiated in response to reappearing postclimactic fragmentation—factional and sectarian, intra- and transnational—within the surviving socio-ideological and political camps. Such fragmentation typically attends and promotes the late stages of a revolutionary process. But faulty strategies could once again delay the consummation, as they did in the earlier Anglo-German context.

The two grand revolutions were not only successive but also interrelated. They were related operationally in both directions: in one, by the exacerbating role that heightened socio-economic class differentiation and price fluctuations played in the last stages of the religious conflicts; in the other, by the both exacerbating and legitimizing role that religious differences played in the earliest stage of the politico-economic revolution—when Protestant sea powers (Dutch and English) spearheaded the onslaught on Catholic Spain's at best amphibious (primarily land-based military and only secondarily maritime) power overseas. The revolutions were related also symbolically, as the overseas colonial realms replaced heavenly horizons as the critical "world beyond," the object of imaginary compensation for what was too well known and of too little comfort "here and now." And, insofar as the later revolution provisionally completed the process of forming the modern state and the paraglobal international system, the two revolutions were also related functionally.

Moreover, in the latter respect, both political revolutions unfolded to the accompaniment of several interlocking functional revolutions, and with their support. Prominent among them was a series of military-technological revolutions (from early-medieval stirrup and missile weapons to contemporary nuclear missile launchers and projectiles); they prompted adaptations and extensions in both military and political strategies and both social and political institutions, the latter beginning with the feudal order. Another revolution, this one commercial, extended from thirteenth-century Italy northwestward, laying the bases for modernized seapower and, beginning with the eighteenth century, for Britain's industrial revolution. Yet another, and closely related, was the bureaucratic-administrative revolution. It rationalized the collection of revenues and management of resources, initially for war.

But, again, such functional innovations did not revolutionize politics overnight. They were lastingly significant for the pattern of activities only after they had been diffused within the system and had elicited correctives—either material or in adjusted strategies—to their initial impact and potential thrust. Only then were they assimilated—particularly by hegemonical interstate contentions—into preexisting political patterns. The final margin of stable and effective change was thus much smaller than might have been apparent or seemed likely when the diffusion-and-adaptation process began.

Assimilation of innovations matches postrevolutionary restoration in limiting the impact of change. Both types of revolution (political and functional) advance the crystallization of individual states and their configuration in the kind of interstate relations that are sufficiently regular and predictable to amount to a system. Neither revolution explains all. That same system is continuously and incrementally evolved also by routine interactions of power politics that follow their own "laws."[2] Thus promoted, the systemic framework in turn constrains the impact and reduces the effect of either of the two revolutions. There is thus a circular cause-effect or stimulus-restraint interplay between politico-ideological and functional revolutions on the one hand, and the structural evolution of a multistate system on the other. The interdetermination also alternately shapes and reflects the changing values of politically relevant moods and mentalities.

As part and parcel of the structural evolution, the typical state-actor was either aggregated from lesser prior units or individuated out of larger conglomerates; its increasing internal cohesion and projectable capability were progressively matched by a close contiguity between powers. Physical contiguity grew with the elimination of both insulating belts of territorial fragmentation and complicating cross-linkages of political (e.g., feudal) obligations. Its progress produced an uninterrupted network of the readily transmitted, assertive and counteractive, impulses that are requisite for system-type interactions of the equilibrium-maintaining type. Furthermore, in the absence of a common authority, the attributes of a system evolved *pari passu* with the stakes of competition becoming increasingly identical for all actors, themselves essentially identical because territorial states. The resulting setting was intrinsically homogeneous, though one hierarchically layered as to power if not authority and differentiated in terms of secondary features.

Selection of viable powers thus went hand-in-hand with their socialization into increasingly self-conscious rules of the game. Further, the structuring of the system entailed its subdivision into central and subsidiary or peripheral

2. For more on these "laws," and their relation to issues discussed here, see chapter 6 and Conclusion.

segments, as a function both of different system-wide and system-dominant conflicts and the different individual capacity of each actor to sustain conflicts materially, to enact and manage them militarily and politically, and to resolve them uni- or bilaterally, without recourse to third-party arbitration. As this happened, the policy-relevant scope of the system expanded physically as well as functionally, in terms of both the reach and the dominant types of power. And its historic depth grew perceptually, as foreign-policy traditions accumulated and were integrated into overall political intelligence.

While all this, and more, was taking place by fits and starts, by progressions and regressions that are only in retrospect reducible to a continuous evolution, a slowly but prodigiously evolving Euro-global international system tended to outstrip the capacity of the political man for psychological and normative, even more than for instrumental or intellectual, adaptation. The religio-political revolutionary phase of evolution was impressed with material scarcities. The cleavage and tension typical of that phase were between authoritarian statism and antiauthority sectarianism, the first expressed in action programs and coercion and the second in aspirations and evasions. The politico-economic revolutionary phase unfolded in conditions of an expanding physical universe and rising material affluence. The issue of political authority was correspondingly focused at first in the challenge that individualist-cosmopolitan liberal economism offered to the conservative, community-centered emphasis on politics first, biased toward mercantilism and veering toward militarism. Only gradually was that issue to relapse into an updated version of the earlier cleavage and tension.

Areas of possible change and how to discount it

We have now a basis for examining more directly the interconnected questions of change and persistence in significant patterns. Even a view of change as a process unfolding in cycles and by stages does not imply rejection of cumulative evolution. But such a view does inspire proper reserve about too readily perceiving and asserting sudden and irreversible radical change.

One linear sequence, implicit in some of the historical facts and in more of contemporary anticipations, is an extended and internationalized version of a celebrated thesis veiwing society in terms of progress from status to contract. When applied to relations *among* states, the sequence becomes one from hierarchical empire-type ordering of interunit relations to status-egalitarian, balance-of-power politics, structured by contractual alliance undertakings and regulated as much by interallied as by interadversary transactions. When projected *beyond* status and contract, the sequence culminates in some form of solidarity: within a welfare state internally and by way of economic interdependence internationally, the first ensuring social justice and the second underpinning world order. Such a terminus may not necessarily prove for all time to have been an ever-receding mirage, bemusing the weary traveler in the harsh desert of enemy-controlled or poisoned wellsprings, the latest shape of the recurring daydream of man's infinite perfectibility and progress. But, before accepting it as something more than either, it is meet to consider further caveats. The first to be considered has to do with the various ranges and areas of possible change in the international system.

Among the ranges of change, at least three must be distinguished in time or scope: long-range revolutions of the kind already described; middle-range fluctuations in the intensity and location of crises; and relatively short-range or lowest-ranking revisions in instrumental techniques of policy implementation.

Regarding the first category, not much can be affirmed with confidence. It is uncertain whether the second, politico-economic, revolution in the Euroglobal system is actually coming to a close. The close, if such it is, may herald the end of revolutions in favor of the benign evolutionary growth of all equally and cooperatively or signal instead the beginning of a third major revolution around changed stakes—perhaps as defined by the South-North contest, with the third world as one major and in some way revolutionary party. Or the current détente may be merely a prelude to renewed crisis within the ongoing second revolution. The latter could rebound between the current major-power (American and Russian) adversaries or be relaunched with new intensity by the militant insertion of a rising new party (China) to the land-vs.-sea power schism—possibly as a preliminary to the "third" revolution.

Whereas the present era and pattern of international politics can thus be located no better than tentatively within the politico-revolutionary cycle of the overall evolutionary trajectory, they can be more reliably situated within the shorter- or middle-range cyclical fluctuations. These are the cycles of politico-military crises as each gathers strength, reaches climax, and fades into postcrisis lull, the latter coinciding with the build-up of materials for the next crisis round. A temporary recession of a crisis will automatically propel into conspicuous evidence previously latent or secondary relationships: it will impart an apparently causal or determining role to so far merely instrumental transactions. The latter are chiefly institutional and economic, the first keyed to provisionally restoring the system on a level of reduced propensity to conflict, the second keyed to either restoring materially the individual actors or to generating functional substitutes for the temporarily reduced resort to massive force.

Among the efforts and partial and provisional achievements in the institutional category are the unequally holy leagues and multiple alliances marking the peace settlements of Lodi in the Italian system, of Utrecht and Vienna in the European system, and of Versailles (and Helsinki?) in the budding global system. There *are* tides in the affairs of men; even interstate conflict cannot rage all the time at the same height of fury as to means and of optimism as to achievable goals. As powers rise and decline in expansive energy, the changing of the guard will involve some ceremonious marching and countermarching, while crack troops retire temporarily to the training grounds. We are currently descended into one of the valleys of relative quiet, after scaling the peaks of conflict in World War II extending into the cold war. But who will be hardy—or reckless—enough to predict confidently that we will be forever able to tend that valley's pastures in peace with the only help from proliferating transnational organs and cross-national functional alignments?

This brings up economics. There may be times when its relation to interstate politics is summed up in the relation between full treasury and surprise aggression, and times when politico-military crisis troughs are deepest and last longest when coincident.economic stability and prosperity are at their highest. But precedents justify skepticism about either the depth or the assured longevity of economic infractions of the primacy of power politics and, relatedly, domestic infractions of foreign-policy primacy. It ought to suffice in this connection to recall the relatively brief period after the Napoleonic wars, with its "free trade," and the still briefer 1920s, with their unchecked economism and domesticism.

It is only after discounting the change that has apparently surfaced within the compass of both the long- and the middle-range crisis cycles, only after situating a moment in time within a longer historical flow, that one can begin to ponder seriously the scope and significance of effective change at any one time. So long as the state system continues, the argument is bound to stipulate, reliable change is likely to be confined to the lowest-ranking, instrumental dimension—and even there only after manifest, formal differences have been exposed to the test of functional equivalence. The scope of meaningful change is limited if continuing transactions—enactment and resolution of conflicts, support of politico-military strategies and goals with economic weapons, consolidation of alliances, and the like—are carried out not so much differently as more elaborately; when they are carried out with the aid of more institutions or with greater apparent sophistication than was the case in more primitive settings for parties with fewer material resources.

There *is* a measure of difference and change between papal mediation of a conflict or imposition of truce and similar efforts by the League of Nations or the United Nations; the latter in particular marks the thus-far ultimate stage in institutional hypertrophy internationally. Buying impressed recruits with subsidies differs somewhat from promoting political presence with economic or military aid. And trying to consolidate (and often exacerbating) alliance ties through dynastic union of royal bloods is not altogether identical with doing the same through organizational integration of regimental batallions. But more fundamental patterns of interstate relations are changed only as much as are the motivating intentions of actors and the relative efficacy of genuinely alternative (e.g., forcible vs. nonforcible) instruments.

Discounted change and surviving power politics

Thus discounted, what are the residual changes in patterns in the key areas of interstate politics? I shall consider the structures of power and motivation; the incidence of unilaterally usable force and of balanced power; and the relationship of economics to militarily backed politics.

The basic structure of power has always tended to fluctuate between the bipolar and the multipolar pattern: a two-power contest commonly generates fresh reserve, and a multipower contention erodes some of the engaged, power; an important role in the transition often fell to triangular interactions. Moreover, in the early stages of every major system phase, motivation tends to be more than usually impressed with ideological differences—for example, at both the beginning of the successive schisms and the peak of the related revolutions—only to revert gradually to pragmatic modes of competition. Polarization of preeminent powers and ideologies was more than once combined. Thus, superseding the earlier polarity between the Roman and post-Roman western and eastern empires, the Catholic Habsburg was pitted against the Moslem Ottoman empire, while a less intensely or differently ideologized triangular contest—involving Spain with France and England— vied for salience with the bipolar one. A series of full-blown three-power contests over wealth and power followed from the midseventeenth century on, determining policy for the parties involved in the contest and structure for the system. Against the backdrop of Spain's decline, the Dutch-English-French triangle was then the first to fully incorporate, and contentiously span, the spectrum extending from a purely maritime-mercantile (and increasingly bourgeois-capitalist) state, society, and economy to the mainly continental-military (and residually feudal or quasi-feudal and unevenly mercantilist) counterpart.

This triangle was superseded by the analogously differentiated Anglo-German-Russian triangle before World War I, while the latter was in turn replaced by the contemporary U.S.-Soviet-Chinese triangle. The latter conditions once more the enactment of the land-sea power schism between the superpowers. It pits the navally ambitious (Soviet) land power against the preeminent maritime power (the United States) in pursuit of overseas aims from a continental base, that is itself potentially endangered by the more completely or strictly continental state (China) in its rear. The current international system is thus anything but fundamentally original as its ideological-bipolar features fade into increasingly pragmatic and variably postbipolar characteristics, impressed with issues peculiar to a triangularized enactment of the dominant schism.

It can be legitimately counterargued on behalf of change that the present system is unprecedented in key respects. It is constrained by an excess of (nuclear) military power. It is conditioned by novel limitations on the politico-diplomatic implementation of balance-of-power statecraft. And it is modified by an unmatched ascendancy of economic means over politico-military ends within and among the three great powers and, *a fortiori*, the developed European and developing third-world countries. Or is it? And if so, how much?

Diffused nuclear power admittedly constrains not only the ends but also the means of international politics. But nuclear deadlock, in addition to upgrading the nonmilitary leverages, also intensifies resort to lower levels of force and violence. This fills the instrumental vacuum; there just may be present an invariably constant sum of force over definite periods of time in the political universe, more or less dispersed as to kind and concentrated as to use. Nuclear weaponry slowed down the rate of, and evened out the war-peace extremities in, political transactions revolving around equilibrium and hegemony; it has not eliminated them. Likewise, it is true that balance-of-power politics now lacks the easy recourse to war and to automatic reversals of alignments, often held to have existed without restrictions in great-power relations. But power is still being redistributed and realigned in its organic dimensions. And the mechanics of balancing are still being implemented, if only by such second-best devices as proxy wars among great-power clients, arms-control negotiations, diplomatic normalizations, economic growth races, and economic-or-military aid allocations.

If the balance-of-power system no longer has the British balancer, it has finally acquired in nuclear weapons an alternate reserve power, usable *in extremis* to redress a fatally tilting balance. It has also profited from a resuscitation. In the guise of the Chinese Middle Kingdom, it now has again the opposite of the volatile peripheral intervener: the relatively passive but impregnable central power, the *Land der Mitte* of Holy Roman Empire memory. Such a power is not so much intervening as one way or another interposed between—and unevenly weighing down—the unevenly more forward and reciprocally more vulnerable wing powers.

If the structures of power and motivation, the role and incidence of force, and the balancing mechanism are not fundamentally altered, what about the relationship of economics to militarily backed politics? Economics seems to triumph over politics; it is tempting to postulate its undisputed and final ascendancy over a strategically contrived setting. But to do so is as facile and questionably convincing for the present era as it is to see an early "world order" as being tied up with the Portuguese role in the far-eastern spice trade and the Dutch role in either high finance or the carrying trade; this ignores the degree to which that order was suspended between, say, the steadfastness of the Spanish *tercios* and the flexibility of the Franco-Anglo-Spanish balance of military power. Nor was a more recent, nineteenth-century order anchored solely in British textile, merchant marine, and insurance monopolies. After reverting to the outcome of the mid-eighteenth-century Anglo-French wars, that order was tied up at least as much with the Royal Navy and its changing— and in the long run fatally deteriorating—relationship to the distribution of military power and the diffusion of naval capabilities among alternating continental and rising extra-European powers.

A history limited to kings, wars, and frustrated hegemonies cannot be usefully replaced by the history of merchant princes, trade routes, and fragile trade balances only; nor can political realism be suddenly dispossessed by planetary humanism or yet cruder economism. The role of mercantile Venice in the international politics of the balance of power is not co-equal with territorially vaster and militarily stronger Britain's, any more than Britain's has been merely enlarged in scope by America's. Similarly, today's multilateral corporations have not underpinned either the American empire or the related world order (rather than being sustained by both) any more than the far-flung banking operations of the Fuggers were able to transcend the political framework of the Habsburg continental empire. The Genoese traders and bankers did not encompass all there was to the Spanish empire overseas. Nor is the OPEC oil pumped out of the desert sufficient by itself to create great power; it is no more enough, if met with old-style opposition to one-power or one-factor tyranny, than the silver from the mines of the Indies was enough to sustain Spain's imperial might indefinitely on its own. Conversely, imperial Germany was not the only—any more than Soviet Russia is necessarily the last—power that substituted, with some effective-ness, military for relatively weak economic capacities (in either high finance or advanced technology), also at the peripheries of the central system.

The relationship between economic and politico-military power always was, and remains, as complex as that between domestic politics and foreign policy. It must be analyzed, as regards either essential priority or operational causation and interdependence, under specified scenarios that take into account structural settings and evolutionary phases. It cannot be one-sidely simplified because arms are temporarily silent, because the West's material resource happens to exceed its political will, or because the new science of economics has caught up with the older science of statecraft. Even if economics has outstripped politics in theoretical refinement, it has not made statecraft subservient, because no longer necessary, in practical application. It will take more than a contrary belief by political science converts to the primacy of economics to abolish the laws governing movement within the earthly cosmos.

It would make melancholy reading today to scan the depictions of allegedly new international politics produced in the West in the late 1940s and immediately after. The essence of that politics was supposed to be conflict over ideologically formulated ends between two hostile creeds in a nuclear setting precluding any kind of military conflict short of Armageddon. In such conditions, national interests were supposedly undifferentiable as more or less vital; either unlimited freedom (if the United States prevailed) or unrelieved darkness (if Soviet Russia asserted her sway world-wide) was implicitly the terminal end-state of such politics and, incidentally, of history. How different is today's (or is it already yesterday's?) academically regnant image of international politics! Power is seen as infinitely diffused; so are the several cross-cutting functional alignments spanning the various chessboards of action, equivalent in political importance among states with different kinds of power as well as magnitudes of power. Chiefly economic (when not hardware-military) means are seen to triumph again and more than ever over not only ideological but also traditional political ends; creeds are replaced by greeds, themselves contained only by interdependent material needs; and both so-called superpowers are reduced to various forms and degrees of impotence.

The contrast in images between then and now, over no more than two to three decades, is too great to be easily overstated. Even if historical evolution has picked up speed, it has not accelerated at so dizzying a rate! In any case, the contrast ought to give pause to imagination and force the mind to investigate the foundations of the politics among territorial states before it sets about building castles in the air.

New entrants and traditional adaptations

The argument as so far developed suffers from a formal contradiction: on the one hand I have argued that patterns are recurrent and radical change is limited and often only superficially apparent; on the other hand, earlier I contrasted the norm of international politics with the postnorm stage and portrayed the latter as one more like, if invertedly, the prenorm stage. The contradiction is resolved when the portrait of the postnorm stage is seen correctly. It is in part a construct and in part a description of international relations as increasingly perceived in the West and to a lesser extent practiced by western policy makers in the current lull period. The lull occupies the aftermath of a politico-military crisis in the central system, and a détente interlude within a socio-political revolutionary cycle or between two inter-locking such revolutions. It so happens that the revolutionary pause is also the tail-end of one major evolutionary stage, from the Italian to the European and Euroglobal international system. The crisis lull is thus a possible take-off stage into an authentically global international system. If the possible becomes actual, the postnorm of Eurocentric international politics will have been the prenorm of global politics, pending its evolution into a matured norm-type international politics on a world-wide scale.

A process continuing within an ever-expanding scope unavoidably involves a succession of lateral entrants into the system. The issue of such entrants is the last to be raised here. It supplements and rounds off the others in militating against the many ostensible changes in international politics being viewed as fundamental, final, and (if only on balance) favorable.

The most striking late entry of fairly recent memory was that of unifying Germany into the European system, in the period from the 1860s to the 1870s and beyond. It too was preceded by in appearance a permanently becalmed state of international politics—the 1830s and the early 1840s: the "federative (interstate) polity" of the liberal historian, replete with social values epito-mized in the "get-rich" slogan of the Bourgeois King. The lull was fittingly followed, after the social upheavals of 1848, by the recrudescence of Realpolitik, punctuated by a chain of wars presumably terminated only recently. The reversion was to a modified *ancien régime* in international relations: it restored the essentials, while enlarging the scope and augmenting eventually also the ferocity, of the conventional equilibrium-hegemony politics previously disturbed by the French revolutionary upheaval—itself not unrelated to the Bourbon monarchy's last effort (in North America) to resolve the land-vs.-sea power schism to its advantage at crippling cost.

The crisis period following the lull also marked, significantly, the end of a European system in which the structure and dynamic had been determined by its founding members: France, Spain, and England, along with the papacy, the Italian states, and the Holy Roman Empire. The system had evolved as they—and the first three in particular—moved through differently motivated and manifested sequences of policies and policy moods that were alternately expansive and consolidating or contracting. Among the lateral entrants, tsarist Russia had preceded Germany while the original powers were still able to adapt; Germany was followed by Japan and the United States in conditions of steadily lessening elasticity. The later entries both signaled and speeded up the passing of international politics shaped by the saturated or also senescent powers, compulsively self-assertive when not displaying withdrawal symp-toms; they accelerated the rate at which preeminent economic *and* politico-military power migrated northwestward from the eastern Mediterranean toward and beyond the Atlantic, and eastward across the Eurasian continent.

The power flows—the main interoceanic current and the intracontinental undertow—may or may not continue to apply; the trajectories may or may not intersect in Eurasian space, projecting Soviet Russia or China, or the two in succession, to their spell of expansive dominance. But Soviet Russia and, most recently and conspicuously, Communist China clearly do represent fresh entries into the international system after periods of eclipse or ostracism for both. They head a long, straggling line of third-world aspirants to that same role and status.

One can only speculate about the effect of this third major wave of entrants (following tsarist Russia and imperial Germany as the first wave and Japan and America as the second wave) upon the terminal unfolding of the politico-economic revolution and, as part of it, the current lull in international relations. Will China follow Soviet Russia (and Germany), against all precedent in traditional Chinese statecraft, in reaching out for overseas imperial role and presence? Or will she head a new revolution of third-world countries and civilizations, updating the modes of the first, religio-political, revolution by enhanced material content? And, in such a case, will the West as a whole be able to go on playing a part in pragmatizing the revolutionary process, or will it follow Europe's westernmost Hispanic outpost into eclipse? Or will the modern global Northwest (relative to the South and East) complete the trend Holland started for the gradually enlarging European Northwest, and withdraw from active international politics into only economic existence?

If it does, will the new Northwest take shelter behind the shield erected by the last vital military power that can be at all assimilated to the West (i.e., Russia), or will it vegetate on the sufferance of a stalemated balance between two (or among several) nonwestern military powers? Or else—a preferable outcome—will a genuinely global international system reach, without major upheavals, the norm stage of a restored balance of power and a concert of powers? Might not such a norm stage concretize and consolidate the resolution of the land-vs.-sea power schism and its related revolution in the guise of four to five continent-wide powers of West and East, all equipped with symmetrical military, naval, and mercantile capabilities and outlets?

To such questions past patterns of evolution suggest a very limited range of variably hopeful answers, while the postulated new patterns of international action supply none or only variably illusory ones for the West. It may do for a while to postulate as the new norm of a coming world order an old one, which preceded the orderly conflictual interstate politics wrongly dubbed international anarchy, at the limited cost of inverting the givens: ideal into material features of transnational universalism, excessive goals into excess of means, and hypertrophy of external ambitions into that of domestic concerns. It may even do for a while to mistake a temporary lull in politico-military conflict on a grand scale for an open-ended horizon, with peace and plenty beckoning for all. But it will *not* do to mistake the preferences of a weary civilization for a model of goals, and not only of means, irresistibly attractive for thus-far frustrated and again reviving nonwestern political civilizations.

The spark of state and system formation had been miraculously preserved in the ashes of the burnt-out Roman empire. It was, after a number of abortive beginnings, fanned into a blaze of political creation that spread from Europe even farther outward. The flame is not reliably extinct in the world at large, while burning low at its source. Also not extinct, we have reason to suspect, is the explosive mixture of political passion and religiosity—authentic or substitutive—that makes men reach out for worlds beyond the unsatisfyingly familiar. The "world beyond" of the modern age has come to be called the "third world." It was an object of discovery and initial development by western man in his prime; lately, it has been converted into the main object for a critique of the West, in not too different ways, by a Marxism-Leninism that lacks an international theory and by a western liberalism that lacks self-confidence; it begins to look past critique to forms of conquest.

Barring a nuclear holocaust, the future is infinite. Within such a future, that same third world, headed or not headed by a non-western major power, will claim the role of an active subject in both the globalization of the system and the world-wide migration of power—beginning, but not necessarily ending, with the economic. It would be sad, indeed, but in a way also in keeping with patterns that do *not* reliably change, if the civilization hailing from ancient Greece could do no more and no better at such a time than supply another Polybius for describing the ways of power wielded by others.

Location and ranges of apparent and effective change

I am ready to conclude. The patterns that change most concern the make-up of powers *qua* actors in the international system. The at any stage representative individual powers do change internally, and so do individual and collective mentalities; the history of the evolution of the international system is to a large extent the history of changes in organizing and projecting separate capabilities. Thus the rise of postindustrial society has undoubtedly coincided with the waning of political nationalism, erosion of the authority of the state, and atrophy of the willingness to use force; they are all related to a new sense of individual and collective security, the combined nuclear-and-welfare umbrella shutting out fear as something that stimulates at least as much as it oppresses. These and related developments have altered key patterns affecting international relations, but only within western societies and not reliably elsewhere.

Less marked than changes in the representative pattern of actors have been changes in the dominant patterns of action. Powers do not develop evenly, and their maturation and decline will be again and again offset by the formation and rise of others. Changes of key actors will limit both the changes and the possible ranges of variety in interactor configurations and in related ways of responding to power configurations. The least demonstrable change has so far been in the pattern of system change itself: the rise and fall of individual powers and political civilizations, the relationship of various revolutions to evolution, the alternation of troughs and peaks in politico-military crisis, and the succession of new entrants into the system, each new wave relieving the receding generation of the power, labor, and rewards of sustaining a system.

Constituents change more reliably than configurations. If interstate relations are altered less reliably than are individual states, this is because the structures of national economies, or even of the international economy, change more than the relationship of economic to politico-military power does; because military technologies change more than the process of neutralizing new weaponry through adjusted politico-military strategies does; because the identity of late entrants into international politics changes more than their role in expanding the scope and rolling back the tone of international relations does. The level of available resources rises on the whole over time, and the make-up of resources is functionally diversified as a system crystallizes, expands, and (within successive core areas) ages. But hegemony can be attempted, and stalemate is historically more frequent than its opposite, at different levels of military and economic capabilities and in different generations of weapons technology—even as political conduct and concept are technically refined, but not fundamentally revised, along with, if less slowly than, increased resources.

Amid the constants of international politics some are demonstrable, some only putative (e.g., the unchanging level of differently expressed violence); amidst suggested changes, some can be regarded as provisionally established, others but prospective. But the range of *assured* change is limited, and its relevance for essential international politics is questionable. How could it be otherwise in an international system which is perpetually agitated on the surface but has displayed over many centuries only a limited range of persistent regional issues (such as the Eastern question), protracted conflicts, and stable alignments? The rate of socio-economic and political changes that affect intergroup relations within states may have accelerated; shifts in relationships of antagonism and alignment among states have seemingly decelerated. What will be the long-term net effect of the inverse rate change, especially if the tendency of contemporary governments to turn functions inward were to lose its basis in the seeming manageability of economic crises and the seeming stability of social-class relationships? States, and especially great states, appear more solid in their material foundations, including public finance, than they were before. But, are they not still pitiful creatures in peacetime? And was not their capacity to mobilize in and for war always immeasurably greater than in peace and most of the time impressive, even if at the continuing risk of financial or social bankruptcy?

Has economic interdependence really grown immeasurably in scope and in its effect on interstate relations? Or are only the provisional, and conditional, hindrances to the military conquest of economic dependence increased? What is the difference between the West's current dependence on Middle East oil for its industrial and war machines and its earlier dependence on Baltic timber and eastern grain? Supplies depended then, as they do now, on the economic self-interest of suppliers and were, as they are now, subject to interruption as part of conflicts indigenous to the supply area. Has vulnerability to interruptions increased? But so has resource substitutability. Are complex economies more delicate? But they are also more resilient and immune to earlier sources of disaster: is deficiency in "black gold" worse than the overdose of Black Death, at a time when economic miracles grow more than ever out of violent material dislocations?

Another apparent novelty is small states gaining international importance from a single material asset. However, their spectacular rise only revives a condition that was briefly suspended in the age of mass mobilizations. Moreover, a well-rounded, multifactor, power aggregation will still prevail if brought to bear on a narrow-based leverage. Nor are multiple chessboards a novelty if they mean no more than the fact that, pending polarization in crisis, states interrelate differently on different functional issues in peace, or even in limited-protracted conflict. The Dutch traded with Spain while fighting and despoiling her at the same time. Why shouldn't contemporary international relations come back to normal?

Our view of what is normal in international relations has been critically skewed by the brief interlude of a century, begun in the 1860s after a brief dress rehearsal in the 1790s. Total commitments had conclusively proven their worth in the American Civil War and the German unification wars; total mobilizations then continued to reflect total intra- or internation animosities, intensified by ideological certainties. Whenever these appear to fade, the result has been to read as change what is often but resumed continuity, as progress what is a partially felicitous regression.

Contemporary preferences and prognoses must be exposed to longer stretches of time past if we are to peer more than myopically into the vastness of time and theoretical possibilities ahead. Only historically sophisticated strategies can exploit, for attenuation of crises, the opportunities introduced into the continuing—or reemerging—patterns of power and conflict by the expansion of managerial instruments, or by a temporary extension of related timetables for the "decisive" confrontation. Skepticism about the extent of possible change may become a self-fulfilling prophecy; euphoria about affirmed changes that permits moral or material disarmament may be revealed, too late, as having sired a self-defeating prognosis. International politics remains the art of averting the worst outcomes for and among states, so that the *good* life may be striven for within communities with a minimum of derangement from the outside; it is not yet the science of social engineering, applied to creating a planetary—or only regional—framework for the *easy* life.

Irony can write the preface to tragedy. It *is* ironic that, at the very moment when they commit themselves to the concept of system in theory, too many scholars discard as either obsolete or obnoxious the key features that give the international system coherence and endow it with manageable dynamics. We may stand at the dawn of an authentically global international system. Such a beginning is typically also the era of false starts. As the 1980s begin and bring near the year 2000, the *fin-de-siècle* malaise of some contends with the end-of-millennium expectations of others. The malaise is of a kind that also marked, amidst a gathering economic crisis, the transition from the first to the second great revolution and from one to another cosmology at the end of the sixteenth century.

It is not the intellectually or practically best way of approaching our predicament to give way to unease. Neither is it, however, profitable to overindulge in millenarian utopias. This is true even if paradise is looked for in the cessation of world politics, as rediscovered and perfected over the past thousand years, and not in the end of the world itself.

INDEX

Adenauer, Konrad, and Franco-German relations, 13
Africa: and "African century," 8, 36; Soviet-Cuban alliance and, 16, 36–37, 42; U.S. peacemaking in, 38; western European approach to, 25; western military intervention in, 18, 20, 21, 41–42, 122–23
Algeria, and de Gaulle strategies, 11–12, 131
Alliances: consolidation of, 177–78; and land-sea power interplays, 150; relation to international order of, 114, 175, 179. *See also* Atlantic alliance
Arab states. *See* Middle East
Atlantic alliance (and community): vs. Atlantic confederacy, 18, 28, 41; and Communist seizure of Czechoslovakia, 66; economic aspects of, 24, 45, 64; and western European unification, 22, 28. *See also* West, the
Australia, and land-sea power interplays, 137
Australia. *See* Habsburg empire

Balance of power: and concert of powers, 167–68; and nuclear weapons, 179; as type and stage of international order, 114–15, 119, 157, 167–68, 179; and types of "balancer," 179; and U.S.-Soviet relations, 37, 39. *See also* Equilibrium
Begin, Menachem, and peacemaking, 18 n–19 n, 39. *See also* Middle East
Berlinguer, Enrico, and Eurocommunism, 16
Bismarck, Otto von: and German unification, 26; and *Weltpolitik,* 79
Brandt, Willy, and *Ostpolitik,* 13
Brazil, and land-sea power interplays, 137
Brezhnev, Leonid, place in Soviet evolution of, 112
Byzantine empire: and East-West interactions, 58–59, 80, 134; and institutional diffusion, 62; and land vs. sea power, 58. *See also* Roman empire

Cambodia. *See* Indochina
Capabilities (military): vs. economic, 180; and hypothetical scenarios, 25; vs. military action, 18; and U.S. hardware fixation, 17. *See also* Intervention (military); Nuclear weapons
Carolingian empire: and power gravitation, 57; present relevance of, 12–13, 16; and rise of territorial state, 160
Carter, Jimmy: and peacemaking, 35, 38–39; political values and postures of, 33, 38, 48–49, 50–51, 84, 109
Castile. *See* Spain
China: American connection and, 20, 28, 41–43, 84, 106, 151; and East-West interactions, 64, 104, 122; internal changes in, 110, 121; and land-sea power triangle, 64, 81–82, 112, 121, 129, 136, 137, 140, 151, 158–60, 176; and nuclear equations, 20; and power gravi-

tation, 57, 121, 137, 138, 183; regional orbit of, 147; relation to third world of, 112, 119, 121, 122, 183; and sea power, 183; and triangular diplomacy, 3–5, 20, 37, 41, 106, 138; and tsarist Russia, 7, 59 n; and Vietnamese imperialism, 123; and western Europe, 28. *See also* East-West interactions; Third world
Chirac, Jacques, foreign-policy Gaullism of, 14
Cold war: American experience of, 39; and détente, 36, 111–12; dynamics of, 151; fading of, 96; and Munich, 66; and political vs. economic rationality, 25; revival of, 37. *See also* Soviet Union; United States
Comenius (Jan Amos Komenský), and political exile, 31
Conservatism: implications for U.S. foreign policy of, 8, 23, 106, 163, 173; and liberal challenge, 175; types of, 7–8
Containment strategy: alternatives to, 5, 36. 46, 77–78, 105, 124–27, 152; historical antecedents of, 104; and isolation, 98. *See also* Strategies
Cosmologies (pre-Newtonian and Newtonian), applied to international politics, 145, 153–56, 161, 187
Cuba, and Africa, 16, 42
Czechoslovakia (the Czechs): compared to France, 66; historical situation of, 65; and the Soviet Union, 66

De Gaulle, Charles: and Algeria, 11–12, 85, 131; and Atlantic integration, 28; compared with Bismarck, 27; as Nixon's model, 52–53; and social normalcy, 47–48; and western European unification, 12, 21–22, 26, 29, 141
Détente: case for, 105–6, 112, 139–42; misconceptions of, 7 n–8 n, 90–93, 124; rules for, 37, 42–44, 98–99, 125–27; U.S. attitude toward, 4, 17, 35–37, 41; viable definition of, 36–37; and western European unification, 27. *See also* Soviet Union; Strategies; United States

East, the: invasions from, 60, 160; political dynamics and values of, 130–31; as power center, 122; third world as part of, 64, 119. *See also* East-West interactions
Eastern Europe: characteristic traits in, 16, 69–72, 163; and East-West divisions, 45, 46, 60–64; German minorities in, 67; and nuclear equations, 20; relation to western Europe of, 15–16, 28, 46; Soviet dominance in, 3, 5, 28, 67–68, 77, 119–20, 125, 147; and the West, 6, 30–31, 60, 65–67, 69–73, 131. *See also* Czechoslovakia; Poland
East-West interactions: contemporary aspects of, 45, 64, 71–73, 80, 105, 110, 120–21, 129,

transnationality, 88, 113, 115, 143; views on, 35, 97–98, 170; and welfare-state solidarity, 114, 175–76. *See also* Utopias; World order
International system (global and general): academic meanings of, 156; continuity vs. change in, 158–59, 165–67, 175–81, 184–87; and crisis-lull fluctuations, 176–77, 182; evolution of, 50, 83, 105, 110–13, 128–29, 156, 158, 161–62, 167–87; functional equivalents in, 177–78; vs. "international anarchy," 166, 183; late entrants into, 152, 182–83, 185. *See also* State system (European)
Intervention (military): political aspects of, 20; by Soviet Union, 36; western role and capacity in, 18, 41, 122–24
Iran: and oil supply, 93; as regional power, 26, 110; revolution in, 43–44, 97; and U.S. client support, 43; and U.S.-Soviet détente rules, 43–44, 123, 124
Israel. *See* Begin, Menachem; Middle East

Japan: and Atlantic confederacy, 41, 45; and land-sea power triangles, 137; and mercantile-maritime issues, 64; position on East-West axis of, 45, 64, 74, 119, 122; and power gravitation, 57, 121, 137, 152; and Russia, 139; and world economy, 81
Johnson, Lyndon Baines, and western European unification, 26–27
Jones, Jim (Reverend), and politicized religiosity in America, 48–49, 85

Kennedy, John Fitzgerald: and western European unification, 26; Winston Churchill as model for, 52

Land-sea power schism: contemporary characteristics of, 45, 79, 80–81, 139–42, 173, 183; and East-West divisions, 63, 105, 172–73; and economism vs. militarism, 78, 84; historical manifestations of, 58–59, 61, 78–79, 128, 129, 135–36, 139, 161, 171; and Marxism-Leninism, 141–42; possible resolution of, 128–29; and secular-spiritual schism, 61, 62. *See also* Triangular interplays
Liberalism: challenge to conservatism of, 175; and East-West divisions, 60; effects on U.S. foreign policy of, 8, 17, 18 n, 22–23, 25–26; and land-sea power interplays, 137, 138, 139–40, 141–42; and power politics, 79

Mao tse tung, and social normalcy, 47–48
Marxism-Leninism: and Anglo-Saxon liberalism, 139, 172; eastward diffusion of, 62; and international relations theory, 22, 141–42; and Soviet Communism, 132
Middle East: and Iranian revolution, 43;

peacemaking in, 18 n–19 n, 35–36, 38–39, 123; and Soviet Union, 19 n, 94; war and oil in, 18–19, 35, 41, 94, 186; western European approach to, 25; western military action in, 20. *See also* OPEC
Moslem powers: and East-West interactions, 63, 171; and power gravitation, 62; and sea power, 58. *See also* Ottoman empire

Nationalism: condition in West of, 84–88; and state power, 172; and world economy, 87; world-wide diffusion of, 62, 110
NATO (North Atlantic Treaty Organization). *See* Atlantic Alliance
Netherlands, The: and land-sea power triangles, 81, 135–37, 147–48, 150, 173; and power gravitation, 135, 148, 183; and sea power, 59 n, 61, 139; and world economy, 79, 81, 180. *See also* Land-sea power schism; Triangular interplays
Nixon, Richard M., pathos and tragedy of, 52–53
North-South relations: and economic interdependence, 35, 44, 91, 94, 98, 183; in medieval Europe, 134–35, 138, 149; within the United States, 39, 117; and U.S.-Soviet relations, 5–6, 129, 138, 140. *See also* Economic factor; Third world
Nuclear weapons: and defense of western Europe, 19–20, 23; and equilibrium-hegemony politics, 179, 185; manageability of, 95; and triangular diplomacy, 138, 160, 179; and violence, 179, 185; and western political civilization, 19, 45, 87–88, 162, 184. *See also* Capabilities (military); SALT

OPEC (Organization of Petroleum Exporting Countries): compared with MLF, 23; as "great power," 180; and the West, 16, 17, 23, 25, 35, 90, 93, 100; western responses to, 12, 41, 79, 98, 102 n. *See also* Middle East
Ottoman empire: and East-West divisions, 60, 80, 104, 134; and Ottoman-Persian-Habsburg triangle, 142 n; and Russia, 7; and sea power, 58 n. *See also* Moslem powers

Papacy (Roman): and East-West divisions, 58; and Galileo, 156; and peacemaking, 155, 177; and power gravitation, 134–35; salience of, 111. *See also* Secular-spiritual schism
Parity (U.S.-Soviet), aspects of, 37, 82, 91–92, 126–27, 139. *See also* Equilibrium
Patton, George S.: martial values of, 51; and Richard Nixon, 51–53
People's Republic of China. *See* China
Persia (premodern), and Ottoman-Persian-Habsburg triangle, 142 n